Foreward by Dave Kolpack

ISBN-10: 1530455170

ISBN-13: 978-1530455171

Front cover photo by David Samson, dsamson@forumcomm.com

Cover design by Rob Beer, rbeer@forumcomm.com

Back cover photo courtesy of the Southland Conference

About the author photo by Becky Thrash

North Dakota State logos, trademark used with permission from Bison athletics, 1300 17th Avenue North University Drive, Fargo, ND 58102

For more on the author, visit www.inforum.com or www.bisonmedia.areavoices.com.

To contact the author: jeff@kolpack.com. Twitter: @FGOSPORTSWRITER

First edition. First printing: 2016

Printed in the United States of America

Horns Up

Inside the Greatest College Football Dynasty

JEFF KOLPACK

For mom and dad.

Contents

I.	Say it's so, Joe	1
II.	No. 11	13
III.	Show me the money	25
IV.	Taking on the big boys	35
V.	Those little guys in green	43
VI.	Dear Brock, I was truly impressed	51
VII.	The magic men	65
VIII.	Planes, trains and automobiles	79
IX.	A season on the brink	94
X.	Gateway to a dynasty	104
XI.	Signing day secrets	116
XII.	Frisco	126
XIII.	ESPN and the Bizon	147
XIV.	The Laramie project	155
XV.	Culture club	174
XVI.	The fourth quarter	191
XVII.	Epilogue: the Xs and Os	201

Foreward

The English language was revered in the Kolpack household, where the daily dinners at 5:30 p.m. sharp turned into accelerated grammar lessons led by my mom, a one-time English teacher, and my dad, a lifelong newspaper reporter. On one occasion when the oldest of three boys asked one of his younger brothers to please pass the "sturd," a slang version of mustard, it nearly sent all three boys to their rooms without supper.

"That's laziness," my mom snapped, not the least bit amused.

After dinner, when one of the boys said that "me and Joe" were going to the playground, it came with the obligatory scolding question of, "Is Joe mean?" Sorry mom. "Joe and I" are going to the playground.

Although all three boys could fashion a sentence worthy of putting dinner on the table, two of them were destined for other careers. My mom always believed that Bruce, the oldest, was the best writer in the family, but he was headed to North Dakota State University to study electrical engineering and computer science. Jeff was going to be an architect.

Before the twists and turns to Jeff's journey are explained, it should be noted that in addition to words, the other passion in the Kolpack family was Bison athletics. We were fortunate enough to have a ringside seat to every event while my dad, Ed Kolpack, covered Bison teams for more than 30 years. He, of course, was required to be fair and unbiased. My mom was not.

She put a bumper sticker on the family car that read, "Motherhood, apple pie and the Bison." She never missed listening to a game on the radio, while at the same time keeping an eye on three boys and making sure they didn't mix their metaphors. She even recorded some of the games on cassette. When late 70s-era Bison basketball player Steve Saladino hit a buzzer-beater to win a game in the North Central Conference holiday tournament, my mom can be heard in the background gleefully exclaiming, "Jeepers!"

My mom was deathly afraid of flying and there was nothing that could get her in an airplane. Well, there was one thing. Her one and only ride on the friendly skies came when the Bison football team qualified for the Camellia Bowl in the late 1960s, which was considered the small school Super Bowl. It's a stark contrast with her husband and two sons flying hundreds of hours throughout the country to cover the Bison.

When one of her sons who shall remain unnamed opted to attend the rival university, one that legendary Bison football coach Rocky Hager often referred to as "up north," it did nothing to alter my mom's loyalty. Returning home after that first freshman semester, a fancy sweater with that school's logo seemed like an ideal Christmas present. It stayed in the box. The NCAA would be proud.

The maiden name of my mom's mother, by the way, was Horn.

My dad retired from the newspaper business in the late 1980s, and joked at the time that it took two Kolpacks to fill his shoes. While Jeff was attending NDSU and dreaming of designing blueprints for buildings, he was persuaded by journalism instructor Lou Richardson to report for The Spectrum, the school's student newspaper. It wasn't exactly a recruiting coup on the scale of Carson Wentz, but it was a success nonetheless.

Jeff worked his way through the North Dakota newspaper circuit, from the Jamestown Sun to the Bismarck Tribune and finally to The Forum, where he eventually took over the Bison beat. These days that includes real-time blogs, tweets, TV programs and radio talk shows. My dad would be floored.

Ed Kolpack's final project was to document what had been the most successful football program at the NCAA Division II level. The book "Bison Football: Three Decades of Excellence," begins with the story of a fan calling the NDSU ticket office in the early 1960s and asking what time the football game was scheduled to begin. The answer: What time can you get here?

It has been a wild ride since. Bison football, in essence, has evolved into six decades of excellence, punctuated by an incredible last six years and, thanks to Wentz, a whirlwind last six months. This sequel will take you from the practice fields of north Fargo to the pre- and post-game discussions in the bowels of the Fargodome to the program's second home of Frisco, Texas, to Wentz's ascension to pro football phenom.

You won't be able to put your horns down.

Dave Kolpack
The Associated Press

I. Say it's so, Joe

The car shouldn't have been on those dirt roads around Theodore Roosevelt National Park near the historic little town of Medora, N.D., but the Mazda RX7 with two Kolpack brothers in the front seat was checking out the outdoor side of life. Earlier in the day, we hiked in hot weather, for seemingly endless miles, to find this "petrified forest" that caught our curiosity.

It was in the late 1980s, mind you, when there was no thought of GPS or cell phones. We saw a map somewhere, and started walking from memory and probably motivated more by the music of the times, and in this case "The Smiths." The dirt trail that was very pronounced for the first hour or two gradually became more of a dirt path and eventually morphed into hardly anything at all.

There's something about western North Dakota that is cleansing to the soul, if you can somehow stay away from the oil scene. Wild horses. Elk. Fox. Deer.

And in the case of the RX7, it was about coming across a herd of bison. The first and lasting impression of the Badlands was staring down a couple of the large fellas and time will never let the lasting feeling go astray. It was fear.

Stay calm, Tatanka.

Before that moment, I had read somewhere how big, round and cumbersome these animals are, but in reality they are rather quick. I really wasn't in the mood to find out how agile that day, but the potential was in my mind. Just don't do anything to get the herd off their rocker and turn the silver RX7 into a silver tin can.

It's not in their modus operandi. American bison are herbivores and their diet consists mainly of grasses. The interesting fact is they have no real predators, mainly because of their size. The young can be at risk to the prairie hunters like wolves and mountain lions but by and large, they do what they do.

Still, there's just something about the look -- the beard, the horns and the thick coat that screams strength. I grew up on the corner of Fifth Avenue and 17th Street South in Fargo, although a rural state, it was still considered an inner-city upbringing. I don't remember the first time I saw a farm but it didn't happen very often, so getting out in the open beauty of the west was a great experience. But somehow, our family was never afraid of seeing what's out there. As a kid, we took our pop-up camper across the country. Dave ran a marathon. I ran five of them – Grandmas in Duluth, Minn., Twin Cities, Chicago, New York and Marine Corps in Washington, D.C. – and still really not sure why, but count one of my biggest life's failures as being on pace in Chicago to qualify for the Boston Marathon, only to hit the proverbial wall in the last few miles, crash and burn. But I still finished.

Bruce grew up in Fargo but Seattle is home and certainly is the family leader in adventure and guts. He's climbed the highest peak on three continents and saw his share of challenges in doing so, including a 20,000-foot peak in the Himalayas. The one rule at home was to never tell mom when he was about to embark on a climb or else she would worry non-stop. Take a trip to Alaska, for instance.

By the time he and his two climbing partners set up their tent on the knife-edged West Buttress of Denali, they had been on the mountain for 12 days. Five days earlier down at Windy Corner, they had made it through the "one bad storm" that every team endures when climbing Denali. Their supplies were plentiful having cached a load at this spot the day before. They were strong and in good health, and the view from this barren camp of rock and ice at an elevation of 16,200 feet was awesome. The airy location of this camp was certainly beautiful, but with 2,000 feet drops on either side, it was also very exposed.

After a hot meal, they settled into their down sleeping bags with thoughts of reaching the summit in two or three days. The arctic night this time of year in the Alaska Range was never dark as the sun only dipped under the horizon for a couple hours. But as the sun was going down, the wind was picking up. By 2 a.m., it sounded like a bison stampede.

The three of them sat in a triangle with their backs against the tent walls to keep it from completely flattening. The looks they gave each other said it all. Not good. The situation was grave. One by one, while the other two held the tent up, they got fully dressed and put on their boots and crampons. One of the four tent poles was already lost, so they had to prepare to bail at any minute. It was time to be strong, like that bison I once saw in Medora.

They were ready to strike camp and head for a more protected location, waiting for the first rays of sun to hit the tent. After a brief debate, the team decided that they didn't want to give up the hard fought ground to get this high, so the plan was to move up to the better protected camp at 17,200 feet known as the "Crow's Nest."

They got out of the tattered tent and surveyed the damage. Since the tent was no longer usable in these conditions, the plan was to dig a snow cave for their next shelter. Or better yet, find an abandoned snow cave at the Crow's Nest. They also discovered that a much-needed backpack and a shovel had blown away. Regardless, they decided to move on ... except for one problem. The wind blowing down the mountain was too strong. They could simply not walk uphill, much less risk the possibility of getting blown off the more exposed sections. A strong cumbersome, bearded animal would have made it, but not these humans.

The team had no choice but to descend. They would spend the next three days down at 14,200 feet, hanging out in an abandoned igloo, regrouping for another attempt. A duffel bag was converted into a makeshift backpack. The tent was to be left behind in favor of cold and cramped (but windproof) snow caves. Tatanka would not quit, nor would they.

Granted, making it out of Denali is much tougher than making it out of an uneducated venture into the Badlands, and we eventually did get back to the historic town of Medora, but not before those thoughts of the bison were permanently etched in my mind.

Bison. Strength. Size. Fear.

I thought I knew "tough" through Bruce and his ascents of some of the tallest peaks in the world. I thought I knew tough by running five marathons. In reality, however, that definition of tough took a backseat to some of these football players who were part of the dynasty. Real toughness was when, halfway through the 2013 season, defensive end Cole Jirik was brushing his teeth and his shoulder fell out of joint. Pain. Slumped to the bathroom floor; hurting like hell.

Three days later he was in the starting lineup.

Maybe that's why North Dakota State won five straight Division I Football Championship Subdivision titles from 2011-2015.

They were farm tough. Some literally so, hardened by a youth spent helping the family make a living off the land. Then they took that work ethic to college. And they did it with a buffalo version of size; they may not look elite fast, but make no mistake, they had speed.

In 2003, Craig Bohl was named the head coach at NDSU and brought his vision of physical football to Fargo, the largest city in the state located on the eastern border. I'll never forget that day because the fan favorite, the favorite with the other NDSU coaches, administrators, current and former players was Casey "Gus" Bradley.

Bradley had the pedigree that athletic director Gene Taylor would want in a head coach. He won a Division II championship as a Bison player in the 1980s. He was smart, one of those all-academic guys. He went on to be a head coach at the Division II level in Colorado. He returned to Fargo as an assistant and was considered an intelligent and masterful defensive mind (this was later proven true when he ascended the ranks in the NFL as an assistant at Tampa Bay, defensive coordinator with Seattle and head coach at Jacksonville). His wife was a great athlete in Bismarck and this couple had Mr. and Mrs. Bison written all over them.

But Taylor went with Bohl.

I was walking into the Bison offices after a basketball game that night when I saw Bradley hastily leaving the building. He looked pissed. Other assistants, most notably Todd Wash, had evidence of tears. One assistant simply gave me the thumbs down and left. Taylor had just delivered the news and a press conference was scheduled the next day to introduce a coach who was previously fired as the defensive coordinator at Nebraska. That day, that night, was a major crossroads in the start of the Division I football journey that morphed into the greatest dynasty in the history of college football. Amazing, if you think about it.

University President Joe Chapman was very frank when he met with Bohl on what needed to be done. When Bohl walked into Chapman's office at Old Main, he showed him a list of schools like Kansas State, Colorado State and Clemson. They were Land Grant institutions just like NDSU, but obviously had higher profile athletic departments. Chapman told Bohl that if NDSU was ever to be viewed in the same academic light, it had to get better at athletics – especially football.

Bohl, privately when looking back at the dynasty, said the marching orders were given. Chapman no longer wanted his school to be viewed as a regional institution and the football program was going to lead the way out of that distinction.

The Bison were 2-8 in 2002 before Bohl got the nod over Bradley. This in a program that won three national championships in the 1960s, five in the 1980s and one in the 1990s. It was those two, Bohl and the freshly scorned Bradley, who would eventually team up to form the nucleus of the reclassification Bison.

It didn't come overnight. Bohl, in searching for assistants, immediately targeted Bradley, but obviously had to win him over. They met constantly over the course of three days, sometimes at obscure, various places around Fargo-Moorhead. They spent time in the skyway that connected the Radisson Hotel to another downtown Fargo building, just the two of them sitting there discussing football philosophy with an occasional beer to whet the appetite. They met at Paradiso Restaurant in south Fargo, where Bohl was amused that Bradley ordered a strawberry daiquiri rather than something like a Jack Daniels on the rocks, you know, a tough-man drink. Bradley was a linebackers coach, after all and with a nickname like Gus, you just don't think strawberry daiquiri.

Gus was a player in 1984 when Bohl was a fledgling assistant coach at NDSU, where he spent just one year. They talked football. They talked personal stuff. Bradley outlined some of the limitations he saw in the program. It didn't take long for Bohl to realize that he had to keep the assistant coach who he got the job over. The program was not in a good place – 13 years removed from its last national title and almost extinct from its national championship glory -- and it needed an overhaul. Bohl knew he needed Bradley to help construct a plan to return NDSU football to prominence.

The bison, remember, went from numbers in the millions in North America to almost extinct at one time. That's darn near what NDSU football felt like to its fans after 2002 – almost extinct. And in some minds, the looming Division I football transition would mean certain death, extinction, to a once proud program.

It wouldn't be the first time. Some programs in NCAA history thrived for a period of time and then just disappeared. The University of Chicago was a founding member of the Big Ten Conference and featured a running back, Jay Berwanger, who was the first recipient of the Heisman Trophy in 1935. It won national championships in 1905 and 1913.

Chicago was coached by Amos Alonzo Stagg, whose name to this day adorns the NCAA Division III championship game.

In 1939, the program was dropped.

Why? As the story goes, the university president considered football and athletics to be a distraction to the student body. Having *athlete* being part of student was just not part of what he saw college being about. He prohibited the head coach from recruiting football players and, well, it wouldn't take long to get the snot beat out of you with that philosophy.

While NDSU fans were hardly thinking measures as drastic as that, the writing was on the wall that the program was in danger of becoming very ordinary, at best. NDSU drew an average of 10,622 fans in the 2002 season. The 18,700-seat Fargodome was quiet. Boring, quite frankly.

But on Aug. 30, 2002, it all changed. That is when Taylor, with Chapman behind him, stepped to the podium at the brand new NDSU Alumni Center and announced the school was going to pursue Division I athletics. Little ol' Fargo was going to give the big arena a try.

As the beat writer for NDSU football since 1995 – and who had been following this program since Ron Erhardt called my father an asshole in front of the entire crowd at a booster club meeting in the late 1960s – I was all for it. I had seen, ever so slowly, the program dwindle from the heyday as I really remember it in the 1980s, with the reduction of scholarships the main culprit.

At one time the Bison were at 45 full rides, which at the time was probably miles more than most Division II schools of that era and a reason for NDSU's dominance. The NCAA slowly chopped that into that 45, however, with the maximum down to 36 in the 1990s. NDSU's talent level dropped accordingly.

Yes, the big, bad Bison were now on the same playing field as many of the other Division II conferences across the country. The tipping point for me was in 2002 when the Bison hosted Augustana College at the Fargodome. You could hear a schnapps bottle drop on the concrete steps of the Fargodome. The place was literally half empty and the atmosphere was worse than that.

The days of Jeff Bentrim, Chad Stark, James Molstre, Mike Favor, Chris Simdorn, Tony Satter, Phil Hansen and all those players who built the Division II dynasty at NDSU was a distant memory. The legendary Hager fell with the

Division II times. He was eventually fired after the 1996 season for not signing a much-publicized "loyalty clause" set out by athletic director Bob Entzion. Those were rough times. It was fascinating to report, but they were some of the low points in program history. Bob Babich did his best taking over the program in 1997, but again, Babich didn't have the full deck of cards that head coaches Don Morton, Earle Solomonson and Hager had in the 1980s and early 90s.

Things had to change. The fact was, the program was suffering, ever so slowly. So slow that many of the big hitters in the NDSU Team Makers booster club refused to acknowledge it.

They were the big, bad Bison after all. Or at least they still held on to that hope.

Isn't a program supposed to be on the "up" when it announces a Division I reclassification? There were those who laughed. There were those who mocked the decision. And after NDSU finished its 2-8 season three months after the announcement, well, let's just say there was a lot of work ahead, not to mention doubts.

It was a five-year transition with 2003-04 being an "exploratory period," meaning if a school wanted to remain in Division II after that season, it could do so without penalty. The first year of Division I post-season eligibility for football was to be 2008 and the general thought in 2002 was that if the program wasn't embarrassing itself by then and was somewhat respectable, well, all the better.

Also consider this: Fargo, North Dakota is geographically isolated in the world of Division I athletics. The closest big time school was the University of Minnesota located 250 miles to the east in Minneapolis. The closest to the south at that time was the University of Nebraska – a seven-hour drive. The closest to the west was Montana State, an entire day's drive. To the north is Canada.

It's not like the long-time boosters in Fargo had a reference point. At the time, the city, the school and its fans had what I called an inferiority complex, mainly because it really had no idea about the level of Division I athletics and I-AA football. Over the course of the reclassification, about 90 percent of the time when we would return from some I-AA destination, the prevailing opinion was usually universal: this is a pretty good place we live in.

"I always saw it as a gem," Chapman said. "In the northern plains, there is nothing that even comes close to what Fargo offers. You have the venue. The Fargodome, the institution, there is no limit where that institution can go in terms of the football program. All of that is crucial to the future of the institution."

Not everybody was on board with Chapman's future. Taylor remembers being in a board room at Pepsi-Cola Inc., and trying to sell the Division I vision to the top Pepsi administrators. Pepsi was a big backer of NDSU. Taylor said Dick Solberg, the CEO of State Bank of Fargo, another staunch Bison backer, was not in favor and Taylor had a couple of meetings with Solberg to try and explain NDSU's dream.

"He was not happy about it," Taylor said. "Some of our staunchest supporters today were adamantly opposed to it. But we just kept telling the same story and talked a lot about the same things Joe did."

And the theme was simple: "Say what you want about athletics," Chapman said, "but we would not been able to gain a national reputation without it, and thereby recruiting students to come there. It all came together."

It came together, especially in football. The one possible reference point, a 2001 game at the Fargodome against Division I-AA University of Maine, was cancelled because of the 9-11 terror attacks. How was this school, this football program, going to compete? NDSU made the move without a conference, meaning it was going to jump in the ranks of being an independent. That's like rowing across the Atlantic in a canoe; independent status is the ticket to mediocrity, at best.

That's why Sept. 6, 2003, was so important. That is the day Division II NDSU traveled to Division I-AA University of Montana, the powerful Grizzlies, and upset them 25-24 on a miraculous second half rally. Before the game, Chapman said he was taunted by some Montana fans, saying it was 25 steps down to his seat and 200 steps out.

"They kept saying that over and over," Chapman said. "I'm behind the bench watching the game and when the game was over, coach Bohl came over and gave me the thumbs up. I turned around and the stands were empty. It wasn't 200 steps out, it was only five."

Over 10 years later, Chapman, retired in Colorado, said that victory over Montana was the turning point for him.

"Absolutely crucial," he said.

When Chapman was privately looking into Division I athletics, from essentially his first day on the job at NDSU, he turned to Montana president George Dennison for guidance and advice.

"He said the first thing you have to do is to get Division I teams to play you," Chapman said. "He said, 'We'll play you.' Then he said, 'We'll kick the crap out of you but we'll play you.'"

Chapman eventually relayed that story to Bohl – the night before the game.

"He said that to you?" Bohl said.

"Yeah," Chapman said.

"We'll see about that," Bohl said.

It was a bizarre game, really. The Grizzlies led 24-2 at halftime and had the look of a team ready to add to its lead in the second half. NDSU, meanwhile, had to get some things done yet to use the trick play they'd been practicing that week. Trick plays are best when their success leaves a mark on a game and the Bison were at least a few scores from the potential pivotal moment.

During a Friday night team meeting with the field goal unit, assistant coach Jeff McInerney went over a fake play where holder John Bonicelli was to flip the football to Rod Malone coming around from the left end. At that point in the meeting, Malone asked McInerney how he would know if he was to run or throw.

"We trust you Rod, go by your feelings," McInerney said.

Bohl, who was standing in the back of the room, thought the appropriate answer was whatever avenue it took to get the first down, which usually is a run-first option, but Bohl reluctantly chose to stay silent and let McInerney do the coaching. The next afternoon, down 24-19 late in the fourth quarter, Bohl called for the fake. The ball had to be on the left hashmark, and it was. Just as he was told in the meeting, Malone came around end and took the pitch from Bonicelli. The Bison running back had plenty of room to run in front of him, but instead, pulled up to throw.

Jamel Thomas, the wide blocker on the right side, was wide open on short flat route, but Malone wasn't thinking short. On the sideline, Bohl just dropped his head, thinking the play was destined for failure. He probably thought back to the Friday meeting when he should have voiced his objection to McInerney's "go by your feelings" advice to Malone. Run, Bohl thought, run the ball on that play.

"But Rod went for the money," McInerney said. "When we practiced it, Rod wasn't the most accurate thrower. It goes to show that at game time, he was the type of kid who could make a play."

The ball sailed to the back of the end zone, where tight end Mike Wieser went horizontal to the turf and dove for the pass. He caught it. Bohl didn't see the catch – and all he heard at that moment was a deafening silence of the hometown crowd. If the win over Montana turned the tide of the Division I momentum for NDSU, that play – that fake field goal -- was the source of it. You can make the argument that NDSU's Division I transition was for all practical purposes launched with 2:13 remaining on the clock at Washington-Grizzly Stadium, with the assist of a last-second Montana missed field goal.

It will never be lost on the Bison players of that era the contributions of Wieser, who died much too young from complications of Wilson's Disease. Perhaps his legacy is the guy who made the play that morphed into an FCS dynasty.

When the Bison returned from Missoula that night, Wieser, riding on the team bus that was leaving Hector International Airport, texted Shane Evert – his roommate who had finished his career a year earlier.

"Did you see that?" Evert said, quoting Wieser's text. "I can't believe it came down to that catch. I just laid out there and it was in my hands and all of a sudden we're ahead."

Wieser got home "and he gave me a big hug," Evert said. "They weren't supposed to win that game. We got down and it looked like we had no chance. Then a trick play, not only a trick play but Mike gave every inch of his body."

Every inch that will have a legacy for years. A signature play in one of many NDSU signature wins, but perhaps that was the biggest that got the Division I train moving.

"That game really brought a lot of people who were opposed to the move to at least being on the fence," Taylor said. "And those who were on the fence were clearly in favor of it because people expected us to go in there and get it handed to us. When we won, I don't want to say it solidified the decision but at least it made it look like it was not that far of a stretch."

In the many months leading up to that game, Chapman battled negativity on the Division I move all over the state, especially at the state legislature. Athletics was part of his quest to move NDSU to an elite research institution on the academic level. Athletics provided visibility and Chapman wasn't interested in the school having a profile only in the Red River Valley.

At a special hearing on Division I athletics with the legislature in Bismarck, one representative got up and chastised Chapman for even thinking about making the move.

"President Chapman, this body is so proud of everything going on at NDSU, we don't want to waste one bit of your precious energy of this silly Division I stuff," he said.

Chapman said he remembers looking at Taylor, as if to say, "Oh no."

"When I look back, that was an important moment," Chapman said.

So Chapman paused, thought about it, and then stood up and addressed the group.

"Mr. Representative, there's good news," Chapman said. "Because I have lots of energy."

At that point, Sen. Dave Nething promptly closed the assembly. Nething was an ally of Chapman and the Division I move and was especially supportive of the fledgling NDSU technology park.

"Bam, that was the end of it," Chapman said. "Those were crucial things."

Also crucial: the state Board of Higher Education keeping its nose out of athletics, something it threatened to do with all of the Division I talk. Chapman said Chancellor Larry Isaak swayed the board to stay away – or the Division I move may never have happened. North Dakota is a conservative state and change does not come without opposition, if change comes at all.

Taylor remembers his part in the lobbying on behalf of the athletic department was rather scripted "because Joe didn't want me getting off topic. We made the promise we would not ask for more state dollars and so I had four or five points that I emphasized. Joe did the majority of the talking. We didn't have a conference and people kept asking what are you going to do about a conference? Things were different back then. We had to prove to everybody that we were serious about this."

That conference problem was a several-year issue, with Chapman initially trying to sway the entire North Central Conference to make the Division I move as a group.

A pinnacle meeting was convened in May of 2002 at Arrowwood Resort hotel in Alexandria, Minn., when representatives from NDSU, South Dakota State, Northern Colorado and the University of South Dakota argued their case for the whole league to move up. Northern Colorado had already announced its Division I intention. The Forum threatened legal action to have the meeting open to the public, but we ultimately backed off, mainly because private schools Morningside and Augustana could argue they're not subjected to open meetings laws.

Anyway, at one point, an unidentified president turned to Northern Colorado president Hank Brown and said, "If you guys plan to do this, then just get out of here." Brown gathered up his papers, closed his portfolio, stood up and said, "You're right. Goodbye." He walked out of the room.

Bam.

Just over three months later, NDSU announced its intention to move to Division I. It took somebody like Joe Chapman who wasn't afraid of change – to make a change.

"He was an aggressive leader that changed the face of North Dakota State forever," said Pat Simmers, NDSU associate athletic director and executive director of Team Makers booster group. "He changed it athletically and he changed it academically. When you insist on change, you're not always popular."

Chapman was the driving force. I'm convinced he'll never get proper credit for what he did for that university, perhaps because of his last year or so in office and the presidential house fiasco that was so damning in the media that it almost erased what he actually did. I'm not here to defend that section of his presidency; it wasn't good.

"The politics were spinning out of control and I'm sure he would admit some of that was on his shoulders," Simmers said.

Chapman became so popular with the students during a stretch of his tenure that they held a "Don't Go Joe" rally when he was considering a position at another school.

"The 'Don't Go Joe' rally steeled him a bit," Simmers said. "You have body armor, you feel you're untouchable and nobody is untouchable. Did I notice that? No, but that was a comment I heard."

Under Chapman, the school raised its academic profile for a research university immensely. It added academic programs, especially at the post-graduate level, at a break-neck pace. Athletically? NDSU won five straight FCS football titles because of Joe Chapman. There is no arguing that. The dynasty is a result of somebody coming into the power chair known as the NDSU president and daring to make change.

"When we first got involved in getting this going, I heard all the time what an incredible record we had in Division II," Chapman said. "I had to spend a lot of time explaining that it was a wonderful legacy but we're going to be coming on the national scene in a way we've never done it before. Even when we got into the Summit League there were still people who thought this was a bad idea; that you're just taking away from the institution. I just tried to talk people through it."

Still to be determined? How to be successful at the Division 1 level. Good luck with that was a prevailing opinion anywhere.

On Jan. 9, 2016, NDSU won its fifth straight FCS championship (Division I-AA changed its name to FCS while NDSU was in the transition). By doing so, it became the first team in the modern era to win five in a row (Yale won six straight from 1879-84). The previous high in FCS was the three in a row won by Appalachian State from 2005-07. It topped the four in six years won by Georgia Southern from 1985-90. There were references to UCLA basketball and the University of Oklahoma, which won 47 straight games from 1953-57. When the national media started getting wind of NDSU's string of titles, it would frequently refer to the Bison as the "Alabama of the FCS." The Crimson Tide went 91-16 and won four national championships from 2007-15. From 2011-15, the most wins in NCAA Division I football were as follows: North Dakota State 71, Alabama 62, Florida State 58, Oregon 57, Clemson 56, Ohio State 56, Stanford 54 and Michigan State 54.

I can't imagine what my father would think today. He wrote the book "Bison Football: Three Decades of Excellence" that was published in 1992. Like me, dad was the beat writer who covered the team from A to Z. He was thorough, he was fair, he was tough if he had to be, he worked hard, he was well respected and he was well-liked. He passed away in 1993 and there were so many times over the years that I wish he was around as a quick Bison football library reference.

In the last few years, my two brothers would from time to time needle me to write the sequel. I balked, but the mountain of resistance started to cave in the weekend of our mother's funeral in October of 2013. Bruce and I went to the Illinois State game – the first and only time I tailgated like a fan (i.e. had a few beers) – and I think it was somewhere in there I felt the family loyalty and obligation in his voice. At that point, I gave the following ultimatum: I'll write the sequel, but only if this team wins four in a row, thinking that the odds of the Bison winning four straight at that point were OK at best.

Everybody knew the train was on its way to Frisco in 2013, and when the Bison got there, title No. 3 arrived much suspense. One year later, both brothers attended an FCS title game for the first time – Dave driving down with a high school classmate and Bruce flying in from Seattle to hang with a couple college friends, who insisted he make the trip.

It was a remarkable game, of course, with NDSU coming from behind to beat Illinois State – the same team that was part of the initial book inspiration – and later Saturday night, I found myself at Scruffy Duffies pub in Plano with the two bros. The conversation went something like this: "All right you little accident (I was the unexpected child), you said if they win four in a row that you were going to write the book. Right?"

I had no answer.

They were right.

So a week later, it started. This project is an attempt to write the sequel -- the Division I sequel. How this program went from 2-8 as an NCAA Division II school in 2002 to an FCS dynasty will forever blow me away. It wasn't supposed to happen. It wasn't supposed to be the next Marshall, Georgia Southern, Youngstown State or Appalachian State. No FCS program was supposed to go 8-3 in its first 11 games against FBS competition, but that's precisely what NDSU did. That included victories over Big Ten and Big 12 conference teams.

So how did it happen?

II. No. 11

It was an odd entrance for the Jacksonville State football team on Jan. 9, 2016, when it took the Toyota Stadium field in Frisco, Texas, in the FCS title game. The Gamecocks came out of their mini-tunnel in single file and it took a fair amount of time before everybody was out. It stalled to the point that the NDSU entrance started before every JSU player reached the field.

Why? Because some of the Jacksonville players were jaw-jacking the Bison players behind the Toyota Stadium stage, where both teams came out of the locker room complex. Probably not a smart move to push the buttons of a four-time champion. As one Bison player put it: "There is only one staircase down to the field from the respective locker rooms in the stadium. Jacksonville was on the way down and we followed closely, within five to six steps. It was a linebacker from Jax that started yelling and talking shit. And they kept yelling and talking smack and it pissed everyone off. All the seniors were in the front so it really pissed us off. Nobody could really understand what he was saying, it was just the fact that he was trying to talk shit before we walked on to the field. I was in the front row and heard him talking shit which really made me mad."

"It just pissed our players off," echoed one Bison coach.

NDSU came out and played like it was pissed off. It was 17-0 before Jacksonville figured out it was in a game. It was 24-0 at halftime and a question that we wondered all week was answered: Will the difference in the level of competition between the Ohio Valley Conference and the Missouri Valley Football Conference be noticeable?

One person close to the program figured NDSU would be able to outcoach the Gamecocks, citing JSU head coach John Grass being just three years removed from the high school level. It appears all factors had some truth to it; JSU adjusted to NDSU's physicality in the second half but by that time it was too late. Final: NDSU 37, Jacksonville State 10.

For the fifth time, the Bison throng stormed the Toyota Stadium field. They had one more night to turn the bars in Plano like Ringos, Scruffy Duffies and Wild Pitch into their personal party spots. It was a strange visiting crowd for Jacksonville, which brought a fair amount of fans to the game, probably about 5,000, but not once did I see anybody wearing red and white wandering around sampling the suburban nightlife. A big reason is by then NDSU fans had long ago figured out how to commandeer all the hotels within the two suburbs. Whatever the case, the win put NDSU into the history books of college football.

"To do this in Division I football is probably one of the more remarkable things that any of us are ever going to see," said Tom Burnett, the commissioner of the Southland Conference that hosts the FCS title game. "To see a program do this at such a high level, it's almost like they are programmed for this regardless of maybe a stumble or two during the regular season. It's almost a shrug of the shoulders that we expect them to come back. They are a remarkable story."

Make no mistake, there were a couple of stumbles during the regular season. A loss to the University of South Dakota in the middle of October was striking in that the Bison didn't give away the game because of turnovers like they did in 2012 when quarterback Brock Jensen threw two pick-sixes in a loss to Indiana State. NDSU was actually a plus-two in that department. No, the alarming thing was the Coyotes just flat-out beat the Bison and for the first time in 26 games, NDSU lost at home. For the first time in a long time, the Bison were acting like a more normal team than the juggernaut of the previous four seasons.

The defeat dropped the Bison to 4-2 overall and for the first time since 2010, they had lost more than one game in a season. The result was a snapshot of just how spoiled a good section of the fan base had become. Klieman was getting emails that were not kind. I got three emails and an actual real letter blaming my column the day before the game for firing up USD, a piece where I said the school's late entry into Division I athletics combined with the strength of the Missouri Valley was poor timing and made success a tough proposition. I pointed out a couple of facts to back up the statement: the Coyotes won just three league games since it joined the Valley in 2012. It was on a 14-game conference losing streak. There is no chance that column was the impetus for USD upsetting the Bison that day in the Fargodome, but if it was, then head coach Joe Glenn owed me a word of thanks.

"Congratulations Kolpack! You just joined the ranks of Mike McFooley (McFeely). Why don't you write a column every week that the Bison's opponent can put on their locker room bulletin board for that extra boost of motivation. Be sure to tell them that they suck and they will never be more than they are. What a moronic thing for you to do. Why don't you crawl back into the hole you came out of, you asshat munchkin."

That same letter writer would strike later in the season, calling me a munchkin cueball, a phrase that I tried to get trending on Twitter.

Anyway, the reason the Coyotes beat the Bison were twofold: NDSU had just finished three straight rivalry games of sorts with the first meeting with UND since 2003, the Dakota Marker game at South Dakota State and the always fierce game with Northern Iowa. The UND game, of course, was the renewal of the rivalry that last played in 2003. We did so many pre-write stories on the history of the game that I got bored with them by Friday. I swear hardly a day went by when a local TV station didn't replay that Jim Kleinsasser touchdown pass in 1995 that showed the big UND tight end pulling away from the Bison secondary at the Fargodome.

As for the USD game, Klieman said he could see a possible upset "from a million miles away." And, for the first time since 2010, the Bison were a young team that was susceptible to being inconsistent.

Susceptible -- even with Carson Wentz at quarterback.

The news got worse on Sunday when Wentz got confirmation that a bone in his right wrist was broken. Initial X-rays taken in the Bison locker room complex after the game didn't reveal much, but the better technology at Sanford Health revealed otherwise. I first heard something was up on Sunday night, but couldn't confirm anything. Rumors hit the Bison fan site on Monday and I started getting text messages and emails wondering if they were true. The rumors varied from Wentz getting hurt duck hunting to punching a wall in the locker room after the game.

The reality is he fell on it wrong the second series of the game after throwing a pass, something he dismissed as a sprain and played through it. It turned out to be the most-often asked question for the remainder of the season. When will Carson return? Will he be back for the playoffs? Will he be back for the national title game?

His surgery with Sanford hand specialist Jason Erpelding was a day a lot of folks at the hospital won't forget. It was becoming obvious by now that those in the medical field who were dealing with Wentz were handling a player who had NFL promise and the hospital knew it. Before Wentz entered the clinic, hospital officials held a meeting telling everybody who would be around Wentz that day to not advertise who was coming in for surgery.

"You're supposed to act like he's not here," said one employee. "It was just different that day. It was quiet. It was not a normal day."

In the break room, there were employees watching the news on TV, with one of the stories being Wentz's surgery. A few took note that the surgery seemed to take longer than usual, which didn't seem like a good thing.

"The guy was kind of a big deal," one employee said.

NDSU, meanwhile, had to forge on with freshman quarterback Easton Stick.

The kid could move, there was no denying that. He burned Indiana State and Southern Illinois with his legs in his first two games and then he led a last-minute touchdown drive to defeat Youngstown State, a game in which YSU head coach Bo Pelini lost his cool.

Pelini came to Youngstown after getting fired by Nebraska the previous season with the reputation of blowing his lid at any point. That's exactly what happened on a pass interference call on the Penguins that set up the Bison touchdown with 35 seconds left, one that Pelini took issue with by getting in the face of the officials. He drew two unsportsmanlike conduct penalties, making for an easy column for Forum sports editor Kevin Schnepf. When asked in the postgame news conference what he thought of the pass interference call, Pelini said in a cold-faced manner: "It's pretty obvious, isn't it? After a long pause, Pelini then looked at Schnepf: "What were your thoughts on the pass interference call?"

When asked if the officials gave him an explanation, Pelini said: "No .... they didn't give me an explanation on anything. There is no explanation." When asked why the officials flagged him for the two unsportsmanlike penalties, Pelini said: "They didn't like the way I was talking to them. Because I told them ....well, I'm not going to get into it."

Pelini had proven his loose cannon status. Earlier in the day, WDAY sports director Dom Izzo and I had the Nebraska beat writer on our Kolpack & Izzo radio show, and he went on to describe Pelini's time in Lincoln as dysfunctional, a word he repeated three or four times. The guy can coach, but other parts of the program were a bit off kilter, he said.

So, I was curious to see him in action. And we got the full Monty. The problem with his tirade is he prevented his team from a chance to rally. The Penguins returned the ensuing kickoff to their 30-yard line and had 29 seconds remaining to get in field goal range. Two medium-range pass plays – and that team had the athletes to do it – and you can give your record-setting kicker a shot.

But Pelini cost his team 15 yards before the first play. On fourth down, Pelini got flagged for another 15-yarder. Not only was the head coach going nuts on the ref, but assistant coach Carl Pelini, Bo's brother, was doing the same. You would have thought perhaps some level-headed assistant would have pointed to Bo to calm down and give the players a chance to decide the game.

It wasn't long before one of my favorite Twitter writers -- @FauxPelini – posted this: "Have you ever had one of those days where you get 2 personal fouls in the last 30 seconds of the football game you're coaching." FauxPelini is the fake twitter account of Bo Pelini, run by a man nobody really knows, only that he is a Chicago-based lawyer who once gave an interview only by his middle name: Michael. He gave an interview to ESPN, but only if his name was not given and his identity concealed – like one of those TV interviews with a mobster in the witness protection program.

Anyway, the Missouri Valley reprimanded Pelini, a move that I'm guessing was met with a chuckle from Pelini. The 27-24 Bison win in the next-to-last game in the regular season set the Bison up for another Missouri Valley title and a postseason run, thanks to a high seed that would mean home field advantage in the playoffs. But before postseason even began, the Bison learned on selection Sunday the FCS playoff committee was going to make it as difficult as it could on NDSU, and the Missouri Valley in general. All five league teams selected for the 24-team playoffs were put on the same side of the bracket, a direct uppercut at league teams NDSU and Illinois State making the title game the previous year.

There were some real head scratchers, like UND being left out of the field despite an FBS win and a 7-4 record, while Eastern Illinois getting a bid with the same record despite not beating anybody. It was a day when we were introduced to the "quality loss," such as Jacksonville's overtime loss to Auburn and Illinois State's loss to Iowa. NDSU won the Missouri Valley autobid by virtue of a tiebreaker and beat the highest common opponent in South Dakota State while the Redbirds lost to the Jackrabbits. But ISU got the No. 2 seed and NDSU No. 3. It didn't make sense.

Getting a top two seed is huge because the home field advantage in the playoffs is so statistically stacked. From 2009-15, no FCS champion ever went on the road. And if NDSU was to win a fifth straight, it would first have to go through Montana, then probably Northern Iowa and finally a semifinal game at Illinois State. The first two happened; the third scenario did not.

***

Wentz uncharacteristically went dark with the media in the playoffs, with either he or the coaching staff, or both, denying requests to be interviewed. I didn't like it but there was nothing I could do about it. Klieman liked playing that will-he-play-or-not game, making it tougher on an opponent to prepare for the Bison. He liked the fact that Jacksonville State had to think about two quarterbacks in advance of the title game.

Adding spice to the theory: Would Wentz's NFL handlers even want him to risk an injury? Privately, one prospective agent said he wanted him to play in the championship game, so he wouldn't be rusty for the Senior Bowl at the end of January. Even those folks close to the program who didn't mind leaking a hint or two were tight-lipped about whether Wentz was even taking reps in practice. Klieman said he wasn't involved in Wentz's dealings with the NFL folks, leaving that up mainly to Doug Wentz, his father.

Privately, his agent-to-be – Ryan Tollner of Rep 1 Sports in Irvine, Calif. – told Carson that he thought it would be in his best interests to play the game.

"He asked my opinion about it," Tollner said. "I felt like he should go for it. I know there was a lot of risk and it might sound counter-intuitive, but ultimately through the draft process you never know what will happen. I said, look, if you go back to that championship game and win the game, that's something nobody can take from you. I also think it's a statement to NFL teams what you're all about. You don't play the game for money or recognition; you play for the love of the game, your teammates, your coaches and the fan base. Go win a championship; let that define you."

Two weeks before the title game, Wentz looked full-go, with the only remaining hitch a CT scan scheduled for the Monday prior to the title game. It came out clean, but publicly, NDSU still was not naming a starting quarterback. How you keep those things quiet in this day and age of social media is beyond me, but the Bison did one fine job of it.

"It's extremely difficult," Klieman said. "It's interesting. Our kids are pretty savvy and pretty smart. We didn't emphasize it to the team, don't say anything about that or don't say anything about this. They know. That's why a lot of the kids are in the program here for four and five years. The kids that are in the program like a Joe Haeg, will tell a young kid, 'This stays in here.' That's why you close the practice and stuff, why you want to make sure when you're in the bubble, nobody can get in there anyway. With closed practices, you can do a lot of things. I wanted to make sure it wasn't a media circus for the guy, so he could do the work and get ready to play."

The head coach was under no mandate to release his starting lineup or injury report, unlike the NFL. Grass said he would have done the same thing. JSU prepared for both Wentz and Stick, so it's not like they would be caught off guard, but perhaps they spent more time on Stick than maybe they would have liked? It's the game behind the game in football. The good news was at least I didn't have to ask the question anymore. I was tired of it. Klieman was tired of it. "You know, it's been a little tiring," he said. "There's no question about that. I think everybody understands the realm of when he was cleared to truly throw was back — or come back to practice and throw was I think the first playoff game with UNI. He was throwing. You guys realize, he was doing just what we said. He was throwing at that time. Then each week he probably progressed a little bit more. Even to the point of the last doctor's appointment. Those were all planned out that he had had for months. We knew if we could get through the semifinal game, there was a great chance that he would play or be able to play. We won the semifinal game, had a couple of days before Christmas that he and I visited." Wentz was his usual self in the title game, completing 16 of 29 passes for a touchdown and running for two more, one a nifty move to the sideline where he sidestepped a Jacksonville defensive back and dove the last five yards to the end zone pylon. It reached a point during the game that Dallas Cowboy fans in the area were tweeting Jerry Jones to draft Wentz in the first round.

Wentz's last ode to his college days came that night when he flew to Irvine with a tweet that got a lot of traffic:

"First off, I have to thank the good Lord for the many blessings I have in my life. Next, thank you to my family. They have always been my biggest fans and I wouldn't be where I am without them. Thank you coaches. Every single one of you deserves more credit than you receive. Personally, you've all pushed me to be the best that I can be and most importantly, you believed in me. That can trump anything and I am so grateful for the coaches I had at NDSU – and the coaches of my younger days. Thank you teammates. You guys that have been my teammates at some point in the last 4.5 years, I love you guys. You guys are my brothers for life. I'll miss going to battle with you. And lastly, thank you Bison Nation and the Fargo community. You guys truly are the best fans in the world. The support you provide us is unbelievable. You make the game so much more fun and provide us the energy we need on game days, and the support and encouragement we need every other day. Fargo, you have been awesome,

4.5 amazing years of my life. I wouldn't trade it for the world. As I go on to the next chapter of my life, the one phrase that keeps ringing in my head is, 'Once a Bison, Always a Bison,' and it couldn't be more true. Thank you everybody and God Bless."

The fact Wentz flew right to Irvine was testament that there was no waiting around. That was the M.O. of Bison pro prospects in the five title years: after the game, it was immediately off to a training destination. There would be no partying with the guys in Fargo.

Signing with Rep 1 was the culmination of about 12 months of research and work by Doug Wentz. It wasn't long after the 2014 title game when Carson asked his dad for assistance, sensing the load of prospective agents was getting too much to handle.

"Carson at that point said, 'Hey dad, I need some help, do what you can,'" Doug said.

There were plenty of agents who wanted a place in line. Doug said he got so many calls that he wasn't able to return all of them. Tollner was one of two finalists and the fact he had such a strong quarterback pedigree made him a good fit for Wentz. Among his quarterback clients at the time were Ben Roethlisberger of the Pittsburgh Steelers, Marcus Mariota of the Tennessee Titans and Blake Bortles of the Jacksonville Jaguars. Tollner's uncle, former USC and San Diego State head coach Ted Tollner, was long known as a guru-type level of quarterbacks coach.

It was a strange season in NFL hype for Wentz, who in August and September was considered by most draft experts as a second- or third-round pick and the fifth-best available quarterback coming out of college. Then he missed almost three months and his stock actually went up. By the time he signed with Tollner, guys like Mel Kiper Jr. had him going in the first round. It was still early in the process however, with the Senior Bowl and NFL Combine up ahead yet.

Those two events went off better than expected. The kid from Bismarck, N.D., was all of a sudden the hottest thing in the NFL Draft talk. And the stock of offensive lineman Haeg was also going up. A walkon from Brainerd, Minn., turned in a productive NFL Combine performance and was getting his name in the draft circles.

There used to be an off-season in this job of covering the team. No longer. Bison football: The story that kept on giving.

***

It was an amazing journey for both Haeg and Wentz, really. Wentz went from a projected middle round draft choice his junior year to being considered as a possible No. 1 overall pick in the weeks leading up to the draft. It was a national story -- even international for that matter.

It goes to show that good guys can finish first and the state of North Dakota could not have hand-picked a better sports ambassador. The rear-window decals that once adorned his silver Chevrolet Silverado pickup were probably all you needed to know about his inner circle. An NDSU logo sat on the lower left corner and a depiction of a duck was on the lower right. In the middle, and significantly larger than the other two decals, was a cross.

Wentz's schedule since that FCS title game was nothing short of CEO-hectic for the star quarterback, who flew across the country more than once and talked with more NFL coaches and administrators than he could probably count. They dissected practically every year of his life and looked under every rock of his background, leaving nothing to chance. He faced more questions than a congressional hearing.

His name was now second nature to millions of football fans, and he went from being able to wander around a sporting goods store unabated in Fargo to being recognized through a door window in some obscure hotel in Los Angeles. He was on a first-name basis with the state of North Dakota. Through it all, three things remained a constant and he saw them in his rearview mirror in college every time he got in his pickup:

Bison.

Hunting.

Jesus.

Quarterback is a complex position but the man at center stage in this case led a simple life.

Perhaps a major reason he got there: a spiritual enlightenment his freshman year at NDSU when this kid from Bismarck took his faith to another level thanks to some Bison football players. "You raise the young man to go to church, but a little light came on his freshman year," said Doug Wentz. "He tackles that just like he does buying a hunting dog. He learns and he digs."

I normally don't write about the faith thing with athletes, mainly because it comes up more often than you think and you're never certain of the sincerity factor. Some players seem to talk about playing for their Lord because it sounds like something they should say. I never sensed that with Carson, mainly because he kept it to himself for the most part.

He wasn't carrying a Bible around when he first arrived to Bison football fall camp as a freshman, but it didn't take long before his spiritual path veered that direction. He remembered the day, almost to the minute, when then-senior quarterback Dante Perez struck up a conversation while both were stretching before practice.

"My head was spinning, I had just learned new language in install meetings and Dante says, 'Hey, ever read the Bible?' " Wentz said. "I'm like, 'We're at football practice, not right now.' Then we started talking, ended up meeting and he kind of mentored me in my faith for about a year. Dante was huge, I owe him a lot."

The two would spend several lunch hours in fall camp talking about religion. In retrospect, Perez said he didn't think Wentz at the time had an NFL look to him by any means. "But where I liked this kid, where I thought he was going to be special, was when you looked deeper into him than just football," Perez said. "I saw a genuine heart as a person. His character, that's what stood out to me. He obviously had the physical talent with his height and stature, but for me, I think that hunger to learn more and want more from his faith is what stood out to me."

Perez came to NDSU along with receiver Titus Mack from California. Mack came back into Wentz's life when Wentz started working out in Irvine, where the former Bison receiver happened to be living. Quarterbacks are always in the need to find receivers to throw to and Mack was still trying to make a go of it in the pro game. In Mack, Wentz reunited with somebody he could trust. "I personally reminded him, 'Listen, don't get caught up in all the hype' and he knows this," Mack said.

Meanwhile, back in Bismarck, hardly a week went by in those few months when somebody from outside of North Dakota hadn't flown in to look into this FCS quarterback who hardly anybody in the NFL circles knew a year earlier. Ron Wingenbach, his head coach at Century High School, talked to about 10 NFL teams and several national media outlets who were doing background work on Wentz. A couple of NFL teams and several national media outlets phoned his Century basketball coach Darin Mattern.

"It's funny, it seemed like no matter who, they were all trying to find mud on Carson," Mattern said. "My answer to that was consistent. You're going to be looking for a long time, because I don't think there's anything out there. Carson has always been able to keep an even keel. I'm so proud of how the kid has been able to stay humble. He hasn't changed his humanistic values."

Reporters would have had a hard time finding an overdue library book on the kid. Doug Wentz said he was not surprised, considering the national scrutiny that his son had faced those three months and will in the future. As a reminder of staying the course, Carson has a "AO1" tattooed on the underside of his right wrist, which stands for "Audience Of One" in reference to playing for his Lord. Ironically, he had it done a couple of weeks before he broke his wrist against South Dakota.

"It was kind of a motto I picked up early in my career, and I finally put it on my body just to live the Lord as my audience," Wentz said, "whether it was playing football, going to school or whatever I'm doing in my life."

Wentz was debating whether to attend the draft in Chicago for the longest time, but ultimately made the decision about two weeks before the event. By then, a couple of moves cemented his decision to do so: the Los Angeles Rams making a trade with the Tennessee Titans for the No. 1 pick and the Philadelphia Eagles making a move for the second overall selection.

It was also becoming obvious that Cal's Jared Goff and Wentz were going to become the top two taken, since no team makes those types of moves to draft an offensive lineman. In Wentz, the most often-asked question was how did he get to that standing?

The answer is he passed every test. He led his team to two national titles. He handled himself like a leader at the Senior Bowl. At the Combine, he crushed the Wonderlic Test, threw well and ran a 4.77-second 40-yard dash, not bad for a guy who was almost 6-6 and 237 pounds. At his Pro Day at the Fargodome, he was spot-on with ESPN and the NFL Network in attendance. One month later, he was a featured player at the NFL Draft.

Those two days in Chicago were something else. Wednesday was more of an appearance day for the 25 invited players. The West Chicago City Center was the appointed media hotel, where I ran into one of 30 employees from Nike who wanted to know about the client it had just signed the previous week.

Later, an Eagles fan plopped himself down on the bar stool next to me like only an Eagles fan can, and proceeded to ask about this Carson Wentz fellow from North Dakota State. He was told one of the quarterback's favorite hobbies is to hunt.

"So he uses a gun and shoots things," the Philadelphia fan says. "I like him already."

Philadelphia takes its Eagles seriously. It's blue-collar. It's a working man's team. It's Vince Papale from the movie "Invincible." And when it came to the Jared Goff versus Carson Wentz mystery on which team will take Goff and which will take Wentz, it really wasn't a mystery in my mind. Goff was the California blond who looks like he should play in California with the Rams. Wentz was the rural-state redhead whose hard-working reputation fit in much better with the Philadelphia fans. Certainly, those attributes were something the Eagles took into account when they traded up to the second pick, said Mike Mayock of the NFL Network.

Mayock knows the Philadelphia fan base because he lived it – his father was a high school and college coach in the city. "They're passionate and they care, and I think Carson Wentz is going to appeal to them," Mayock said. "He has that

Midwestern value and work ethic. He'll come in and give you an honest day's work."

I heard that work-ethic question a lot being on radio shows across the country. Every sports show wanted to know about Carson and the beat guy was an easy call. The Philadelphia radio and online folks wondered about his work ethic.

My standard response: Let me tell you something about work ethic. These kids get up at 5:30 in the morning during winter when the temperatures can be well below zero. They do that in the summer, too, when a lot of college kids party until the middle of the night.

"Just the summer in general I think was the toughest time to go through and is what breeds the attitude we had," said Mike Hardie, a defensive lineman and former teammate of Wentz's. "I always saw stories leading up to the draft about guys who say they had to take three classes in the summer and work out and it was the hardest times of their life. They also have rent paid for them, meals cooked for them, and weight rooms with AC. Most of our players' summer went like this: 5:30 a.m. workout, work from 8 a.m.to 4 p.m. Run at 5:30 p.m., then 7 on 7s until 8:30. Not only did we have 15-hour days, but we were expected to do all that while cooking our own meals, paying for our own groceries, and paying our own rent. I always worked a second job on the weekends at a bar or restaurant so I could buy groceries and get free food while I worked. That was the time of year where you get toughened up I always thought."

Hardie worked the graveyard shift one summer at Perkins Restaurant, usually between 8 p.m. until 4 a.m., meaning he probably slept an hour at the most before getting up to lift. So Hardie wasn't surprised that Wentz looked more like a seasoned FBS guy at the draft than a so-called small-town QB.

The Auditorium Theatre at Roosevelt University in Chicago looks and smells like history, with ornate columns and architecture that looks like it would have taken 20 years to build more than 100 years ago. Walk into the place when hardly anybody is home and you can almost feel the ghosts. Wentz will never forget it.

What went down that Thursday night was historic – just like the theater where NFL Commissioner Roger Goodell, after the usual chorus of boos for him, announced the Bison quarterback as the second pick in the draft by the Eagles. Wentz joined the likes of Fargo's Roger Maris as legendary state sports figures – and he had been an NFL player for less than a day. That's how big this draft is. What was really bizarre: Almost four months of working out for NFL teams came down to 10 minutes – the amount of time each team gets to pick.

"It was surreal, it went really quick," Wentz said afterward. "It was so cool getting that phone call and talking to everybody in the organization and hearing how excited they are. And to think what happened for them to get to that spot and believing in me that much. I'm all smiles now."

The Eagles traded several draft picks to move from No. 8 to No. 2 and get in position to take what they believe will be their franchise quarterback.

"I couldn't ask for a better place to go," Wentz said.

In his first interview immediately after the pick, in an on-stage two-question exchange with Deion Sanders, Wentz said the phrase "go to work" twice – something that will endear him to a blue-collar fan base.

"They're going to see a competitor who is passionate about the game," Wentz said. "The hardest worker out there. You'll see a leader and a guy who knows what's going on. I'll be the first one in and the last one out."

There are three types of people at an NFL Draft: the well-dressed (the players' parents), the very well-dressed (the players) and the FANatics who wear NFL team jerseys and are already wondering how good of a fantasy quarterback Wentz will be. I've never been to an Academy Awards but this had to be pretty close, especially with the red carpet entrance that started at 4:45 p.m. and lasted until about 6:15.

The fashion statements were entertaining, with the likes of Ohio State running back Ezekiel Elliott cropping his buttoned-down shirt in half – it was concealed by his suit coat – because that was his uniform style on the football field.

Wentz? He went the more conservative route with a charcoal gray suit, yellow tie and green handkerchief, the latter two probably a tribute to his school colors. It was tailored at a cost of around $3,000 and considering he was part of a JC Penney endorsement commercial with Michael Strahan on Twitter earlier in the day was a pretty good clue to his retail taste.

"It's a game day atmosphere right now in the state of North Dakota," said Bison head coach Chris Klieman, who also got the red carpet treatment. "It's a great day. They're going to get a first-class guy."

It was a first class story.

The text message conversation was struck with former Bison quarterback Steve Walker a week before the draft: Who would get their number retired first: you or Carson Wentz? Both wore No. 11.

"Well, that is a great question my good man," Walker replied. "My mom would say me. My guess is she may be in the big time minority though."

Yes Steve, I'm afraid she is.

But you certainly had your day.

III. Show me the money

The Fargo Country Club has been around for much longer than Carson Wentz and Steve Walker combined and has seen its share of nostalgic moments in the history of Fargo. For instance, one of the pioneers of professional women's golf, Beverly Hanson, grew up in Fargo and got her start at the Country Club. She went on to win 17 professional tournaments and three majors in the 1950s including the first-ever winner of the LPGA Championship in 1955. Unfortunately and somewhat tragically, time forgot about Bev until Jim Dixon walked into The Forum one day in 2014 and said she died the previous week in California and, as a former high school classmate of Bev at Fargo Central, wanted to pay for an obituary.

My first response was simple. Who? In retrospect, it was very embarrassing to my newspaper in general and me in particular to not know who Bev was and what she accomplished. The Country Club also forgot about her, relinquishing a portrait of her to a small, out-of-the-way hallway.

Let's hope time doesn't forget Art Bunker.

Like Beverly, Art was a pioneer of sorts only his contribution was in a field that NDSU desperately needed: fundraising. Art and Erv Inniger were on the 17th tee box of the Country Club one day when the hole was stacked with golfers, so they had to wait in the golf cart while others teed off. Erv, ever the opportunistic fundraiser, thought it was the perfect opportunity to ask his friend for a big gift.

"I think you can give NDSU a million," Erv told him, throwing it straight at him straight up without much warning.

Bunker chuckled.

After a pause, Art turned to Erv: "You're not kidding, are you," he said.

There was another pause.

"What do I get?" said Bunker, gazing at the fairway and who by the way is not one for the public eye with such ventures and therefore probably didn't care what he really "got" for a financial gift.

"The (Physical Education Building, formerly the Old Fieldhouse) needs to be named after you," Inniger said.

Bunker eventually agreed to the $1 million donation on the premise that his old college basketball coach at NDSU, Chuck Bentson, be part of the deal. Then-President Jim Ozbun agreed and told Inniger that Bentson Bunker Fieldhouse "sounds good to me."

A short while later, Art Bunker became NDSU's first-ever million-dollar donor to athletics.

There was more where that came from and Inniger, as the associate athletic director for external fundraising, was a driving wheel. So was Team Makers' Pat Simmers. So was Jim Miller, the executive director of the NDSU Development Foundation and NDSU Alumni Association. So was Gene Taylor. So was Craig Bohl. You just don't go from 36 scholarships to 63 in a matter of three years without a handful of motivated worker bees doing the heavy lifting.

"The toughest five years of my life were the five years we went through the transition," said Inniger, a successful NDSU basketball coach before moving into the administrative world. "Right behind that, they were also the most rewarding. And I coached a lot of big wins."

Inniger was tough to turn down. And he was relentless. When he spurred the movement for naming rights to the new minor league baseball park in Fargo in the mid-1990s, his first 22 asks resulted in rejections. Also know this about Inniger: when somebody says no, his first question is: When can I come back? Of the 22 people who turned him down, the 15th was advertising billboard magnate Harold Newman. After coming across some capital as the result of selling a venture, Inniger said, Newman came back to him. And that's how Newman Outdoor Field became a summer staple for Fargo-Moorhead RedHawks fans for many years thanks to $1.5 million paid over three years by Harold. Sadly, he passed away in 2014 but if you were to walk up to any of the Newman family members today they would tell you it was one of the best investments they ever made.

***

Pat Simmers grew up as one of 12 children in Grand Forks, N.D. in a house that didn't have 12 bedrooms, and certainly not a bed for every kid. What he did have is three meals a day, a roof over his head and somebody to fight with.

Simmers' wife, Susie Simmers, could light up a room with her eyes and smile from a football field away. Wheelchair-bound with multiple sclerosis, her husband was always by her side. If NDSU was looking for a Team Makers executive director to help guide the program through a transition – someone who understood unwavering loyalty and devotion -- he was the right guy. It took some toughness to raise funds for scholarships and Division I athletics. Making it tougher still was the recession of 2008 that jabbed eastern North Dakota, generally considered recession-proof because of the agricultural and manufacturing economy. From 2008 to 2010, the United States Department of Labor documented a loss of 8.7 million jobs. We felt it at The Forum, laying off around 30 percent of the downtown building and most of it happened in one frightening day.

They don't want to hear that in athletics, but the Bison decided to make the big Division I financial move instantly – even if they were struggling for money at the time. The athletic department had a nice cash cow going in para-mutual horse racing that produced about $400,000 a year. So in 2004, the books looked to be on the verge of being balanced despite the D1 framers making the decision to go from the Division II maximum of 36 scholarships to the Division I-AA max of 63 as soon as possible.

"Then came the Susan Bala debacle," Simmers said. "That balanced budget automatically became a significant deficit."

The simulcast company Fargo Racing Services, of which Bala was president, was under federal investigation for under-reporting bets and back taxes. The North Dakota Attorney General's office removed Bala from day-to-day operations of the company, essentially ending NDSU's tie to racing funds as one of the two main charities. Bala was eventually indicted for taking in $99 million in illegal horse wagers.

NDSU, meanwhile, needed to find other sources of revenue and find it fast. So it came up with Circle of Champions campaign with the hope of finding donors to immediately fund athletic scholarships, which at the time were $9,700 a year for a full ride.

There are no ifs, ands or buts; you don't build a Division I football dynasty on the cheap. There was to be no dipping the big toe into the water and gradually getting wet. It was an all-out head-first dive with no reservation. NDSU was going to get to 63 full scholarships as quickly as it could.

It sounds simple, but for a Team Makers booster group that was stuck somewhat in a rut at raising about $750,000 a year for several years, the task seemed even more daunting. And it just wasn't Team Makers, either. This was to be an all-out effort by the NDSU Development Foundation led by Miller, Inniger and his resources and Simmers and, well, the entire football program in general.

***

At least early in his Bison coaching career, Bohl thought nothing of sitting down with boosters, anywhere, to raise funds for scholarships. More often than not, if a booster gave $1,000 to the program, Bohl was able to double that in the name of Division I football. Originally, when Bohl took the job, the plan was for NDSU to reach 63 scholarships within five years. Bohl, however, wanted to reach the Division I-AA 63 in just two years.

He got his wish. And he worked at it, too.

"Craig could work a room better than anybody," Inniger said. "That was the D1 mentality. Most of them know they have to fundraise because if they don't it will be hard for them. Craig was the master of masters. He could get in your pocket. A lot of times, I didn't need Craig to ask, I just needed him to be there so I could ask. If I brought Craig in a room, are you going to say no in front of

Craig? Those are the things that we used. I didn't ask if I were getting say a $1,000 gift but if I needed a big gift? To this day he stays in close contact with some of those donors. One of them gave him a horse when he got the Wyoming job. Craig would tell me that if he was recruiting out in Dickinson or Minot that he would be available if there was a donor he needed to see."

Those stories were common everywhere within the department. And speaking of being everywhere; that was Inniger. The one fact nobody realized about this Division I move is it opened up the rest of the country to fundraising. In the Division II days, nobody in Arizona or Florida really cared to donate because they never saw the end result. They got some mail from NDSU, but that was about it. With Division I, specifically ESPN and internet streams, football games in the Fargodome suddenly were directly connected to the donors anywhere in the country.

Inniger was in charge of raising funds for the athletic endowment, but he got stretched in other avenues with the Division I move. In the second year of Division I athletics in 2004-05, it was looking like that the athletic department was going to be about $250,000 short of breaking even (this was separate from the Team Makers goal of funding scholarships). Certainly, the loss of the horse racing funds didn't help. On the department's annual Arizona fundraising trip in February, Inniger and Taylor asked Bunker for $100,000 more.

"Art said, 'You got it, but don't come back,'" Inniger said. "Of course, I went back."

Once back in Fargo and still short, Inniger and Taylor arranged for a luncheon of about 25 donors like Goldmark founder Jim Wieland and longtime booster Ed Tyson at the Fargodome. Inniger said they raised $200,000 that day and for the most part, the athletic department never ran in the red again during its formulation and implementation of the FCS dynasty.

Inniger didn't do it alone, frequently taking his wife Linda along to help with the fundraising strategy. They got good at it, too. She would help run golf tournaments. She would help the spouse of a male donor in the kitchen while at somebody's home for dinner. She would help run interference if Erv needed to be alone with a donor to ask for money.

"I would tell her I need you to distract the spouse because I need to get to him," Erv said.

She knew if Erv was struggling with a name of a potential donor, so she would introduce herself to that donor. In the first two years of Division I fundraising, Erv once spent 21 days in Arizona, came home for three days, and then left for another 15 days. On average in 2004 and 2005, he figures he was gone 12 out of 14 nights. It didn't matter where, either. Erv developed key relationships in Florida with powerful attorney Irv Meyers and his brother, Frank Meyers. The first time he traveled to Orlando, Fla., and talked with Irv was fruitful. "I walked into his office and he wrote out a check for $10,000 even before any discussion," Inniger said.

Chapman, certainly, was not far from the fundraising trail, either. Inniger is on the side that Chapman was the best thing that ever happened to North Dakota State, both athletically and academically. Whenever Inniger needed an assist from the president, Chapman never hesitated.

"I could bring a donor in and we would have lunch in his office," Inniger said. "I think we were 99 percent successful. He was never a cheap date. He was always willing to do stuff like that. I had to do the asking, but if I brought you in Joe's office, do you think you would get out of there alive?"

NDSU's athletic budget went from $6 million to $7.7 million in 2004. At $7.7, NDSU had the third-highest budget of the previous 12 schools that officially landed in Division I, in an analysis compiled by The Forum. By comparison, South Dakota State's budget that year, also its first in Division I, was projected at $5.5 million. Northern Colorado, which just finished its first season in Division I, projected its next year's budget at about $4.5 million. Both were frequent NDSU opponents. Compared with the eight established schools in the Big Sky Conference at the time, NDSU's budget ranked third highest behind the University of Montana, at $9 million, and Montana State, at $8 million.

Taylor said finding revenues in the $7.7 million range for a Division I program was a better proposition than raising what he would estimate to be a $6.5 million budget if NDSU remained in Division II. Total spending on athletics – including tuition, salaries and scholarships – went up in the largest increments in the athletic program's history. Total scholarships went from 91 to 140½. Football, of course, got the largest boost going from the Division II maximum of 36 to 54½.

Translated, the scholarship cost to Team Makers took about a $670,000 hike to $1.6 million. The department budgeted for $713,000 in added operational costs, with most of that being travel.

It was guys like Inniger who went out to find the funds.

"The guy was pounding on everybody's door," said Tyson, a 1956 NDSU graduate. In Phoenix, Fargo car dealer Tim Corwin took care of the automobile rentals for Inniger and Taylor. In Florida, Inniger stayed with boosters Bernie and Rhonda Ness for a few nights while on an extended trip. There were not many five-star hotels, if any, in the cross country ventures.

Irv Meyers, a 1954 NDSU graduate, said a February meeting that included Taylor and Chapman was received favorably by Bison boosters living in the Florida area. "And I think a pretty good percentage put their money where their enthusiasm was," said Meyers, who said NDSU's Division I move rekindled his interest in the athletic department. "Erv was really selling the message. He was a very good salesman."

With Division I football came more exposure. Not right away, mind you, but it did come. At first, just getting the NDSU score on the ESPN scroll was considered a big deal. Don't laugh. That was one of Chapman's selling points.

I remember being somewhat amused myself in 2004 after the first Division I football game against Valparaiso, an event I dubbed "Valapalooza" because of all the hype. By then, a better handle on the competition was reaching my desk and I picked the score in our Saturday predictions at 49-7, much to the surprise of a lot of people. Mike McFeely tabbed it 38-10. I was more accurate; the final was 52-0.

The hype before the game was tremendous, with a large banner on the north side of the Bison Sports Arena seemingly so big that pilots on final approach into Hector International could see it from miles away. The athletic department increased its marketing budget from $50,000 to $80,000 and between the university and its contract with Flint Communications the race was on to get the Division I label in everybody's head. Bartenders and waitresses around town wore Bison football jerseys with the No. 1, to signify the Division I move. Car stickers and lawn signs became popular. It was a marketing score by the Bison athletic department. It was also the first experiment in opening a tailgating lot for alcohol.

Getting that through was like pulling teeth without Novocain. One of the problems with the beginning of Division I football is a lot of people didn't understand the tailgating atmospheres of Division I football because they had never seen it. I wrote this in a column on the Valpo game day: "If done right – i.e. the University of Montana way – NDSU will eventually need more tailgating space, perhaps opening up another paved lot." We all know how that turned out.

In all, it was our first lesson in Division I FCS football both off the field and on, and in the difference between the 63-scholarship leagues and the non-scholarship conferences like Valpo's Pioneer League.

"The Valparaiso game was eye-opening to me," said Phil Hansen, a former Bison great and a member of the radio team that day. "I remember driving home thinking that's a Division I team? Granted, they weren't a great Division I team. You can talk about the coaching and players but the fans kept contributing and coming up with the extra scholarships. Everybody got on board and everybody contributed – it was very much a regional thing. Looking back at that, I didn't know if it was going to be a close game or they blow us out or we blow them out. You didn't know where you were. The thing I've learned through it all as a guy who's watched football his whole life is the difference between the top of Division II and the bottom of Division I isn't monumental. The difference between the best college teams and the lower pro teams isn't something you can't overcome. Football is football and that's true in high school, college or pros but we put these barriers to entry on there and for the Bison, I don't know how any team could have done better than what they've done."

In 2004, the Bison weren't quite at the full 63 scholarships, but it wouldn't take long. The reason: FBS schools required FCS programs to average 60 scholarships over a three-year period for the FCS team to be labeled as a D-I counter. NDSU wanted those FBS games because they routinely provided guarantees in the $300,000 range if not more. Plus, if you're going to compete, you need the funds to recruit players. NDSU's recruiting budget at that point was already over $100,000.

"The best decision we made was to fund the program early," Simmers said. "We threw money at it, strategically in the right places. Whenever you build a business, which we were doing, you need capital. How many businesses are successful without enough capital? What we did well is we funded it early and then we caught up."

Meanwhile, Chapman was busy fighting the legislative fight in Bismarck, continually telling lawmakers state funds would not be used for the Division I reclassification.

"We were very careful to keep as little of state money out of it as we could," Chapman said. "Everybody was watching that. They were hovering over that."

Simmers credits former NDSU vice president for business and finance Dick Rayl for coming up with the Circle of Champions idea to immediately fund scholarships.

"We were not going to make it on minimum donations," Simmers said. "We needed people to invest. We needed people to understand that we needed to pay the day now and reap it tomorrow."

Not helping matters was double-digit percentage increases in tuition, meaning every time higher education raised the price, the athletic department had to find equal external dollars to complete the full scholarship. So about a year or two into the transition, instead of tapping into existing donors for more funds, the athletic fundraisers set out on a nation-wide campaign to tell the Division I story.

Inniger tapped into some friends to help him tell the story, like former NDSU football player Bob Yaggie, who helped Inniger open some agricultural-sector doors like Titan Machinery and RDO Equipment Co. With Yaggie along, Inniger got CEO Ron Offutt to fund a scholarship.

"I remember going to Titan and Bob would say, 'Do you want me to buy a combine or not?'" Inniger said. "It was an unbelievable partnership."

Inniger got his start at NDSU in 1978 and immediately instilled enthusiasm into the Bison basketball program. He started a pep band. He instituted an entertaining style of play and it wasn't long before the BSA became the place to be. He took that same energy to the fundraising level. He got good at it. And sometimes, the best thing to say is say nothing at all.

"True story, Gene was talking to me about going to Doolittles (restaurant) and we were going to ask a donor for $100,000. At first, Gene would get nervous when asking for money so here's what I taught him. Once I say to the donor, I would like to have you give us $100,000 for this. And then you have to stop. Now what are they going to say? What happens is so many fundraisers keep talking. You can't talk. You ask and then you stop. You can't say anything else. I once asked somebody, I'd like you to donate $50,000 to the SHAC (Sanford Health Athletic Complex), what do you think? I was honestly sitting there for three minutes sometimes. You have to be silent. A lot of fundraisers keep going and talk themselves out of the stinking gift."

By 2006, fundraising was exceeding expectations thanks to some Bison teams that were turning in milestone performances. When NDSU announced on Aug. 30, 2002 its Division I move, having Team Makers raising more than $1 million per year for scholarships seemed outlandish. The goal in 2006 was $1.5 million.

Beating a nationally-ranked team like the University of Wisconsin in men's basketball seemed impossible when the Bison first talked about Division I, but that's precisely what happened in January of '06. The 62-55 win over the 15th-ranked Badgers was the biggest victory among several notable accomplishments in the first two years of Division I. The football team reached the Division I-AA top 25 poll in its first year with a full I-AA schedule. It cracked the top 10 in 2005 before fading.

Inniger said the No. 1 factor in changing the Division II attitudes of NDSU fans and boosters was that 2003 win over Montana.

"The second biggest thing was that Wisconsin win, that changed everything," he said. "It went world-wide. Montana was big, that was the first step. But beating Wisconsin, they don't lose in Madison. I could tell you, I still get emotional about it now it was such a big deal for us. After that, I felt like that was the point where nobody was looking back. There was no second-guessing anymore. No nothing. Those people wouldn't talk anymore."

***

It wasn't very often that I went with an unattributed source for a story; I could count on one hand how many times. One of those was in 2002 when I got a head start on the release of a financial feasibility study NDSU did on the potential of moving to Division I. The consulting firm that did it sounded more like a board game, but the influence of Convention, Sports & Leisure International on the entire D1 movement was immeasurable. Its favorable projection of revenue potential was a major reason the school went D1. By 2007, it was obvious the Twin Cities firm was right – and then some.

It estimated NDSU's revenue potential for 2008-09 – the first year it was eligible for NCAA championships – to be between $6.7 million and $7.9 million. The school blew that figure out of the water with 2007-08 budgeted revenue of $10.9 million. When NDSU contracted with CS&L in 2002, its budget was $5.1 million. The athletic department had budgeted revenue of $9,529,230 in 2006-07.

Why the sudden increase? Figures released by the university showed revenue exceeded CS&L's high projections in donations, institutional support, appropriated funds, guarantee games and other sources such as advertising, the USA Wrestling tournament, commissions/licensing and radio and television rights. Ticket sales and money from student activity fees were in line with the CS&L report. Only sponsorship revenue was lagging from the 2002 projections.

Jay Lenhardt of CS&L, who worked on the 2002 report, said he wasn't surprised NDSU had surpassed expectations.

"We were purposely conservative in our projections," he said, "so that the university could make decisions based on numbers that they would, at a minimum, meet but most likely exceed."

The CS&L report noted that "on-field performance, marketing efforts, economic conditions or other such factors could impact the revenues estimated herein."

The footnote was right.

The support on campus, however, wasn't real solid with the students. Being the skeptics that students often are, and should be, trusting a study from some firm from out of state just didn't pass the smell test. Adam Jones, then the student body vice president, said "There was a lot of student resistance in general as well as within the student government. Obviously you've heard it before, but lots of talk about this being 'the end' of Bison athletics, NDSU belongs in Division II, etc."

Jones and Student Body President Jonas Peterson were big supporters of the move and had many student senators on their side, but Jones said they really had to sell the idea.

"Dr. Chapman and Gene were really hoping for a show of support from the students, if even as a sales point to those outside of campus," he said. "In the end, we got it through, but the big stipulation was conference affiliation, which we didn't have at that point. The resolution had a clause with that stipulation because the consultants had placed that as a key to success. Regardless, both Jonas and myself assumed that there were going to be some brutal years ahead, which for the most part, obviously never came. We did think that over time, NDSU could and would compete. I never could have dreamed of what ended up taking place, a cliche, I know, but true. My success metrics when looking at the move were to have a nationally broadcast football game from the Fargodome on ESPN, and for the basketball team to make the Big Dance. My hope was that these would happen in my lifetime. That was my serious time frame. We could have never guessed all of this would have happened this quickly. I think at the time, we overestimated the level of play in I-AA football and mid-major Division I basketball, while at the same time underestimating the level of the upper echelons of Division II. That's not a knock to Division I, the perception was just that the jump would be so big. The Montana game certainly did a lot to help everyone's confidence."

IV. Taking on the big boys

It's a statistic that will probably never be equaled. When the 2010 NDSU recruiting class finished its eligibility following the 2014 season and fourth straight FCS title, that group had more titles, four, than losses, three. An amazing feat, to say the least.

Included in the 58-3 record was a perfect mark against FBS foes – 4-0. There is also an element of bewilderment not only in the four straight over the FBS programs, but NDSU's overall record against FBS competition in its first 11 years in Division 1. The Bison went 8-3 against bowl-eligible programs. Even one win over an FBS team is considered rare for most FCS schools.

The roll call of Bison victims encapsulated FBS programs and leagues of all sizes: Ball State (Ind.) in 2006, Central Michigan and Minnesota in 2007, Kansas in 2010, Minnesota again in 2011, Colorado State in 2012, Kansas State in 2013 and Iowa State in 2014. In reality, the Bison were a blocked, last-second field goal from beating the Gophers in 2006, losing 10-9, and a couple of big plays from beating Wyoming in 2008, losing 16-13. The only real decisive loss was 34-17 at Iowa State in 2009 so you could make a case this program was on the doorstep of going 10-1 against FBS programs in that span.

"My eyes opened when we beat Montana and Ball State," said former offensive coordinator Pat Perles. "After those two, it was like, wow, why can't we go after these other (FBS) teams? After those games, it was like: why not dream for bigger things than just the lamb-fed-slaughter-for-payday against Minnesota like most teams. We can beat Montana in hostile territory. We can beat Ball State with Brady Hoke as their coach. By the time we got to Minnesota, we had enough talent to get the ball rolling. It was crazy, but by the time we got there, we realized we had as much talent to win as they do."

Keep in mind that up until 2013, research by footballgeography.com showed FBS schools historically had an 82 percent success rate against FCS teams. Of the 104 FCS schools that were actively playing in 2014 that played FBS opponents since the divisions were split in 1978, only Delaware (15-12) and NDSU posted winning records. Miami (Ohio) was 3-1 and Troy (Ala.) was 4-3 before moving up to FBS.

A few other FCS programs had .500 marks – Lehigh was 8-8 with its last win in 2002 vs. Buffalo; Morehead State (Ky.) was 3-3 with its last win against Cincinnati in 1989; Tennessee State was also 3-3 with its last victory in 1984 against Louisville and New Hampshire was 7-7 with its last win in 2009 against Ball State.

Of the 104 that played FBS programs, only 33 had not yet registered a win by 2014, which seems a bit surprising. The point is this: a lot of FCS schools got that occasional one upset, maybe two and considering the number of bad FBS teams (Georgia State, South Alabama, Connecticut come to mind) out there, that almost should be expected. But not many put multiple wins together in such a short time span as NDSU did.

Nobody in Fargo who was part of the Division II transition saw that coming. Never. Appalachian State, considered the poster child of FCS upsets when it beat Michigan in the Big House in 2007, was just 7-35-1 against FBS schools. NDSU not only reversed that trend, but at times physically handled its FBS opponents.

It got to the point in scheduling that by the time the Bison starting winning FCS titles, nobody was returning a call. Certainly, the Mid-American Conference, which counts Bison victims Ball State and Central Michigan as members, wanted nothing to do with answering the phone from a 701 area code.

That Central Michigan game was something else, perhaps the best performance I saw from a Bison team in the first 11 years of FCS play. The final in Mount Pleasant, Mich., was 44-14 and it wasn't that close against a team that would produce four future NFL players: wide receiver Antonio Brown, tight end J.J. Watt (who later transferred to Wisconsin and was intelligently moved to defense), quarterback Dan LeFevour and linebacker Frank Zombo.

The Chippewas came in as the defending MAC champs, but suffered their worst home loss since Boise State stomped them 47-10 six years earlier. It was a physical mismatch with the Bison dominating the offensive and defensive lines of scrimmage, as well as being more powerful in the backfield. Tailback Tyler Roehl, all 220 pounds of him, had 143 yards and three touchdowns. The signature play came when fullback Tyler Jangula, leading the way for Roehl, blasted a CMU cornerback about five yards backward.

It was one of the many unsung, talented and physical plays by Jangula, who came to NDSU from Williston. He died unexpectedly early in 2015 at 28 years old after undergoing surgery to repair an Achilles tendon and his funeral in Williston drew former teammates from all across the country. I'll always remember Tyler as a 250-pound force on the field but a very nice man off it. Great guy. He overcame two ACL injuries and still had a tryout with the New Orleans Saints, which tells you something about his tenacity.

The ensuing month after the funeral was difficult, especially, of course, for the family. There was no initial cause of death, although it was widely speculated, and in some instances reported, that he passed away from pulmonary embolism, or blood clot. An autopsy was conducted, but results were not immediately released. A week later, we submitted an open records request to the state medical examiner, which is typical modus operandi of reporting by news organizations for the results. A two-page fax showed up on our fax machine two weeks later.

I quickly called Rheanda Axtman, Tyler's sister, who in the immediate aftermath of his death, seemed to be the spokesperson for the family. She said the family didn't want to talk publicly about it. Several minutes later, Randi Jangula, Tyler's mom, called me and essentially asked us not to run the story. That kind of request was out of my jurisdiction, so I referred her to our editor, Matt Von Pinnon. They were not easy conversations. Lawyers soon got involved in the story. A friend of the family called asking me to kill the story. Former players emailed me asking the same.

The official cause of death written by the state medical examiner was opiate drug poisoning caused by a lethal mix of prescription-type drugs, most notably hydrocodone – a pain-killing drug often prescribed following surgeries. Other "significant conditions" in Jangula's death in the report included the use of acetaminophen, bupropion, fluoxetine, chlorpheniramine and dextromethorphan. The medical examiner also found that arteriosclerotic heart disease, or hardening of the arteries, was a significant condition.

So why did we run the story, at the angst of family and friends? Because Jangula was a public figure, one of the best athletes the state produced in NDSU's initial Division I era. Our job is to set the record straight, as painful as it may be. What if the Williston hospital was at fault for prescribing the wrong medication? There are a multitude of "what ifs" and it was our job in this case to make sure proper procedures were being followed. People have the right to know.

It was sad, because on the field the guy was a force, especially in that Central Michigan game. LeFevour came in as the highly-touted guy, but Steve Walker was 25 of 31 passing. The Bison scored on their first drive of the second half, after a Chippewas fumble, and it was 30-7. The announced crowd of over 16,000 at Kelly/Shorts Stadium began to hit the exits.

"They are tough, they're physical, they're strong and they have a good mentality," said Central Michigan head coach Butch Jones.

It was not a good day for Jones, who made us wait an hour or so before showing up for the post-game press conference.

"There was absolutely no underestimating on our part," Jones said. "I told our coaching staff that the way they play the game of football is the way I visualize us playing with a couple of good recruiting classes and a great strength and conditioning program. They're tough, they're physical, they're strong, they run the ball and they have a mentality. We knew exactly what we were in store for today."

Mike McFeely, in his column for The Forum, said the outcome was the furthest thing from an upset.

"Consider it an ongoing education," he wrote. "We thought the move up from Division II was going to be bumpy. Wrong. Then we thought the move up to playing teams from FBS conferences was going to be rocky. Wrong again.

Ball State, Minnesota and now Central Michigan can attest to that. If these teams believe NDSU is coming to town to take a paycheck and a beat-down, like the old days of I-A vs. I-AA, they're sorely mistaken. There would come a time, of course, when the Bison would hit a ceiling. The question is, how high would that ceiling be? Could NDSU win the MAC? Is it a stretch to think they could be competitive in the middle of the Big Ten?"

Jones could talk all day about not underestimating NDSU. And for the most part, I'm sure most of these FBS coaches said all the right things in the week leading up to playing NDSU. But I sense the FBS players, in every case, underestimated the Bison in all eight victories and probably in the three defeats. It's the geographical ignorance factor – FBS players generally were signed and developed to compete against other FBS teams. Not FCS. And, certainly, not an FCS team from a rural and virtually unknown state like North Dakota.

I bet if you were to take a survey of players from those 11 FBS opponents that a good share of them would not have known much about North Dakota. Some wouldn't know where to pick it out on a map. It's that underdog factor that played into NDSU's advantage every dang time.

And to be sure, NDSU was good at finding all types of motivational material. As the decade wore on, Twitter became more universally accepted and before the 2012 Colorado State game, a couple of ill-advised tweets by Rams players found their way to Fargo. In a comical response, before the Bison charter left Colorado after the game, punter Ben LeCompte responded with a tweet of his own: "See you Colorado, the shit was real."

The final was 22-7, NDSU, but the Bison were the far better team after giving up an early touchdown on a 69-yard touchdown play. The Bison had the ball for 39:52 to CSU's 20:08, a decisive time of possession advantage. It was following this game when "Petitiongate" came to a head.

Earlier in the month, four starters – cornerbacks Brendin Pierre and Marcus Williams, running back Sam Ojuri and offensive guard Josh Colville – were among eight current players and one former player who faced misdemeanor voter fraud charges, according to state Attorney General Wayne Stenehjem. Also affected were second string players cornerback Aireal Boyd, safety Bryan Shepherd and linebacker Antonio Rodgers. Receiver Demitrius Gray was redshirting and Josh Gatlin was a former Bison cornerback. In addition, two former Bison players, D.J. McNorton and Don Carter, and one current player, tight end Lucas Albers, were on a list of petition circulators who, state officials say, submitted signatures to the state and later had signatures rejected.

Bohl said he was contacted a couple of weeks prior about the investigation. He said he helped coordinate the players being available to investigators and he said the players complied with the investigation. NDSU did not allow any of the players to comment. Bohl and Gene Taylor said they were going to let the legal process play out before deciding on any ramifications. It was a story that took awhile to go away.

An investigation by the North Dakota Bureau of Criminal Investigation found that some statements submitted to the state were not correct and many of the individuals whose signatures appeared on the petitions had not signed them. According to the statement, investigators believe the forged signature names were lifted from telephone directories and cellphone contact lists of the circulators. Some were simply made up.

The players were hired by a firm called Terra Strategies out of Iowa, which was in charge of soliciting signatures for two ballots for the November election: a medical marijuana initiative and a conservation fund. Because of rejected petitions, both fell short of the signatures they needed to be placed on the ballot. The medical marijuana initiative ended up being more than 900 signatures short of the needed 13,000-plus. The conservation fund, as a proposed constitutional amendment, required 26,904 signatures, and 37,785 were submitted. After losing the signatures the investigation found invalid, the petition drive came up 7,938 votes short.

Ojuri stated he was paid $90 for an eight-hour shift and $45 for a four-hour shift, adding he was told by his employer that if he reached 80 signatures in an eight-hour shift he would receive a $10 bonus. Asked what would happen if he didn't obtain the minimum expected signature count of about 60 signatures per shift, Ojuri said it was his understanding people would be fired if they weren't "up to par."

Here was the problem: the players had very little trouble collecting signatures for the conservation fund, but in a conservative state like North Dakota, not many people wanted much to do with the marijuana ballot. They didn't want their name on that paper and if the players didn't get any signatures, they didn't get paid. You do the math. The players aren't on scholarship in the summer and football is a year-around fulltime job. If you're not getting money from your parents, which some or most of these players weren't, then you need to find a way to eat.

After the game, Kevin Schnepf approached Taylor with the angle of his column on how NDSU used the incident as motivation for its inspired play against Colorado State. Taylor went right to the point in his response: he told Schnepf there were going to be no disciplinary issues with the players.

"Then he started rambling about it," Schnepf said later. "So I said, 'Gene, let me get this straight: you're saying there's not going to be any discipline?' I think there were a couple of things going on there. One, Gene was caught up in the excitement of the win but at the same time you could tell he wanted that issue to be over with. He was very adamant about it. It was almost like he wanted to get it off his chest."

Taylor, three years later, admitted: "I kind of went off on him."

Schnepf also talked to NDSU President Dean Bresciani before the game and Schnepf said Bresciani gave no indication the players were not going to be disciplined.

But Taylor had other thoughts after the game.

"Then my column took a sudden turn after talking to Gene," Schnepf said. "I remember coming back to the press box and saying, holy shit, this is what Taylor just said."

In retrospect, Taylor said if he could rewind time, he would have been more proactive, but said he still would not have suspended the players. He said the NDSU administration was told all along it was nothing more than a misdemeanor.

"I don't know what I would have done because even the prosecutor told me: 'Look, Gene, I probably shouldn't tell you this but I'm getting pressured to do something and legally they have not done anything more than probably get community service."

The issue was finally resolved early the following week. Taylor apologized when 10 players pleaded guilty in Cass County District Court. Ojuri was the only player suspended, one game, but that wasn't because of the petition incident but other factors that involved a violation of team rules, Bohl said.

"I pride myself in handling any media situation with professionalism," Taylor said, "and sticking to the issues in hand. After answering Kevin's question, I allowed my personal bias rather than a professional approach as athletic director. I've always been able to keep my emotions in check, no matter what the situation is, but that particular night I didn't."

The guilty pleas brought a quick end to a legal mess. The 10 players who pleaded guilty were given a deferred imposition of sentence, 360 days of unsupervised probation, a $300 legislative fee, 50 hours of community service to be completed by April 15 and a $25 community service fee. If they met the terms and completed the probation without further offenses, the charges would be cleared from their public record.

"The election laws are important," Cass County State's Attorney Birch Burdick said afterward. "And I think what happened here was very unfortunate. Having said that, our recommendations were based on what the court has done in the past and our effort to try to keep a matter of uniformity to similar kinds of behavior."

I thought NDSU screwed up at the outset by not suspending the players for at least a half or the entire season opener against Robert Morris. Although the players probably weren't aware of the seriousness of voter fraud when they submitted false signatures, it still was breaking the law and there are those who would say it was just plain un-American in interfering with the voter process. The best way for damage control is to get it behind as quickly as possible (something, by the way, that the athletic department was constantly guilty of in the 1990s). By letting the "process play out," this story dragged on.

Plus, the opener was Robert Morris. It wasn't like NDSU wasn't going to beat Robert Morris without a few key players. Bohl and Taylor should have known this. The Bison had a loaded team returning from the 2011 title team and it could have beaten Robert Morris with its entire second string offensive and defensive units. Suspend them for that game, and bam, controversy is over. As it was, the Bison bombed the Colonials 52-0 and a lot of those guys were on the bench in the second half anyway with the outcome already decided.

While Schnepf was putting up with Taylor's outburst, I was on the other end of the stadium getting Jim McElwain's take on the loss to an FCS team. It was his first season as the head Rams coach after coming over from Alabama, where he was the offensive coordinator. McElwain was very diplomatic, perhaps sensing that losing to an FCS program was a product of the poor cards that he was dealt.

That became a theme of NDSU's FBS games: first-year coaches. Whether it was educational guessing on the part of Taylor scheduling FBS schools who were on the verge of losing their head coach, or just plain luck, the Bison had the fortune of playing six FBS teams who had a first-year coach. Two other matchups were against teams coming off losing seasons.

Only two games were against teams coming off productive seasons: Minnesota was 7-5 and reached the Music City Bowl in 2005 before playing NDSU in 2006. Kansas State won the 2012 Big 12 Conference title, but lost its Heisman Trophy-contending quarterback when the Wildcats played NDSU in 2013.

"If an experienced FCS team is playing a team that is young at the FBS level, I think there's a pretty good chance of winning that game," Southern Illinois head coach Dale Lennon once said. "Timing is very important in giving yourself a chance. They might be young. They might have had a coaching change."

Lennon, of course, was very familiar to NDSU fans in his time at UND. He was in charge when the Sioux overtook the Bison for state Division II supremacy, and ultimately DII national title status. But the series changed when NDSU took the D1 plunge and UND didn't – something that Lennon did not agree with.

Jones was a first-year coach at Central Michigan in 2006. Brewster was new to Minnesota in 2007. Turner Gill was in his first game at Kansas in 2010. Jerry Kill took over at Minnesota in 2011 and of course McElwain at CSU in 2012. And with all of those new head coaches came new assistants, new schemes, new philosophies and new players. Moreover, with the exception of the 2007

Gopher game, the Bison played the rest of these FBS programs early in the season.

It made for the perfect FCS storm. The other fact: the Bison over the course of a decade were one of the few Division I programs anywhere to excel at physical football. Remember, this was an age of the spread offense, the pistol quarterback formation and the no-huddle offense. It was all about speed on offense -- and defenses had to counteract accordingly by getting faster on that side of the ball. What those teams forgot, and underestimated in playing NDSU, was the Bison West Coast offense. Bohl was smart in matching his location in Fargo with his recruiting philosophy. In the Midwest, the linemen are just bigger, he said. So the bulk of the offensive and defensive lines were going to be a concentration of North Dakota, Minnesota and Wisconsin recruits.

Speed had to be recruited from elsewhere, although not all the time. Anyway, that West Coast power wore down FBS defenses more often than not. The poster child in that theory: Aug. 30, 2013.

NDSU vs. Kansas State.

That win made NDSU 2-0 against the Big 12. The other one came in 2010 – the game that changed the course of FCS history for Craig Bohl. After going 3-8 in 2009, the Bison ventured to Big 12 Kansas for the 2010 opener.

Of course, nothing got the masses going more than the three games with the Gophers.

V. Those little guys in green

The buffalo vs. the varmints. For starters, never in several lifetimes did I think North Dakota State vs. the University of Minnesota on the football field would ever happen. Moreover, never did anybody think NDSU would have gone 2-1 in those games and should have been 3-0.

Of all the victories in the rise of the FCS dynasty, the biggest perhaps came in 2007 when NDSU marched into the Metrodome for the second straight year, only this time coming away with a 27-21 win.

Before Frisco, there was Gopher.

The five-year onslaught on Frisco, Texas, started on Oct. 20, 2007 in downtown Minneapolis when an NDSU fan base that we know now was sleeping for decades suddenly awakened. If the narrow loss the year before got people thinking what could have been, that victory energized Bison fans across the country. Bison football was no longer a Red River Valley thing; it was a national scene with ESPN taking note that night making it a center stage of its SportsCenter show. It got donors in Arizona and Florida on board.

"You could just feel the energy of the fans after that game," Steve Walker said.

After this game, you couldn't go anywhere in downtown Minneapolis without running into some sort of green or yellow. I didn't realize the slogan "Go Bison" was hip until that day. For many who grew up in the Division II days, it was probably a surreal thought of an NDSU team beating a Big Ten team. While a lot of people will point to the win over Montana in 2003, my belief is the '07 Gopher game was the true start of the Bison fan base that filled Frisco for five straight years. The Forum's headline the following day was "Yellow Fever."

It was the 2007 game that made believers of fans on the fringe; those who really didn't want much to do with Division II but we're officially on board now.

"I think it was a defining moment for the public, press and fan base," Pat Simmers said. "It galvanized them. It told them, 'We can do this' because there were the skeptics. We did not make that move without a lot of prep. There was a lot of research that went into it. I'm that old guy; the best programs in the country (in the 1970s) were Montana, Youngstown and Northern Iowa and we used to beat them all. Was I worried? No, it wasn't a matter of if, but when?"

It was also the one-year anniversary of my debut in the Minneapolis TV market, although it had nothing to do with game analysis. The story:

After I got done writing my stories at the dome in the 2006 game, I went back to my hotel in downtown Minneapolis to drop my computer off, before meeting my wife Ruby and friends for dinner at a restaurant just a couple of blocks away. No problem. I'll just walk. It wasn't late, about 8 in the evening.

I was probably just several steps outside the hotel door when, with a lot of people milling around, I sensed some commotion in my peripheral vision. In an instant, and I'll never forget it, something swinging came at me. At the last millisecond I ducked a bit to dodge what I would learn soon enough was a fist. I still took a decent shot to the jaw.

Down goes Frazier, I mean Kolpack.

I vaguely remember being dazed. I remember a Bison fan, Bill Kiefer, coming over and asking me what happened. Seeing as how I was not really sure what just went on, I said something to him about being fine. With Bill's assistance I immediately ducked into a cab – in my mind to escape whatever danger just hit me. I told the cabbie my destination, which happened to be probably less than two blocks and he looked at me with a puzzled look. I told the driver I don't care; just get me out of here. It turned out to be the shortest, most expensive cab ride ever.

I met my party, including former players Tom Shockman, Hank Klos, Kevin Donnalley, Dan Hare and Wayne Schluchter at GameWorks restaurant, and the first comment was why I was late. I told them I just got punched. Silence. Nobody really believed me, until the red mark on my skin in my jaw started to get more pronounced as I was trying to explain what happened. We were having dinner with Bison players from the 1980s, and let's just say a couple of them wanted to come to my defense immediately and take matters into their own hands. I appreciated the offer, but declined.

So how did this get on Twin Cities' television?

The next day I wrote a blog about the game and wrote the following smartass comment:

"The hardest hit by anybody in Minneapolis on Saturday was not delivered by a Gopher player at the Metrodome. No, it was a young punk who threw a right hook at my jaw a couple of football fields from my downtown Minneapolis hotel after the game. Totally random violence. Not sure if he was getting revenge for a couple of Bison fans passionately yelling at Sid in the press box or what. Or maybe it was a Bison fan thinking I was McFeely."

A Twin Cities TV station picked up on that blog post, and asked the local ABC affiliate, WDAY, to interview me on the incident. That story aired that night in the Twin Cities and the story just took off. I gave this quote to another Twin Cities media outlet: "I've covered a lot of boxing over the years, now I know how these guys feel when they get clocked to the canvas."

One local radio personality wanted me to take the matter to court. No chance. I wanted no part of driving to a Minneapolis court room on my own dime to testify about a sore jaw. The kid who hit me was later arrested; it appears he went around Hennepin Avenue hitting random people, with four known assault victims, according to Minneapolis police.

"The suspect did this deliberately, he chose his victims, he has his own motivations," said Lt. Greg Reinhardt of the Minneapolis Police Department.

A couple of years later, out of curiosity, I searched his name in court records and saw he was charged with a much more serious assault crime. Perhaps I was fortunate. The next year when NDSU returned to the Metrodome, I made sure Phil Hansen was not far from my side. In fact, I appointed Phil, in jest of course, as my paid bodyguard.

The hype started early in the week in Fargo. The Bison were perhaps thinking about the previous year's 10-9 loss to the Gophers.

"It's a big game for our football program and a big game for the North Dakota and South Dakota players on our team," said NDSU defensive coordinator Willie Mack Garza. "But it's especially big for our guys from Minneapolis and the surrounding area."

The Gophers fired Glen Mason after the 2006 Insight Bowl collapse against Texas Tech and hired Tim Brewster. The new coach installed a spread offense, one that had been putting up big numbers, including 580 yards of total offense in a 49-48 loss at Northwestern the week before the Bison game. Yet, the Gophers were 1-6 heading into the NDSU week. Brewster, on that Tuesday, made it clear he did not want to schedule the Bison after that season – something he said the previous spring much to the surprise of his athletic director, Joel Maturi.

"I want to play a nonconference schedule that will help the University of Minnesota in recruiting," Brewster said. "I don't have a problem playing a I-AA team. But North Dakota is not an area where we will go to get a lot of our football players. It's not a negative on them ... it's just the way it is."

Maturi won that battle – the teams played in 2011. Bohl, meanwhile, didn't say much that week but you knew he was burning inside. Maturi interviewed Bohl for the Gopher opening but ultimately decided on Brewster. Why? Not many people could figure that out, although the popular theory is Brewster told Maturi what he wanted to hear. Brewster could talk a good game, but it didn't take long before his used car shtick got old with a lot of folks in the Twin Cities area, most notably the media.

McFeely said Bohl once told him that Bohl and Wisconsin head coach Bret Bielema were hoping the Gophers would give Brewster a lifetime contract because "Brewster would rather go to Arkansas and get a five-star kid rather than take a kid from Minneapolis and develop him."

"NDSU feasted off Brewster's incompetence," McFeely said.

Brewster once referred to NDSU as those "little guys in green," a sentence that made its way on that so-called Bison bulletin board. What kind of coach provides that kind of motivation? Calling a football team little? Bohl couldn't have been handed a better motivational line than if he made it up himself. Brewster was probably joking, but the fact he didn't figure his comment would be taken as condescending (the big school vs. the little school) or a reference to the Bison players being small (again, you just don't call a football player little) was plain stupid.

There was nothing little about NDSU's convergence on the Twin Cities. It wasn't long after the 2006 game that the NDSU staff went looking for a bigger venue. It contacted alumni associations from Iowa State, Wisconsin and the University of Iowa for advice. Sheri Schmidt from the NDSU Alumni Association had never imagined such a gathering of Bison fans was possible. The pre-game party for 5,000 was set at The Depot in downtown Minneapolis.

"I had never seen a sold-out anything," she said, referring to NDSU's first four Fargodome football games that season. "It used to be we were excited to be in Florence, Ala. This is the place to be."

The Depot staff told Schmidt that NDSU's event was probably bigger than those held by Wisconsin and Iowa when the Gophers hosted those two Big Ten schools. At that point, it was the biggest party the NDSU Alumni Association had ever hosted. It also had a post-game party at The Depot and the 750 tickets easily sold out. "People who have never been to Bison games are coming here," Schmidt said. "It's been like watching a drama for a year. All year you've had episodes and now this is the finale."

That was some game for the home fans – and by that I mean the visiting team. Walker will never forget the moments before kickoff when the captains were ushered onto the field slightly ahead of their teammates in order to prepare for the coin flip. On the NDSU sideline was Walker, safety Nick Schommer, linebacker Joe Mays and offensive tackle Nate Safe.

"The Gophers came out with all the firework and we're standing there on the sideline," Walker said. "Then our guys came onto the field and literally the floor was shaking from the noise our fans were making. You could feel the floor of the dome shaking from how loud it got. We had that many more fans behind us."

Game day was electric with The Forum estimating the Bison attendance at the Metrodome between 25,000 and 30,000. The city of East Fargo witnessed another crowning moment in the NDSU Division I magical mystery tour. The 27-21 win before 63,088 fans was more than an FCS program beating a FBS team from the Big Ten. Without the benefit of the playoffs because of its reclassification from Division II, it was NDSU's Super Bowl.

Running back Tyler Roehl set a school record with 263 yards rushing and became a fixture on ESPN "SportsCenter" that evening, especially his 77-yard touchdown run on NDSU's third play of the game. The Bison did it behind 585 yards of total offense and a defense that got better as the game wore on.

Walker's seven-yard touchdown pass to a diving Thor Brown with 12 minutes, 56 seconds left gave the Bison a 24-21 lead.

Minnesota had taken a 21-17 lead on Duane Bennett's 32-yard pass from quarterback Adam Weber with 1:43 left in the third quarter. But from there, the Gophers ran just six offensive plays in the fourth quarter with the big defensive play by Bison cornerback Nate Agbetola, who picked off a Weber pass on third-and-10, giving the Bison the ball at the Gophers 48. The Bison took 12 plays to reach the 9-yard line, but settled for Shawn Bibeau's 21-yard field goal with 7:46 remaining, giving them their 27-21 lead.

The Bison again forced the Gophers to punt after three plays on their ensuing possession. Starting from their own 34 with 5:40 left, NDSU picked up two first downs. Another first down – a pass to tight end Jerimiah Wurzbacher – was called back because of a holding penalty. NDSU stalled with 1:48 left and Mike Dragosavich lined up in punt formation, but Minnesota's Dominique Barber was flagged for a 15-yard roughing-the-punter penalty and, with the Gophers out of timeouts, the Bison ran out the clock.

Walker finished 20 of 25 passing for 191 yards and two touchdowns. Besides Roehl's big day, the Bison got 87 yards from backup Pat Paschall on 12 attempts and 29 yards on five carries from Pete Blincoe. NDSU averaged 8.0 yards per carry on the ground.

Roehl was a beast. Just when it appeared the halftime score would be 14-14 after the Bison took over at their 7 with 34 seconds left, Roehl busted open up the middle and Barber caught him from behind 68 yards later, which was another ESPN highlight. The four-play drive ended with a Bibeau 37-yard field goal as time expired. By then, Roehl already had 200 yards rushing.

Walker ended the game taking a knee on two plays, and then threw the game ball to the Bison bench. The ensuing celebration came in various forms. It included defensive end Christon Dallas simply running by himself to one corner of the Metrodome. It included receiver Shamen Washington high-fiving as many fans as he could find sitting in the front rows. And there was cornerback David Earl, who stood near midfield and raised his helmet to the thousands of fans in the upper deck.

It was a victory for NDSU administrators, who took some criticism in the early days of the Division I move and now had to endure just one more year of the Bison being ineligible for playoffs.

So NDSU was 1-1 vs. the Gophers and with Brewster saying that would be it, many thought it would.

Maturi thought otherwise, saying in 2009 the Gophers were committed to playing a regional opponent and the programs signed a contract for a 2011 game, in which NDSU would receive a $350,000 guarantee, a slight increase from the $300,000 the Bison got in both the '06 and '07 games. In essence, 2011 turned out to be the proverbial rubber match since the teams had yet to schedule a game up to 2020 – and most likely beyond.

Brewster didn't make it to the 2011 game. He was shown the door in 2010 after never coming close to his promise of taking the Gophers to the Rose Bowl. Minnesota took a more sensible approach in hiring his replacement Jerry Kill, a good ol' boy who rose through the ranks of Division II, FCS (his 2005 Southern Illinois team beat NDSU 9-0 in Carbondale) and FBS Northern Illinois.

But like previous years, Kill had to deal with the "overlooked" motivational angle used by NDSU's players from the Twin Cities. Tight end Matt Veldman's grandfather, for instance, was a Gopher season ticket holder for around 50 years. His father used to have season tickets. Linebacker Grant Olson grew up a Gophers fan, right up until the point he committed to NDSU. His brother attended Minnesota, his uncle went there and his grandparents met there. Offensive lineman Billy Turner's uncle went to Minnesota. Growing up 10 minutes from the Metrodome, he and his brother, former Northern Iowa receiver Maurice Turner, had dreams of playing for the Gophers. All three players from the Twin Cities area were offered walk-on opportunities with Turner being offered "grayshirt" status, where players walk on the first year and the school says it will scholarship you after that.

Turner watched the 2007 NDSU-Minnesota game on TV because his family was friends with Weber, the Gopher quarterback who went to high school with Maurice Turner. Olson, from Wayzata, was at the 2006 game and also watched the '07 game on TV while hunting.

"I was rooting for the Gophers because that's who I grew up watching," he said. "The funny thing is, I remember Tyler Roehl and saying, 'Who is this guy running over everybody?'"

If anybody thought the '06 and '07 games were a big party, they hadn't seen anything yet. NDSU outgrew The Depot for a pre-game event, so the Bison found bigger space at the Minnesota State Fairgrounds. An official helping park cars estimated the crowd to be bigger than any other opponent he saw, which of course would include Wisconsin.

With the move to the new TCF Bank Stadium in 2009, there were 13,000 fewer tickets available for Bison fans, which was probably the start of NDSU folks taking to StubHub or other internet sources to find tickets. And unlike '06 and '07, NDSU was not be able to put on football fatigues, sneak into Minneapolis in the middle of the night and end up on the field opposite of the Gophers. Their head coach knew too much about the Bison. For one, Kill was part of the first-ever game at the Fargodome as the offensive coordinator for Pittsburg State (Kan.).

"Rocky Hager was there, and we were both running the split-back veer, and we were the ones that opened the dome," Kill said. "So you don't have to convince me how hard those son-of-a-bucks are going to play. That's a subject that doesn't need to be discussed."

Kill went on to Division II head positions at Saginaw Valley State (Mich.) and Emporia State (Kan.). He missed by one year at Emporia from returning to the dome, which came to Fargo in 1998. But Kill and NDSU crossed paths again in 2005 when the Bison played at Southern Illinois. It was NDSU's first full year with an FCS schedule, a game won 9-0 by SIU. Turning a Big Ten team around, however, was much more complex than winning in Carbondale, Ill., so when Kill was asked about NDSU's roster being filled with Minnesota kids, he interrupted the question.

"I know, I hear about it every day," he said. "I understand. Shoot, I was told I wasn't good enough for this job. So hell, I'm one of those guys. So you bet your tail end they are going to come in here and be ready to play."

He was right.

It was a new venue, an outdoor jewel, and quarterback Brock Jensen handed out over 15,000 invites to his Bison friends and he took along cornerback Marcus Williams as his Best Man. Two sophomores. Two players who had never played better and they did it this time in front of 48,802 fans at TCF Bank Stadium. The final was NDSU 37, Minnesota 24 and you could have taken it two ways: the Gophers had a long way to go to get up to Big Ten standards or the Bison couldn't get enough of the Minneapolis big stage.

"I've never had this feeling before," Turner said. "I was passed up. The feeling I have is the feeling everybody else from Minnesota has."

For the third straight Bison-Gopher game, the visitors were the better team. Here was the prime example: It took until the first play of the fourth quarter before the Gopher defense stopped the Bison. NDSU had three long touchdown drives in that span that ate up a couple of days and a field goal – it was 31-17 heading into the final 15 minutes. The balance was still in doubt until Williams cranked out his second big play – a 40-yard interception return with 2:36 remaining. It turned out the basketball player from Hopkins was a pretty good football player. "It was emotional being from here," Williams said. "People thinking I was not good enough to play here."

Williams was also part of a quirky play at the end of the first half that broke the Gopher spirit. Minnesota was trailing 21-14 with five seconds remaining and had the ball at midfield. On fourth-and-8, quarterback MarQueis Gray heaved a "Hail Mary" attempt downfield, but it was picked off by safety Colten Heagle at the 18-yard line. Heagle immediately headed up the sideline and returned the ball 30 yards before running into Gopher tacklers. "(Then) I saw

Marcus and he was yelling 'Pitch' so I just threw it," Heagle said. "In a game like this, you can't hold anything back."

Williams said he wanted the ball once he saw that Heagle was going to get tackled. "I'm yelling 'Pitch, pitch, pitch' and he threw it back," he said. "It was just a heads up. I've never been in one of those. You see them on TV a lot. I've always said 'I want to be part of one of those." Williams took it to the end zone and the Gophers never recovered from the 14-point halftime deficit.

Offensively, NDSU coaches wanted a higher completion percentage in the 2011 season and they got it. Jensen came within one completion of tying Walker for a team record for most consecutive completions. Walker had the mark at 16 in a row over the course of the first three games of the 2004 season. Jensen hit his first six attempts against the Gophers that brought his streak to 15, but it ended on an attempt to Warren Holloway. He finished 16 of 21 for 197 yards and no turnovers. Walker was 20 of 25 for 191 and no turnovers in '07.

Flawless.

Execution.

NDSU had 24 offensive plays in the first half for 207 yards, a model of efficiency no matter who the opponent is. They were 6 of 9 on third down conversions. And the result: They turned downtown Minneapolis into another green and yellow celebration. The NDSU academic recruiters hit the jackpot again. "It was the same feeling at the end," said running back D.J. McNorton, who was at the Metrodome in '07 as a redshirt freshman in his jersey and jeans. "But I wasn't really a part of it. To play in this was great."

VI. Dear Brock, I was truly impressed

It was a humid, 100-degree day in Manhattan, Kan. The Bison, two-time defending FCS champions at the time, returned another talented team and everybody knew it. At least 5,000 NDSU fans made the trip and if there was ever a question on the tailgating euphoria that gripped Bison faithful during the dynasty, it was answered and then some in Manhattan. Before heading into the stadium, our Bison Media Blog decided to do our pregame show at the NDSU tailgating site, located on a grassy field that was about a 10-minute drive from the stadium. We first drove by the parking lot that normally is home to K-State tailgating, but it was so hot the home fans stayed inside. The asphalt was empty.

Not the visiting fans. It looked like a photo from Woodstock. The Bison players were a tough lot in those years, and this proved the fans were, too. The suffocating heat and humidity did not keep them away. A friend of mine, who came to the game from Cincinnati and who was very familiar with major college football, said this is how the SEC travels and he couldn't get over the green and gold turnout.

"There was a lot of electricity going to Manhattan to play a Big 12 team," said Jim Miller, the executive director of the NDSU Development Foundation.

Miller knew all about K-State; he used to work for the university.

"I don't know how to describe it, I really don't," he said of the swell of NDSU support from across the country.

For K-State fans, it was probably hard to describe what they saw; their defending Big 12 champs struggling to beat an FCS team. I've said many times and I'll say it again: a coach like Bill Snyder can preach all he wanted about respecting an FCS opponent, but kids recruited to Big 12 schools are recruited to play against Oklahoma and Texas; not North Dakota State. The Wildcats, like the rest of the Bison FBS opponents, didn't bring their A-plus intensity game.

For the NDSU coaching staff, this game started the day spring football ended. They put that much time into preparation. As the defensive coordinator, rarely an office day went by where Chris Klieman didn't work on the Wildcat game plan in some fashion. He and linebackers coach Steve Stanard regularly attacked the paperwork at all of the different K-State formations and unbalanced sets.

"It was one of the hardest game plans I ever did," Klieman said a couple years later. "We worked on it all summer long. We knew their quarterback (Heisman Trophy candidate Collin Klein) wasn't coming back but we knew they would run the same stuff. Every bit of extra time I had in the summer, even after playing golf, I'd sit at home and watch two or three hours on a June night just to see if I could find something to help us. I knew we were out-manned a little bit."

The players weren't oblivious to the staff's summer work, either. Because the Bison had such a veteran team returning, they didn't necessarily have to work on blocking, tackling and the fundamentals of football for two or three weeks and *then* work on the K-State season-opening game for a week.

"We didn't have to beat the heck out of each other," Klieman said. "It was to the point where I remember meeting with the defensive backs in early August when in fall camp, we watched a bit of summer practice and then we flipped K-State on."

Still, the attitude of the players the week of the game raised the eyebrows of strength and condition coach Jim Kramer. During a weightlifting session early in the week, he saw a bunch of players who didn't look focused. They appeared downright giddy to him, he said. Kramer talked to Bohl and told him he didn't think the players were very locked in to the Friday night nationally-televised opener on Fox Sports 1. He looked linebacker Grant Olson in the eyes and told him "You're about to play the biggest effin game of your lives and you're not locked into the lifting routine."

Then it dawned on Kramer as he thought back to the week of the Minnesota game in 2011. The players had that same look – not focused in the weight room.

"They were already anxious to play the game," Kramer said. "When we thought about it, maybe it was not a bad thing they were unfocused in the weight room because their focus was already on Kansas State and their focus was on football. We had that class of players and they were seasoned for this. They were seasoned for this game. You felt like it was going to happen."

The Bison coaches knew if they ever had a chance to beat K-State it would be early in the season. The Wildcats lost some key players and were breaking in a new quarterback in highly-heralded junior college transfer Jake Waters.

"They were putting, 45, 50 points on everybody the previous year," Klieman said. "We didn't want to go out there and get beat 59-14 or something and have a miserable night."

It didn't start out miserable for NDSU, but it didn't start out great, either. The Wildcats acted like the defending Big 12 champs, opening a 21-7 lead midway into the third quarter. The Wildcat fans behind the Bison bench were letting the visiting players know about it.

"This is what happens when you play a real team!" some kid shouted at linebacker Travis Beck.

But the Bison defense got stronger as the game wore on. A memorable play: linebacker Beck's Superman-like dive into the K-State backfield to help blow up a play. It came on a formation when Beck wasn't supposed to be in the game because he and outside linebacker Carlton Littlejohn were rotating in passing situations. On the prior play, however, Beck took a knee to the helmet in tackling a Wildcat back for a two-yard loss, but the hit practically knocked him out. It didn't help that he didn't inflate his helmet with air properly, he said, but that's another story.

"I remember Carlton going, 'Beck, you're out,'" Beck said. "I said LJ, I can't see anything. All I could see were dots; it was just black."

Still, with the fog quickly lifting but not enough for Beck to run to the sideline, Olson tapped Beck on the shoulder and told him where to go on the blitz alignment on the next play. So on the snap, Beck took one step and went horizontal with the turf when a K-State player tried to block him low. It was believed landing after the dive was the cause of the first shoulder injury in a shoulder-problematic junior year, but he actually hurt it when he was already on the ground and tried reaching up to grab a scrambling Waters.

"I should have jumped and landed on my feet, I don't know what I was thinking," Beck said.

NDSU responded the last half of the third quarter getting a Kevin Vaadeland touchdown and an Adam Keller field goal to make it 21-17 heading into the fourth quarter.

After the Bison stopped K-State after two first downs, they got the ball back at their own 20-yard line with 8:58 remaining in the game. Certainly, 99.9 percent of the time, a Big 12 power would be wearing down an FCS program by now, especially in that weather.

During the week, the NDSU staff was concerned about the heat and humidity since the Bison rarely practiced in those conditions. But the Bison also had Jim Kramer in their back pocket. Kramer did some cutting edge stuff teaming with Sanford Health to establish a system of identifying which Bison players were more susceptible to cramping by conducting a study using sweat patches and analyzing which players lost more salt in strenuous workouts and which players retained more.

The point being: Losing salt is generally a precursor to muscles cramping.

"We identified those kids and made a list in fall camp," Kramer said. "We tried to determine which kids are more prone to cramping, and we tried to get more salt into those kids."

Getting players to buy into the salt diet was easier said than done, however. That week, NDSU resorted to an age-old grandma's remedy: chicken noodle soup – with an addition of salt. It was a staple menu item for the players. Pretzels and chips were readily available. Salt was also added to sports drinks, although it wasn't a pleasant addition.

"It's not always fun to chug that down," Kramer said. "Salt in Gatorade does not taste good."

The extra-salt diet was no big secret, Kramer said, saying there are several products on the market. The key was to get players to follow directions, and Kramer said that was not a problem with that group.

The diet was prominently used the previous year at the FCS national title game in Frisco. Chicken noodle and tortilla soup were staple items, with additional salt of course.

"But here it is in Manhattan, Kansas, it's 100 degrees and the kids are eating (hot) soup," Kramer said.

One Bison player who didn't particularly take in his salt like he should have was quarterback Brock Jensen. In the locker room following the game, everybody was going nuts throwing water and jumping around – except Jensen.

"I was sitting there with no emotion on my face," he said. "The trainers were putting towels over my face and I think it took me 40 minutes to get up and do post-game. I had zero left in the tank. Beyond zero. I was really dehydrated and physically exhausted. I didn't do the salt in the drink like I should have and coach Kramer just shook his head. He gives me crap about it to this day."

Kramer didn't have to say anything on the charter flight home – Jensen was throwing up from being overheated.

"I did a little of the salt but maybe I didn't take it as serious as the other guys did," Jensen said. "And it paid off for everybody else but me. At least I was able to use adrenalin."

The salt, soup and dietary discipline paid off in the last 8:58 of the game. As the second half wore on, a few Wildcat players were noticeably cramping. On the other side of the field, there was very little to none. Kramer said some Bison players were on the verge of cramping, but nobody locked up. After The Forum ran a story of the salt study and plan, Kramer was deluged with requests from other trainers and conditioning coaches throughout the country. He probably could have gone on a speaking tour.

Then again, he wasn't Jensen driving his team down the field in awe of almost everybody, K-State fans included.

The drive didn't start very impressively and Jensen said the original hope was to just change the field position, thinking NDSU was going to get two possessions to finish the game. Running back John Crockett lost one yard on two carries and the Bison faced third-and-11. But Jensen dumped a middle screen pass to running back Derrick Lang – who was in the game presumably because he was the team's best pass blocking back – and Lang maneuvered his way for 11 yards and a first down. It would turn out to be a huge play – one that Forum writer Eric Peterson would later deem his Play of the Year in our Media Blog season-ending awards. His reasoning: if Lang doesn't make that play, maybe NDSU doesn't win a game that kicked-started the greatest season in the history of FCS football.

Getting out of second- or third-and-longs were commonplace on the drive. On first down after Lang's big play, Jensen lost three yards. But on second-and-13, Jensen found Ryan Smith for 11 yards and Crockett's five-yard gain to the Bison 43-yard line picked up the third-and-2.

But once again, Crockett's run that lost two yards on first down made it second-and-12. How many times could NDSU break out of the long-yardage jail? Jensen's five-yard pass to Trevor Gebhart made it third-and-7. Then, Jensen hit Zach Vraa for eight yards and the Bison kept the chains moving, now in K-State territory at the 46.

There was still 46 yards to go to pull off the shocker. NDSU finally had a productive first down when Jensen's swing pass to Crockett was good for seven yards. And for a change, Jensen didn't have to go to third down with a four-yard pass to tight end Andrew Bonnet at the 35-yard line.

The 6-foot-3, 225-pound Jensen carried a few Wildcat defenders on his back in gaining seven yards. By now it was obvious that NDSU was the superior-conditioned team.

"We were looking at the K-State players and they were going down like flies," Jensen said. "On that last drive, there were a lot of breaks because their players were going down. I remember getting in the huddle and looking at the other guys and they were looking at me. It was a 'I'm good. Are you good? I'm good' type of thing. Once we crossed midfield, I just felt like this game was over and you are not about to stop us. Then I looked at a few other guys and said the same thing: 'You tired? I'm not. We're good. Let's get this done.'"

Crockett followed with back-to-back seven-yard gains and the West Coast offense was at its power best. The clock was now under a minute and Jensen said he was having a hard time hearing himself think at times.

"The crowd got into it on third down, I couldn't hear anything on third down," he said. "The guys would see my lips and mouth moving but they couldn't make out any of the words. The only communication we had was in the huddle of me yelling at the top of my lungs."

The Wildcats stopped Ojuri for no gain forcing a third-and-3 at the K-State 14-yard line – four-down territory for NDSU, though the Bison wouldn't need the extra down; a seven-yard pass to Vraa reached the 7 with 42 seconds left. Jensen finished 7 of 7 passing on the drive for 53 yards and the Bison converted all four third-down conversions with three Jensen passes doing the job.

On a first-and-goal from 7, the take-charge quarterback almost scored, taking a keeper to the right side that reached the 1; he was actually tackled by his own guy, left tackle Billy Turner, which told you something about the offensive line surge on that drive. The Bison took time out with 32 seconds left. Once back on the field and lining up, the Wildcats took time out. The suspense in the stadium was reaching a peak.

As usual, the Bison put the ball in Jensen's hands with the game on the line. On second down, he reverse pivoted, took a K-State tackler head on, blew through him, and scored with 28 seconds left. It was the same play that Jensen came up short on against Eastern Washington in the 2010 FCS quarterfinals. Guard Tyler Gimmestad pulled on the play and took out a K-State lineman. Jensen remembers putting his hand on Gimmestad and kind of throwing him to the side before shedding the linebacker and falling into the end zone.

The Bison fan section on the opposite end of the stadium was hysterical. Jensen gave a shout to the Fox camera; the Bison sideline was pandemonium. Olson sealed it with an interception and the Bison had their biggest win in school history.

"Where we have come the last 10, 12 years, I never would have fathomed this," Gene Taylor said.

"We have a remarkable group of seniors," Bohl said. "We've had these types of wins but never over a program like this. I don't know if our players fully understand the type of program that we played but I knew."

Because it was a night game, the post-game press conference was a shotgun affair. Everybody had deadlines.

"They are an extremely tough football team … they played harder than we did and they outplayed us," said Snyder, who conducted a postseason press conference while scheduled fireworks were exploding outside in the stadium named after him.

The Bison players and coaches hung around for a bit, talked with parents and friends, then proceeded to clear the field. We quickly filed our stories and headed back down to the field to shoot the Media Blog post-game show. We were about the only ones around, except for Bohl who walked onto the field in his suit and tie for one last look. He stared at the empty stadium, seemed obviously emotional, and headed back toward the Bison team bus.

What we probably didn't realize was the personal nature Bohl had with this game. The last time he coached a game at Bill Snyder Stadium, he was the defensive coordinator at Nebraska and his team got blown away. It was the third-to-last game of the 2002 season and the final was 49-13. It was the first of three losses to close a season in which Bohl took a beating from the fans and press for the Huskers' lack of defense – perhaps dating back to the previous season when Nebraska gave up 62 to Colorado.

The popular theory was head coach Frank Solich fired Bohl to save his own skin and Bohl went to the exact spot in the stadium where Solich delivered the news after Nebraska lost to K-State and conducted his own inner payback of sorts. So, 10 years later, with Solich having drifted off to virtual college football anonymity as the head coach at Ohio University, where you could occasionally see his team on a Tuesday night in front of not many people on ESPN's

MACtion, Bohl got some personal satisfaction of revenge in Manhattan. Not against K-State so much, but for getting a big chunk of the blame for Nebraska's problems.

"Coach Bohl broke down and cried in front of his players," said Kasey Byers, the NDSU video coordinator who is allowed inside the locker room. "And coach Bohl didn't do that very much, if ever. Every single person in the locker room was just looking at him. They were soldiers who just fought this war and they did it for this leader and this one man. Some of those guys almost killed themselves in that game for him. They did it for him because they knew what it meant for him. Coach Bohl loved those kids."

Byers took a job as the producer at LoboTV at the University of New Mexico after the 2013 season – in the same Mountain West Conference as Bohl when he took the Wyoming job.

"When we played Wyoming, that's all we talked about, all he talked about was those kids and NDSU," Byers said. "That's why for me it was sad when you hear about those strained relationships. No one can ever take that title away from us. Everyone I work with at New Mexico wants to see my national championship rings. Most people don't give rings to staff members. No one can take that away from me. I think for coach Bohl that was a high point in his life because he felt like he was thrown out by the big schools. Nebraska got rid of him and that game vindicated him as a head coach; that everybody made a mistake on him and he did it with those kids. That was the highlight of my life that night personally; I still can't believe it happened. I think it was the most important win in the school's history. We all did. Everyone felt this emotional connection. Guys played dehydrated that last eight minutes."

Taylor said that Nebraska connection was the reason Bohl got emotional after the game "and he typically was not very emotional after games. Even after the national championships. I just remember how appreciative he was of his players to come out and play like that."

The headline in The Forum the following day was "Manhattan Magic." Our copy editors got pretty good at NDSU football headlines over the years, starting with "Miracle in Montana" in 2003. My favorite was "Golden Boys" after the first FCS title in 2011. When the Missouri Valley Football Conference, in its 30th-year anniversary, documented its top moments in league history, the NDSU win over Kansas State was called one of the top three wins over an FBS opponent.

The after-glow of the victory was impressive; especially from the national folks who couldn't get over that an FCS team defeated the defending Big-12 champs. NDSU was a regular visitor in Dennis Dodd's CBSsports.com top 25 FBS poll, although Dodd used nostalgia along with intelligent rankings. Other samplings:

Sports Illustrated: "Sooner or later, teams are going to stop scheduling North Dakota State, or the Bison are finally going to move up to the FBS level."

ESPN Big 12 Blog: "That's right, Kansas State paid NDSU $350,000 to come into its home stadium and give it a loss. In fact, NDSU, the two-time defending FCS champion, could pay the salary of coach Craig Bohl, who makes $206,000 per year, with the check it received for visiting the home of the defending Big 12 champion."

Bleacherrport.com: "As the Big 12 blog clearly noted in the Week 1 game predictions earlier this week, North Dakota State is not your garden variety FCS team. The Bison have won the past two Division I national championships and their past three games against FBS teams. The foresight ended there when we still picked Kansas State to win big. Whoops."

USA Today: "It was a glum way for the Wildcats to wrap up a festive day on campus. The school dedicated a $90 million renovation to the west side of its stadium in a ceremony attended by Gov. Sam Brownback and Sens. Pat Roberts and Jerry Moran. Along with a ribbon-cutting, the school also unveiled an 8-foot bronze statue of its beloved coach. Snyder even made the rare decision to leave his team on game day for a few hours to attend the ceremony, but joked that if the Wildcats stumbled, 'it's all going to be on my shoulders.' Then again, perhaps the 73-year-old Snyder wasn't joking at all."

NDSU, specifically Jensen, wasn't through from hearing from Snyder. As paranoid as the veteran coach seemed with his bunker-like mentality in preparations, the guy was genuine. The following week, he sent Jensen a hand-written note (yes, hand-written, who in that day and age used a pen on paper?) saying how impressed he was with the senior quarterback.

It read: "I was truly impressed with you and your teammates. You played so very well, virtually error-free and with such poise. Please share my thoughts with your teammates."

The letter went viral within the Bison football fan base. Jensen had actually greeted Snyder before the game when he first came onto the field for warmups. Jensen did that on occasion during his career, often seeking out coaches he knew like SDSU's John Stiegelmeier.

"That was a cool moment with coach Snyder before the game and then a week later to receive that letter … I still got it. It's framed. Oh yeah, it's framed."

***

Whoever would have thought Jensen would turn out to be one of the most important players in NDSU history? He didn't verbally commit until a week before signing day on the first Wednesday in February in 2009. It was a short, three-paragraph mention in a Forum story, but there was much more to his story than just a small-town recruit from Wisconsin.

The kid was in line to get his equipment his freshman year of high school in Waupaca, Wis., as a running back, tight end and linebacker. A coach asked him his last name. "Jensen," the kid replied. In Waupaca, where there are a few Jensens, that didn't exactly narrow it down. "Which Jensen?" the coach asked.

"Brock Jensen," the kid said.

At that point, Waupaca High head coach John Koronkiewicz pulled his head from around a corner and told the coach to issue the kid equipment for a quarterback. At least that's the story that Steve Jensen, Brock's father, remembers.

Whatever the details, it was the genesis of a winner. Brock later led Waupaca to an undefeated state championship his senior year. The ascent continued at NDSU, where he set an FCS record for most victories by a quarterback with 48.

The fact NDSU got him was somewhat a stroke of luck in that he wasn't NDSU's first choice as a quarterback recruit. The Bison wanted A.J. Westendorp from Holland Mich., but Westendorp ultimately chose FBS Central Michigan, where he didn't amount to much. He actually played two games as a tight end as a freshman and spent the rest of his CMU career as a backup quarterback.

NDSU was straight up with Jensen from the outset, telling him he wasn't their first choice. And in the end, that was very appealing to Jensen, who said that approach by the Bison made for a trustworthy relationship.

"They were telling me everything that was going on throughout that time," Jensen said. "They told me exactly where I sat. It's a long process, and they wanted to make sure they got the right guy. It just so happened it worked out and it fit."

He was most serious with Minnesota-Duluth, which was coming off a title of its own in Division II. It's possible Duluth could have said, "Take us now or we'll pull the offer and you can risk losing out on NDSU, too." It wasn't as if Division I schools were lining up outside of Waupaca waiting to talk to Jensen. Obviously, he didn't have the total package they were looking for. Wisconsin and FBS Eastern Illinois offered walk-on status, he said. Division II schools Grand Valley State and Northern Michigan liked him, but did not offer.

"The recruiting process was brutal for me, very difficult," Jensen said. "I couldn't crack that first offer; that's what it was. After that first offer, they usually start to roll in a bit. I couldn't get that in the process."

It was amazing when you rewind to the 2009 recruiting process. Division II schools weren't high on Jensen, yet he went on to one of the most distinguished careers in the history of FCS football, a division that claims Randy Moss, Kurt Warner, Tony Romo, Joe Flacco and Vincent Jackson. Recruiting is a funny business. Eastern Illinois hit on a small-town Wisconsin kid named Romo. It didn't get a kid named Steve Walker. It has a pack journalism mentality – if one publication is hot on a guy, they all are. Keeping external evaluations from polluting your own vision is a must. That's probably how NDSU arrived at keeping Jensen in the loop. I'm not sure what there wasn't to like, unless playing in a lower high school division scared away people. He was big. He was a leader. He was a winner. He's well-spoken and mature. A highlight video on WDAY-TV on signing day showed him running away from people, which meant he was pretty fast unless all those kids that were left in the dust were pulling grand pianos. Bohl, on signing day, said Jensen was an accurate passer – he threw for 1,582 yards and 21 touchdowns and ran for 1,140 and 19 touchdowns.

Jensen said Bison assistant Tim Polasek was the one who was most insistent that NDSU offer him. Polasek continued to talk with Jensen until the Bison offensive staff agreed to a scholarship offer late in the game.

Jensen and "late in games" were good to NDSU.

"I used that, looking back, it motivated me," he said. "I just needed that one opportunity and I couldn't ask for a better place to have that opportunity than here in Fargo and NDSU. It was just totally meant to be. There's a reason for everything I feel like in life and I definitely was meant to be here."

***

The same could be said for Polasek, whose own route from Wisconsin to NDSU was far from typical.

He'd just got off work from the logging fields in central Wisconsin when Bohl called him at 5:05 p.m. one day.

"How you doing?" Bohl said.

"Just getting out of the woods," Polasek replied.

"This is Tim Polasek?" Bohl asked.

"Yeah coach, I log part-time," Polasek said. "I just opened a Miller Lite because I just got done with the day. It was a hard one."

Bohl called Polasek to see if he wanted to interview to be a graduate assistant. The connection happened about a month earlier when Bison assistant Todd Wash was at Homestead High School in Mequon, Wis. recruiting when somebody told Wash he had the perfect candidate for the open position at NDSU.

"I got a guy who doesn't care about making money," the guy said.

When Bohl called, he asked Polasek when he could come to Fargo for an interview. Polasek had certainly heard of NDSU football, but didn't know how far it was from where he was at. Bohl told him about an eight-hour drive.

"I'll be there in eight and a half hours," Polasek said.

It wasn't that spontaneous, but Bohl got the idea of what kind of personality he was dealing with. Problem for Polasek was he was making hardly anything as a graduate assistant with the Wisconsin-Stevens Point football program and didn't have much cash for gas money. So while golfing with a couple buddies, he asked one of them if they knew of anybody who would want to buy his driver. A school superintendent in the district caught wind of Polasek's sales pitch and offered him $280.

So Polasek drove to Fargo and got the Bison GA position.

There was an ironic twist that ultimately became a defining moment in his life: He was also offered $40,000 a short time later to be either the offensive coordinator or defensive coordinator at Stevens Point, but turned it down in favor of the NDSU job which paid $6,000 over a nine-month period. He figures his take-home pay was $290 every two weeks. In terms of the coaching structure at Division I schools, or most colleges for that matter, a GA is about as low as it gets on the ladder.

"Everybody has a bridge they can or cannot cross depending on what they have in choices," Polasek said. "I took a shot. I wasn't going to be denied."

Once back in Fargo in February of 2006, he spent his first three months essentially homeless. In something akin to the movie "Rudy," Polasek slept in various parts of the Fargodome football offices, either on a lounge chair or small couch in the second floor office complex or a futon in the lower level locker room area. A few people in the program knew about it, but nobody said anything, respecting the fact a young coach was doing anything he could to learn the game. Even if it meant living out of a suitcase.

"Just give me a futon and a TV and I could have stayed there for a year," Polasek said. "I didn't think it was such a big deal. Think about it, I got here in February and had to learn a whole new offense and I had a month to bang that out. Then in March we started spring football and then we went recruiting. That was part of the deal. I told coach I'll only come if I can recruit so he gave me 30 schools so I would go out for three or four days. There's no time to worry about where to live. I just thought you have to be vested in football now because you're not going to get this time back."

It's debatable if very many players knew of Polasek living in the Fargodome, or if they even cared. They also don't mind it when he gets in their kitchen over a failed play. Polasek is never shy in balancing constructive criticism with praise. He'll sprint 40 yards to congratulate a player. In position meetings, he would get so animated that they've been known to have more fun than a comedy show.

He's the biggest reason tight end Matt Veldman got a shot in pro football. In his first couple of years, the knock on Veldman was he was not very tough and if there's one thing Polasek wouldn't put up with, it is that. Polasek was moved from running backs coach to tight ends coach after the 2010 season, in part to toughen up the likes of Veldman. Among his first words to the veteran player: "You're a rookie to me," Polasek said. "We're going to get you to be all-league if you trust me. But it's not going to be all sunshine and roses."

He's qualified to toughen players because that's the way he lived. He grew up in a single-parent household, his mother never making more than $30,000 a year. Polasek figures she made less than $19,000 a year when she was raising him as a kid in junior high and high school. He somehow scraped together enough resources to play football at Division III Concordia University in Wisconsin, where as a quarterback he set all kinds of passing records. He got his master's degree from Concordia in 2005. He was never afraid to get to work while almost everybody else in Fargo was sleeping because the thought of working in the logging fields will forever be enough motivation for him. It was dog-like work. He operated a skidder, often cutting the large branches off trees, pulling the logs out of the woods and stacking them in a pile. "We're talking big, monster pine and oak trees," he said.

There was also time spent working at Thyssen Krupp steel mill in Waupaca, Wis. It's the same company that made the escalators in the Fargodome that Polasek took his first three months after waking up in either a coach's office or somewhere in the locker room.

"I know there are people for 348 days a year that are covered completely in black soot, dirt, doing the iron and ladle and shoveling sand for eight hours at the factory," Polasek said. "I did that. I have a great appreciation to have the opportunity to work with kids and coaches."

Assistant Willie Mack Garza helped take care of him, buying his dinner at Buffalo Wild Wings whenever possible.

Bohl knew he had a gem to help mold his physical West Coast offense. Polasek was also the guy who helped changed the punt unit, traveling to Wake Forest University for a week in 2008 to learn a new scheme that has three blockers in front of the punter that form a "shield" with the blockers at the line of scrimmage spread farther apart. It's designed to help prevent blocks. He left NDSU after the 2012 title to take an assistant position at Northern Illinois, but returned a year later when Klieman tabbed him as the offensive coordinator.

This time, he got one of the bigger offices in the Bison Fargodome complex and he was financially fine to not have to live in the dome. His name was etched on the glass door. Yet, the thoughts of working in the factory or logging in the woods are never far away.

"What I make now, it still feels like a million bucks to me," he said. "The days get long and there are days you would just like to take a day off. But you don't get to call in sick in football. Ever. It can be a grind, but there's one thing

… people don't realize when you're not in the playoffs, you're off from Dec. 16 to Jan. 8. We haven't had that break in five years, which we don't want obviously."

The ironic thing about that Kansas State drive was perhaps the coach who has instilled the most toughness over the years, Polasek, was game-planning something at Northern Illinois that night. Then again, those Bison seniors had three years of Polasek under their belts. There were plenty of players on that field who had Polasek's name to it.

Like Brian Schaetz.

***

The first meeting between Polasek and Schaetz was all both of them needed to know. Polasek shook the kid's hand and then looked at both of them.

"Do you work somewhere?" Polasek asked him.

"Yeah, I work on a dairy farm," Schaetz said.

"You have some tough-looking mitts on you," Polasek said.

Polasek knew those tough-looking mitts could translate into a tough-playing defensive tackle. The kid from Denmark, Wis., was yet another example of the walk-on program that NDSU hung its hat on. Denmark was a town of 2,200 people located in the northeast corner of the state.

"I shook Brian's hand and instantly knew there might be a 270-pound body in there," Polasek said. "He is a powerful, powerful kid. Brian is a farm kid from Denmark, and it doesn't take long to realize that when you're around him. The kid has a big heart."

Schaetz received recruiting attention from Central Michigan and Wisconsin, which got interested in Schaetz between his sophomore and junior seasons. Wisconsin eventually went a different direction, which Schaetz said was probably fine with him because he wasn't much for the email and internet recruiting methods anyway. He did not have an email account and Polasek was the only college coach to make his way to rural Denmark. He had a couple of Division II offers, one being St. Cloud State (Minn.). But he was so sold on NDSU that he verbally committed in August as a walk-on his senior year in high school.

"Those kids come in with a chip on their shoulders. 'So and so missed out on me,'" Polasek said. "They are hard-working hungry guys, and you can't have enough of them around. K-State found that out."

How tough was Schaetz? In August before the 2014 season opener, it was uncertain if he was going to be ready to play the first game after suffering a broken foot and dealing with a blood clot issue over the summer. Schaetz had surgery on the foot in June and spent the rest of the summer wearing a protective boot. Then came one evening in July when the pain got to be too much in his calf so he took a trip to the emergency room at about 11 p.m. The blood clot diagnosis was followed by a doctor telling him he'd probably be out two to three months. It took some work, but Schaetz was finally able to see a specialist about a week before fall camp. He was told the clot was highly unlikely to reach his heart or lungs and moreover, he was told it will probably be gone by the start of camp anyway. There wasn't much that was going to keep him off the field. He had the look of hard work the day he walked on campus. It was the way he grew up. The best evidence: he would wake up at 4 a.m., go to Denmark High School to lift weights, come back to do his chores and then go to school. It was that kind of work ethic that got Polasek to make it a priority to recruit Schaetz as a walk-on and that mentality never changed.

Asked before the start of the 2014 season if he felt offended that reports indicated very little to no experience in the interior of the Bison defensive line, Schaetz said he didn't pay attention to that. Plus, he wasn't much for the injury questions, or any type of comments that could be taken as an excuse.

"I don't like to listen to anything what people say," he said. "They can talk all the want and that's not going to bother me. I'm going to come out every day and go to work. I grew up doing that and I'm going to keep doing that."

Plus, there could have been family repercussions if he did. "If my dad caught me saying something in front of somebody like that, if he caught me looking at the media saying something about that, I think he would really be ticked off," he said. "He'd probably tell me to go do some chores, go milk the cows."

VII. The magic men

There have not been that many regrets on the Bison road trips over the years, although numero uno came when the Bison played at California Polytechnic State University, San Luis Obispo, also known as Cal Poly, in 2007. The source of the frustration: the movie "Sideways."

It was about that time when the flick starring Paul Giamatti, Thomas Hayden Church and Virginia Madsen became a cult favorite on my laptop or DVD player, especially on those long flights. It tells the story of two old college buddies going up the north coast of California on a trip to different wineries and restaurants, with the central theme being wine and life.

The movie was shot on location at several places within driving distance of San Luis Obispo, so as I was flying into the city on the Pacific Ocean, the thought occurred to me: the Hitchin' Post in Buellton or the Los Olivos Café in Los Olivos cannot be that far, probably about an hour.

I could take my own Jack and Miles tour of a couple spots and check them out for myself. The problem: my journalistic conscious was telling me to do a Friday story from the campus.

Story. Wine. Story. Wine. What to do?

Not wanting to get in trouble, I did the story on a $21.5 million renovation to Cal Poly's Alex Spanos Stadium, talking to Poly head coach Rich Ellerson and athletic director Alison Cone on a gorgeous Friday afternoon. It was an OK story, but nothing compared to getting my "Sideways" fix.

It was one of the few times that I covered a game solo from The Forum. Kevin Schnepf, Mike McFeely and Trevor Peterson from WDAY took the company plane to Gainesville, Fla., to cover NDSU's first men's basketball game against a major Division I opponent in Florida.

The next morning, I did the Saturday morning sports radio show solo from my San Luis Obispo hotel room, a two-hour tour that was about as hideous of a radio experience as it gets. For starters, with the Pacific time zone, it started at 6 a.m. local time, 8 central, and it took the longest time to hook into the WDAY studio. The signal was bad. I couldn't hear the producer at the station half the time. By the end of the two hours, I was pretty certain the only one listening was my mother, and only because she was my mother and not that she enjoyed the show.

That's the price you pay for doing radio on the road; sometimes the stuff just doesn't work and you're left swimming upstream without a life jacket.

The game later that night, however, was an ocean full of drama. Of all the Division I rallies NDSU manufactured in the decade, none top this one in terms of improbable and miraculous.

Or, in the case of Cal Poly, in the terms of The Big Choke.

The Bison were down 28-9 in the fourth quarter and with it being a night game on the West Coast, I had to cheat the deadline as best I could. The story was essentially done with the following theme: Here ended NDSU's dream of an unbeaten season. It was a nice run, not getting beat until early November after nine straight wins, but the excitement of a new stadium renovation, a packed house and the Bison coming to town was too much to overcome.

Plus, some places are just tough on teams. The only other time NDSU played at Cal Poly in the Division I era was the only time I saw a Craig Bohl team badly beaten. It was in 2005, a game that ended 37-6, and it wasn't that close. Steve Walker was 9 of 18 passing for 89 yards and spent all night running for his life.

On offense, the Mustangs had a receiver so big that when he came out for warmups I thought he was a tight end. Ramses Barden, all 6-foot-6 and 230 pounds, had five receptions and a touchdown and against NDSU's 5-foot-10 cornerbacks Scott Walter and Bobby Babich. He looked like a man amongst boys. It should be noted it was about the only major downfall for the two corners, who played with smarts and toughness as their careers wore on.

"Play after play, they kicked NDSU's living ass," said Keith Corliss, the pilot for Forum Communications. "The train would pull up behind the stadium and the engineer would sit there and watch the game and watch them roll the Bison. Man they pounded them that night."

Afterward, defensive coordinator Gus Bradley was in a hallway in a building where the Bison dressed and had this look of helplessness. Gus knew he had some Division II recruits playing against D-1 guys like Barden and running back James Noble.

"We got beat bad," said Bison linebacker Joe Mays.

And it was looking that way two years later. Ellerson's triple option offense was running roughshod over NDSU's Tampa 2. For one of the few times in Division I football, NDSU faced a noise problem on the road. The last time it happened was the '03 shocker at Montana. All that was needed for my story was 10 more minutes off the clock and, bam, hit the send button at the final buzzer so the layout guys at The Forum can get it in before deadline.

Forum editors already had the deadline extended knowing it was an important game in the Pacific time zone. So what happens?

The deadline gods got to me.

If you thought the win at Montana was a shock, this comeback blew me away. My lede in the Sunday Forum: "The legend of Steve Walker outgrew the state of California on Saturday night."

Walker's swing pass with 10:02 left in the fourth quarter was picked off for a touchdown by Cal Poly safety David Fullerton. The victory party at Spanos Stadium was in full gloom.

Game. Set. But not match.

Walker remembers walking to the sideline and running into receivers coach Reggie Moore.

"Time for that magic," Moore told him. "Let's get it done."

In the previous year, Walker brought the Bison back from a 24-0 deficit at UC Davis, located north of San Luis Obispo, in the biggest comeback in school history.

This rally started with Walker's 67-yard touchdown pass to Jordan Schultenover with 9:36 remaining. A 48-yarder to Schultenover – after the Mustangs went for it on fourth-and-2 and failed to convert on an incomplete pass – put the Bison on the door step again.

"Jordan made big plays," Walker said.

Tyler Roehl's 4-yard touchdown run made it 28-23 with 4:21 left and suddenly what once looked lost was attainable. Up in the press box, my delete-backspace key was getting a workout. My nerves, so calm when it was 28-9, were shot.

NDSU held again, and got the ball back at its own 4-yard line. But there were no time outs and about a minute left.

Walker scrambled for 16 yards to the 20. He killed the clock by spiking the ball on the next play. On second down, receiver Kole Heckendorf ran a fly pattern down the right side, a 9 route was the play call, and Walker hit him stride for the game-winner with 38 seconds left. Eighty yards.

Perles said NDSU took advantage of a routine failure by Cal Poly on film: it never deviated from a lack of playing cover zero or cover one – meaning not much safety help.

"Even in our film study, they never went to soft coverage," Perles said. "They weren't going to change their schemes. We had no choice, it didn't matter what coverage they were in. We were fortunate the coverage broke down and Kole beat the kid. The reality was Kole was really fast, he just didn't look fast on film because he was such a long strider."

Afterward, I ran down to the field and caught Bohl and a couple of Bison players for comments. I glanced over at the Cal Poly bench and saw some reporters beginning to gather around Ellerson.

There was no formal press conference like you see every game these days. Ellerson was accepting of what happened, putting the blame on himself. He even told Bohl in the post-game handshake that he coached a poor game.

Amazingly, on the 80-yard touchdown play, Cal Poly was in man-to-man coverage with no safety help – a question that was asked of Ellerson.

"I let them down," Ellerson said. "That's on me. They should fire me."

I felt like firing him myself for wrecking my story.

Although I'm not able to listen to Scott Miller's play-by-play during games, that had to have been one of his best calls. You can still find it on YouTube with Miller's reaction and it is classic. After Heckendorf caught the pass and shed a tackler around the Cal Poly 40-yard line, Miller shouted "are you kidding me" as the Bison receiver was sprinting toward the end zone. It's captivating stuff.

"Steve Walker," Schultenover said. "The kid is Magic Man."

The result was NDSU was 10-0 heading into the season finale at South Dakota State. The Bison were ranked No. 1 in the FCS top 25 coaches poll despite not being eligible for the playoffs.

Walker was indeed a magic man.

One year earlier, he pulled off the biggest rally in NDSU football history when the Bison came back from 24 down at UC Davis.

I like Davis, the town. I like the bicycle culture, the laid-back approach to life and the location in northern California, not too far from Sacramento, San Francisco and Napa. It was the site of some great playoff games in the Division II days. Ask any player from the 1980s about postseason and they'll forever remember the 19-14 loss in the 1982 semifinals to a Ken O'Brien-led Aggies team. They'll remember the payback a year later in the semifinals, in Davis again, in a 26-17 Bison victory on a team led on offense by freshman quarterback Jeff Bentrim and a defense that held Davis to just 45 yards rushing.

In the 2000s, NDSU and Davis were brothers of sorts in the Division I move. The Aggies made the jump a year earlier and had the look of a program that had big things in front of it. The head coach, Bob Biggs, was a media-friendly guy who the night before the '06 game was casually out for dinner at a local Davis restaurant – he was a Davis kind of guy.

He almost took a scientific-like, high-intelligent approach to football. He chose his words carefully in post-game press conferences, not to guard against saying something stupid but to make sure of the accuracy of his words. He didn't have much to say after the Bison game on Nov. 4, 2006. It was 24-0 at halftime and it looked like it could have been worse, especially after running back Kyle Steffes was stopped on fourth down at the Aggies' 1-yard line in the last 30 seconds of the second quarter.

At halftime, Walker said the players were nervous that they were about to get their rear ends chewed out. It was actually the opposite with Bohl, who Walker overheard tell another coach: "These guys aren't trying to suck, let's coach them up." Bohl also told his assistants that in times like this it's why they're getting paid. He told them to paint a clear second half plan, instill some confidence into the players and give them something to hold onto. The biggest adjustment wasn't technical – the Bison went back to their base defense. On offense, they got their power running game going.

The result: The Bison went 74 yards in 10 plays on their first possession of the second half. The touchdown was a bizarre halfback pass from Steffes to Wurzbacher. That was just the start. A 47-yard touchdown pass to Heckendorf to close the third quarter made it 24-14. Steffes' short touchdown run with 7:04 left made it 24-21.

The game-winning drive took 77 yards in 16 plays, including a couple of heroic fourth down passes from Walker. One was a 14-yarder to Heckendorf on a fourth-and-12. The other, with the Bison facing fourth-and-10, went for 22 yards to John Majeski on a pass that looked like it dropped between the entire Davis secondary. I'll never forget it.

"I don't know how Steve squeezed it in there," Majeski said after the game. "It looked like it went under the defender's armpit."

What most of the players didn't know is Walker got whacked on the prior play and came over to the sideline during a time out. He looked like he was spitting up blood, but it was probably just a cut inside of his mouth. He looked like he had a hard time breathing and Bohl was looking over his shoulder for the backup to get into the game. Walker then turned to Bohl and said, "Don't you take me out of this fucking game."

The winner came with just four seconds left on a 10-yard pass to Majeski in the back of the end zone.

"I was in the booth spotting for Scott Miller and he was going about his usual business, he puts his whole self into games," Corliss said. "I literally thought Scotty Miller was going to have a heart attack. We're in this plywood box of a press box, there's no room to do anything, and if there wasn't a back wall there, Scotty would have fallen back and fainted. It was that emotional of a moment. It would have ended with the usual 'my oh my' and clunk, he would have fallen to the floor. You look at a guy like Walker and he doesn't look like much on paper, but he just wins. He was magic in a bottle. How do you recruit something called heart? He was that guy. What a great quarterback during the transitional phase."

Whether it was a stroke of luck or great recruiting, NDSU was blessed to have calm, cool quarterbacks in the clutch in the first 11 years of Division I ball. For Walker, it was instilled by his father when he was a Little League baseball player, who told his son things are never as good as they seem and they're never as bad as they seem.

"That was a strength of mine, stay even keel," Walker said.

He was recruited by former Bison assistant coach Glenn Caruso, who went on to become the head coach at the University of St. Thomas in St. Paul. Caruso was working under former Bison head coach Bob Babich when the staff made a last-minute decision before Thanksgiving of 2002 to go into Chicago and try to find some players. Little did anybody know that trip perhaps help set the table for NDSU's FCS dynasty.

On the drive there, Caruso phoned a connection and asked him what games to check out in Chicago area. One happened to be a playoff game between Walker's Lockport team and Hinsdale Central. Walker drove his team 90-plus yards in the final minute for the winning touchdown.

"The kid had so much moxie that it was coming out of his pores," Caruso said.

The next day, Caruso went to the Lockport High School and asked to see Walker, who was sitting in an English class.

"The secretary said a coach from North Dakota State wants to talk to you and I had never heard of North Dakota State," Walker said. "I was more excited just to get out of class."

Walker had visits with Eastern Illinois and Florida Atlantic, and took Caruso up on his offer to fly to Fargo. Eastern Illinois had just graduated Tony Romo and that was appealing, but the bigger schools stayed away because Walker wasn't the biggest and certainly not the fastest recruit around – about a 4.8-second 40-yard dash. Caruso saw something in the kid he liked, especially when he sat down with him in his living room when he returned to Chicago for a home visit.

"I got into his home, sat at his kitchen table, look out the sliding glass door and the high school end zone was right out his window," Caruso said.

Also, Caruso said he graded three of Walker's high school games and charted an 85 percent accuracy. In the years 2004-07, that was something Bison fans saw on a Saturday basis.

"And no way had I ever seen a player that commanded his troops the way he did time after time," Caruso said. "On a scale of intangibles, I've never recruited a kid who has what he has. Ever."

Recruiting Walker through his high school coach, Bret Kooi, led Caruso to a couple of other Chicago-area players: Joe Mays and Mike Dragosavich.

"I went in and sat down with Bret and said 'I'm new, I'm only here for a week and a half and I need to scramble up as much business as I can. Where are the good places to go?'" Caruso said.

He drove to Hyde Park High School to meet Mays, whose Division I possibilities were dwindling to nothing. I ran into Joe in Frisco, Texas, at the Bison's Friday open practice before the 2014 and fourth consecutive title game.

I reminded him of that visit, and he laughed, saying he'll never forget what Caruso looked like when he came to the school. Caruso was wearing a long trench coat.

"He looked like he was from the mafia," Mays said.

But Mays listened. Caruso said if Mays blinked once in the hour he talked with him, he would have been surprised. The kid was listening that intently.

Dragosavich is from Oak Lawn, Ill., who came to NDSU as a 6-foot-5 wide receiver. He never made it on the field at that position, instead Bohl seeing him more valuable as a punter. The coach was right.

Dragosavich started a run of punting excellence that directly contributed to the building of the dynasty. He averaged 41.3 yards as a freshman in 2004 and that was just the start.

There is no underestimating the defensive importance of a good punter. The Tampa 2 defense and its quick linebackers, active defensive linemen and intelligent secondary generally make it tough to go 70 or 80 yards on a drive. A poor punting game can cut into that effectiveness.

Dragosavich left after the 2007 season and John Prelvitz took over in '08. The only one-year wonder in the punting bunch, Matt Voigtlander, played a key role in the 2011 title team – and the title game with a fake punt that he took a first down that led to a touchdown. Not wanting to be a backup running back for four straight years, Voigtlander decided to concentrate on punting his final year and it paid off.

Walker. Mays. Dragosavich.

Those three key players in the Division I transition, running back Cinque Chapman plus a couple of others from the Chicago area who didn't stick around, signed with the Bison in February of 2003. The following day, Babich bolted for the NFL and assistants like Caruso were left to find something else.

Sadly, Caruso did all that recruiting leg work and never got a chance to coach those kids for even a day. So when Walker led the Bison to those incredible comebacks and back-to-back 10-1 seasons in 2006 and 2007, never forget a big reason was because Glenn Caruso paid attention on tape to the final minutes of his high school games – and didn't fall victim to the lack of measurables like height and speed.

Certainly, though, there was speed, strength, athleticism and the will to not lose. The Bison pulled off more rallies in that Division I era than anybody could expect.

"I never in my six years there had been a part of more great games than in the combined 19 other years," Pat Perles said in 2015. "There were so many great finishes. Specifically that Davis game. You can put that game on and we had a lot of good players. We had some talent, but if you really want to get down to it, that's the game Steve Walker came to us at halftime."

"Put the game on my shoulders," Walker said.

The coaches let him continue to speak.

"Coach, we're going to come back and get this," he said. "Don't lose faith. I threw a couple of bad balls, just give me a chance."

"I specifically remember him saying that," Perles said. "He was keeping us calm."

Walker wasn't alone in quarterbacks leading NDSU's rise to a dynasty. After Carson Wentz led the last-minute rally in the 2014 title game win over Illinois State, it was rather easy to point to the top 10 fourth-quarter moments for the Bison in their first 12 years in the FCS.

That's almost one a year – an incredible ratio. It should be noted that perhaps before the D1 comebacks, there was the 2003 rally quarterback Tony Stauss engineered at Montana. Stauss provided a nice transition in quarterbacks for NDSU in moving from DII to DI. A former prep All-American in Wisconsin, he started his career at Northwestern. Not seeing the playing time, he came to NDSU and the fact he had big-time experience was probably a big factor in Missoula. In Stauss, you had a quarterback who wasn't freaked out by the packed Washington-Grizzly Stadium. So before we get to the Division I comebacks, perhaps it was Stauss who helped set the table.

Here are those 10 in order with No. 1 being the most compelling of the comebacks:

10. Oct. 5, 2013: NDSU 24, Northern Iowa 23

The drive: NDSU went 76 yards in eight plays to complete a fourth-quarter rally from a 23-10 deficit, scoring on Ojuri's 19-yard touchdown run with 2 minutes, 52 seconds to play. It wasn't the most amazing of comebacks in that Ojuri's touchdown came with plenty of time on the clock. But perhaps the opponent had more to do with this ranking than anything – UNI and NDSU are more of rivals than NDSU and SDSU.

It was a rough weekend for the Bison until the final quarter. Earlier in the week, cornerback C.J. Smith suffered a shoulder injury and starting offensive guard Tyler Gimmestad endured meniscus damage to his knee. Then, on Friday night, starting center Colville was involved in a car accident giving him concussion symptoms. The game was only seconds old when Marcus Williams fumbled the opening kickoff.

"When our top kickoff returner fumbles on the first play, yeah, it's going to be a bad hair day, I can tell you that," Bohl said.

Down 23-10, the Bison started their comeback on their first drive of the fourth quarter, a 68-yard march that took 10 plays. NDSU capped the drive with a crucial fourth-and-6 conversion. Brock Jensen found Zach Vraa open in the end zone on a slant route. That play covered 11 yards and cut the Northern Iowa lead to 23-17 with 10:14 remaining.

NDSU came up with the winning points on its next drive. The Bison took advantage of two Northern Iowa 15-yard penalties on a march that covered 76 yards capped by Ojuri's touchdown.

"I think the biggest thing was looking back at that Kansas State game," said Bison junior defensive end Kyle Emanuel, who had four tackles and three quarterback hurries. "Being in that situation before, we were used to it. We didn't let it get to us."

The Bison trailed by 14 points in the second half at Kansas State in the season opener before they rallied for a 24-21 victory.

9. Oct. 20, 2007: NDSU 27, Minnesota 21

The drive: The only one that didn't involve scoring, the 12 plays that went 46 yards in 5:20 ran out the clock and prevented the Gophers from getting the ball back before just over 63,000 fans at the Metrodome. Included in the drive was a roughing-the-punter penalty by the Gophers on Dragosavich, who admitted later he may have fallen harder than he probably needed to.

This win was not so much an FCS victory over an FBS opponent but more of a celebration of a fan base that came alive in the last couple of years. NDSU came within a blocked field goal of winning in 2006, with the Gophers prevailing 10-9 but not in front of an estimated 20,000 Bison fans at the Metrodome.

NDSU took a 27-21 lead on a Shawn Bibeau field goal and held the Gophers to three plays and out after that. Then came one of the most important non-scoring drives in NDSU history.

Starting from their own 34-yard line with 5:40 left, NDSU picked up two key first downs.

"There were thoughts of last year when we out-yarded them but came up short," Bohl said.

There were more thoughts when another first down pass to Wurzbacher was called back because of a holding penalty. The Bison drive stalled with 1:48 left and Dragosavich came on to punt.

But Minnesota's Dominique Barber was flagged for roughing Dragosavich and with the Gophers out of time outs, the Bison ran out the clock.

After the last snap, Walker heaved the ball toward the NDSU sideline – a ball that is still on display to this day.

8. Nov. 4, 2006: NDSU 28, UC Davis 24

The drive: Down 24-0 at halftime, the Bison used 2:28 to go 77 yards in 16 plays completing the biggest rally in school history with the 10-yard touchdown pass from Walker to Majeski with just 4 seconds left. Walker converted a fourth-and-12 with pass to Heckendorf and a fourth-and-10 with pass to Majeski on the drive.

It's one thing to rally from 24 down at home with the fans behind you, but to do it on the road is another matter.

7. Sept. 23, 2006: NDSU 29, Ball State 24

The drive: NDSU went 92 yards in seven plays, scoring on Walker's 39-yard pass to Travis White with 1:25 remaining, completing a fourth-quarter rally that gave the Bison their first-ever win over an FBS opponent. The pass to White was a thing of beauty, a wide receiver screen in the left flat that caught the Cardinals flat-footed.

Perles said he wanted to call a slow screen in the middle of the field, but assistant Brent Vigen was insistent on the jail-break screen to White. Perles, the offensive coordinator, took his advice. Ball State obliged by throwing a "zero blitz" defensive alignment at Walker, meaning the Cardinals were all in on a sack. It didn't work.

"It was a great pass by Steve, he had someone right in his face," Perles said.

The drive started with a 29-yard pass to White with 4:37 left. An eight-yard pass to White got a first down at 2:37 at the Ball State 40-yard line. After a one-yard run by Steffes, White took a bubble screen pass and found all kinds of room down the middle for the game-winner.

"We will not be underestimated again, I can tell you that," Bison cornerback Richard Bowman said. "We're a program on the rise."

The Bison got a school-record performance by Walker, who completed 29 of 46 passes for 451 yards, three touchdowns and no interceptions. Heckendorf had seven receptions for 95 yards and a touchdown, and White added six catches for 112 yards. The game also featured a 39-yard touchdown pass to close the first half – a "Hail Mary" bomb from Walker to Heckendorf that pulled NDSU to within 14-13 at the break.

The final drive stunned the home-standing Cardinals crowd in a matchup of an 85-scholarship program and a 63-scholarship team.

"It's another huge step for our program. We just keep going out and competing against programs that have more," Gene Taylor said. "It's been an amazing little streak. It says a lot about our kids. They just continually get it done. It's been impressive. It says a lot about our athletic program. We made some decisions financially that we were going to do this the right way. We were going to fully fund scholarships, pay coaches and give them dollars to recruit. I think it's paying off for us."

6. Nov. 10, 2007: NDSU 31, Cal Poly 28

The drive: Bison, down 28-9 in the fourth quarter, rallied with three touchdowns. The last covered 92 yards in three plays with no timeouts to work with. False start penalty moves NDSU to its own 4. Walker scrambled for 16 yards to the 20. On next play, he hit Heckendorf down the right sideline for an 80-yard TD with 38 seconds left.

5. Sept. 15, 2007: NDSU 41, Sam Houston State 38

The drive: The Bearkats scored with just 26 seconds left to take a 38-34 lead and a bunch of Fargodome fans headed for the exit. But the Bison grabbed a squib kickoff at their 46-yard line and were somewhat in business. A 27-yard pass from Walker to Heckendorf reached the Bearkats' 27. Walker threw an incomplete pass, but with seven seconds left, he connected with Heckendorf in the front corner of the end zone for an improbable rally.

I'll never forget the thought of hundreds of fans who had already left the dome after Sam Houston scored. With Walker, you never left anything until the final buzzer.

4. Dec. 6, 2014: NDSU 27, South Dakota State 24

The drive: After the Jackrabbits took a 24-20 lead on a touchdown with 3:18 left, the Bison drove 76 yards in eight plays with Wentz leading the charge. A 29-yard pass to R.J. Urzendowski was the second-biggest play behind the 12-yarder to Urzendowski in the corner of the end zone with 54 seconds left in the FCS second-round playoff game.

When SDSU quarterback Austin Sumner hit Jake Wieneke with a 3-yard touchdown pass with 3 minutes, 18 seconds left, the Jackrabbits led 24-20. Like a kid in his backyard, Wentz grabbed his helmet with the chance to engineer a winning drive. It's not that easy. The Gate City Bank Field fans, especially those with tickets to Frisco, were on the verge of nerve overload. NDSU, keep in mind, was the three-time defending FCS champion. The opponent was an inter-state rival. The Jacks, for the most part, had the look all day of a team ready to finally win after losing six straight to the Bison. Wentz shut all of that out.

"He was the same cool, calm kid he is all the time," Klieman said. "Whether it's in practice or the locker room, there's no panic in him."

True to this game, a holding call set the Bison back to a first-and-20, but Wentz erased most of that with a 19-yard strike to Carey Woods. Wentz's four-yard run got NDSU a first down at midfield with 1:41 remaining.

The next play took seemingly forever before it was resolved. SDSU was called for pass interference, but the call on the field was Wentz's pass was tipped at the line of scrimmage, and therefore interference was null and void. It was overturned after an official review, basically because nobody got within two feet of touching the pass.

"Penalties came throughout the game, and there was controversy on a number of them," Wentz said.

With 1:05 remaining, it only added to the paranoia. Another addition: Woods dropping a pass in traffic in the end zone and a Bison illegal motion penalty that set them back to the 12. That's when the magic happened.

"I was just trying to stay calm," Urzendowski said. "We ran that play a few times, and I got the same look."

He was one-on-one with SDSU linebacker Dallas Brown, and the Jackrabbit sophomore had decent coverage. But Wentz lofted it right over the outstretched arms of Brown, and Urzendowski made a twisting, falling grab. The visual evidence captured by Forum photographer Dave Samson showed it was not an easy catch.

"We practice that situation every week," Urzendowski said. "We're all comfortable with it, and you just have to stay calm."

3. Dec. 14, 2012: NDSU 23, Georgia Southern 20

The drive: Taking over at their own 47-yard line in the FCS semifinals, the Bison needed seven plays and took the dramatic route for the lead on Jensen's five-yard touchdown run on fourth-and-3 with 3:05 remaining in the fourth quarter.

It set an unofficial record for the most suspenseful game in the 20-year history of the Fargodome. "Those are the situations you live for," Jensen said. "I'm proud of all of our guys."

For a while, it looked like NDSU wouldn't get to Frisco again. GSU quarterback Jerrick McKinnon had 168 yards rushing against a Bison defense that was giving up an average of 64 yards rushing a game. The Eagles led 20-17 when the Bison got the ball with just over six minutes left in the game.

The touchdown came one play after Jensen ran five yards to the 5-yard line. There was a lot of debate on the fourth down play call on the Bison sidelines. With back-to-back time outs buying them some time, Vigen finally made the decision – and he wasn't about to let somebody else other than Jensen handle the ball. It took a while to get to that point, though.

During the last time out, Bohl went into the middle of the Bison huddle near the sideline.

The conundrum centered on whether to run a play NDSU had been running all game: quarterback power with Jensen carrying the ball. The Eagles' defense was yelling it as Jensen came up to the line of scrimmage. GSU head coach Jeff Monken ran on to the field to call the first time out, knowing what NDSU was about to do.

"Everybody in the stadium and everybody and their grandmothers knew what was coming," Jensen said. "We ran the same formation every time. I sent the same guy in motion every time. But coach Bohl said 'we're coming at your ass' and you have to respect that. They knew what was coming but we didn't want it any other way. Power is our game. I remember vividly the last time I went over to the sideline and I still get goosebumps thinking about it. Coach Bohl was looking at all the other guys and hit me without looking at me. The guys looked at me. I was looking at them. I just smiled and said let's get it done fellas."

After the time out, the Bison decided on the same play. Polasek shouted over the coaching headsets that he wanted the fullback Lang out of the game in favor of a tailback. Several coaches were questioning the play call most likely because of the predictability. That's when Vigen slammed his hand on the table in the dome coaches' box. It was an unusual display of emotion for Vigen.

"I'm telling you coach, it's the right play," he adamantly told Bohl.

Jensen took the snap in shotgun formation, got a great kickout block from Gimmestad, shed a linebacker near the line of scrimmage and bulled his way into the end zone. The drive took seven plays with a personal foul penalty on the punt return on GSU giving NDSU the ball at its own 47-yard line. Jensen gained 23 yards to the Eagle 40. Perhaps the big play was a roughing-the-passer penalty on GSU standout Brent Russell that gave the Bison a first down at the 12-yard line.

The game was still not over on a Friday night ESPN2 telecast. The Eagles responded getting in position for a 50-yard field goal attempt, but it was blocked by Carlton Littlejohn with 34 seconds left.

2. Aug. 30, 2013: NDSU 24, Kansas State 21

The drive: NDSU traveled 80 yards in 18 plays on national TV to defeat the defending Big 12 Conference champion in front of 53,351 fans, scoring on Jensen's 1-yard run with 28 seconds left.

"To me, it still ranks as the flagship victory of this whole run," said Mike McFeely. "Minnesota, and all those other teams; you knew they were not good teams and that's why NDSU scheduled them. But Kansas State, you go down there and you see how big it is – this successful program. You can talk championships and everything else, but that was the one that put them on the ESPN map. The national map. That victory made them the darlings of FCS football. That changed the whole discussion and it turned out to be a pretty good K-State team."

This one was historic in so many ways. It was the debut weekend for Fox Sports 1 and it couldn't have gone any better for the visiting team. It was miserably hot from kickoff until linebacker Grant Olson's interception to seal the victory. That 18-play drive was a thing of beauty, both in terms of an FCS team handling K-State at the line of scrimmage but also in the poise and patience of NDSU.

1. Jan. 11, 2016: NDSU 29, Illinois State 27

The drive: The Bison went 78 yards in six plays, although the march actually covered 83 yards because of an early penalty. Wentz carved his future completing three passes to R.J. Urzendowski including a 33-yarder that reached the 5-yard line.

Wentz scored on the next play.

Adding to the suspense: it came right after the Redbirds had the game won when quarterback Tre Roberson scored from 58 yards out with 1:38 remaining.

More on this game later, when Frisco became a yearly destination in early January.

VIII. Planes, trains and automobiles

Every weekend in the fall, it's as if there are two families in my life: the one at home and the one in the press box. The first one requires daily maintenance in all things life. The second one requires daily maintenance in all things life.

Never a dull moment.

First, let's get one thing clear: the fact the NDSU football program has a media contingent of several follow it across the country in the Division I football years is not the reason a dynasty was born. We did not raise money, we did not recruit players, we did not coach them, we did not assemble a coaching staff, we did not train them and we did not motivate them.

That being said, having a Forum Communications Company private plane certainly doesn't hurt the profile of a dynasty, either. That just doesn't happen in FBS let alone FCS. Mike McFeely tells the story of Los Angeles Times columnist Bill Plaschke calling him one day in 2005 for a story on the Heisman Trophy race, where USC running back Reggie Bush was one of the favorites. Why McFeely? Because he ran into L.A. Times college beat writer Chris Dufresne on the beaten path somewhere when the subject of the Heisman voting come up. Dufresne, despite covering USC football, was not allowed to vote for the Heisman because his newspaper had a conflict of interest stipulation that prohibited him from voting for anything on a team he covered. I get it. It was old school journalism and I respected that. So Defresne went on to ask McFeely why he was going to vote for Bush.

"Isn't that funny," Defresne told McFeely. "You're a Heisman voter in Fargo and I cover USC. Why did you vote for Reggie?"

"Because he's clearly the best player," McFeely said.

So Dufresne later told Plaschke about his conversation with this columnist/Heisman voter in Fargo, North Dakota. It wasn't long before Plaschke called McFeely, with his angle being a story on how a Heisman voter in Fargo can have more of a say than a guy like Dufresne who actually watched Bush play. Plaschke's reasoning: if some writer in Fargo is voting for Bush, then he probably has the award wrapped up.

"Why did you vote for Reggie?" Plaschke asked McFeely.

"Because he's the best player," was his reply, a standard response by now.

"How many games have you seen?" Plaschke said.

"Full games?" McFeely said. "None."

"Wow, what do you do on Saturdays?" Plaschke said.

"I write a column and cover North Dakota State football," McFeely said.

"So you spend Saturdays driving in a car or waiting in airports to fly out somewhere," Plaschke said.

"No," McFeely said, "we have a private plane. Forum Communications has a private plane that we fly to all road games."

That response floored Plaschke, who works in one of the biggest newspapers in the world yet the thought of flying private was, well, never a thought.

"You have a private plane that you fly to all road games," Plaschke repeated. "How many does it seat?"

"Ten," McFeely said.

"Really … " Plaschke said.

The discussion then went back to Bush and why McFeely voted for him. Bush was having a monster year and finished with 2,611 all-purpose yards and 18 touchdowns and captured the essence of being a Heisman front runner. Then Plaschke interrupted McFeely on one of his answers and piped in with a comment something like this:

"Wait a second, you fly in a private plane to football games?" he said. "Your company flies you to football games in a private plane? Wow. That's amazing."

It is amazing, actually. In all my years of covering Bison football, I never saw a traveling media party like ours. Nothing close. Everywhere we went, with the exception of that 3-8 season in 2009 when nobody really cared, we would bring a media crew of at least six to road games. On the flipside, the only time I ever saw media covering a visiting team at the Fargodome bring more than one person was the Grand Forks Herald, the Sioux Falls Argus Leader and a couple of newspapers that cover Northern Iowa football. And they would bring two reporters, with a photographer at the most three.

Keith Corliss, our pilot since 1993 who's probably been to almost every major and mid-major private Flight Base of Operations in the country, said he's never heard of media guys going private. He hears it from other pilots all the time: You're flying who?

"Credit Mr. Marcil," Corliss said of former Forum publisher Bill Marcil, who handed off reigns of the business to his son, Bill Marcil Jr., in 2013. "This was put in place before me, by (pilot) Bill Freeland and the relationship NDSU had with The Forum. They had no problems supporting our sports reporting crew going to these games. It helps having the synergy of WDAY and at the time radio and TV. We came in with that 1-2-3 punch like nobody else could and that made aircraft sensible."

WDAY radio long had the rights to Bison games until Radio Fargo-Moorhead got the bid in 2010, ending a run of 43 out of the previous 46 years

Forum Communications had the contract. Still, that didn't stop us from our mobile reporting army. Now, instead of radio, we take a video guy or two for our pre-game and post-game web shows, productions that by 2014 started to reach WDAY's digital TV channel. The same-day travel is also essential for WDAY-TV, so Dom Izzo can do his Friday night 10:20 sportscast and then catch a flight in the morning to wherever NDSU plays football, mainly to Youngstown, Carbondale, Macomb, Brookings, Vermillion, Springfield, Normal, Cedar Falls or Terre Haute. Those are the towns of the Missouri Valley Football Conference.

Yes, we were spoiled.

Well, mostly spoiled. We also took a scare in the first year of the Division I transition when the Bison played at Nicholls State in Thibodaux, La. The trip started like all the rest; we met at the Fargo Jet Center, loaded the King Air 350 and headed for the south.

But somewhere around Sioux Falls, the sliding door to the cockpit opened and Corliss pointed to the windshield; it was cracked and starting to form multiple spider webs. Jack Michaels and Phil Hansen looked at each other and said the following: "So this is how it's going to end."

"A loud snap, it gets your attention in a hurry," Corliss said. "I can't see anything through the window and you say to yourself this is going to get interesting. The Beachcraft manual will tell you it's not a dire emergency but who wants to fly around with pieces of glass falling into your lap? We had the option to continue but we thought it was just wise to turn around and not drag it into something worse."

I wasn't too alarmed because some of us had already gone through this once; a cracked windshield on the way to the NCAA Division II women's basketball tournament in Pine Bluff, Ark., several years earlier forced an emergency landing in Springfield, Mo. We got the full treatment on that safety measure, with fire trucks and an ambulance already on the runway as we came in. Anyway, with the latest problem, we flew back to Fargo at lower altitude for safety's sake.

But here was the problem: it was game day morning and kickoff was later in the afternoon in Thibodaux.

"I remember descending from like 30,000 feet to 10,000 pretty quick," Hansen said. "But Corliss is a good guy and we were in the best capable hands we could be in."

Thanks to some quick thinking by co-pilot Craig Holly -- he was the lead pilot for Black Gold Potatoes based in Grand Forks -- the powers that be negotiated some sort of trade out and the new plan was to take the Black Gold plane to the game in Thibodaux.

But even that included complications: the Black Gold plane was an hour north in Grand Forks and we had to return the King Air to Fargo.

Let's just say after we landed that the speed limit on Interstate 29 to Grand Forks exceeded 75 mph. We reached the private aviation quarters in Grand Forks, reloaded and headed once again for Louisiana. Time was of the essence and the person that was most affected was Miller, the play-by-play announcer.

I loved Scotty, the guy was as genuine as they get, funnier than a chicken but also a perfectionist on game day and had the need to get to the stadium plenty early. I felt bad for him because anxiety was setting in and Scotty does not like to let down his listeners.

There were other problems before we got to the stadium, however. Thibodaux did not have an airport, so we had to land in Houma, La., located about 19 miles from Nicholls State.

These were 19 twisting and turning miles, much more frightening than the cracked windshield at 29,000 feet, because the passenger van we got at the Houma airport had deficient breaks.

"The van with no brakes," Hansen said. "Scotty was just beside himself."

"The saddest man in the world was Scotty Miller because his lifeblood is calling NDSU football games," McFeely said. "We were driving in the back roads of Louisiana in a Scooby Doo van where the brakes didn't work with the game on the radio and the Nichols State radio team calling the game. Scotty was looking like a kid at Christmas who didn't get any presents."

Michaels from WDAY started to figure out that pumping the brakes seemed to work better, or perhaps he just let off the gas 100 feet before a stop sign to make us feel better. We arrived at the stadium somewhere just short of halftime.

It was 14-0, NDSU, when we reached the press box. We missed a 10-yard touchdown run by Steffes and a 36-yard touchdown pass from Stauss to receiver Allen Burrell. It still wasn't the worst of circumstances for a writer; I could always catch up at halftime and after the game ask players if there were details to fill in. Plus, the second half is when most games are decided anyway.

No biggie.

It was 90 degrees and very humid, some rain in the area, with little wind. By the time the Bison players were walking off the field following a 24-14 win, they were exhausted, almost too tired to celebrate the first legitimate win over a Division I-AA program. I'll never forget the look of the players outside the locker room trying to regain a sense of normalcy.

"The heat was brutal and we were feeling it," Stauss said.

Our work, of course, was not done. Mike and I still had to file our stories and we still had this plane issue to deal with and a van with brake problems. The original plan with the King Air was to stay in a hotel in the area, but Holly didn't want his Black Gold plane to stay at the Houma airport overnight because it wasn't a secure area. So the nearest FBO was in New Orleans.

The way this day went, I was all for a visit to Bourbon Street. So was everybody else.

"We're only here once, let's check it out," McFeely said.

We got there around 11 p.m. Dinner was a shrimp joint in the French Quarter. Dinner and beer and whatever else we threw down our throats to settle the nerves that were frazzled most of the day. A very large cockroach taking a stroll on the floor of the restaurant made for a nice local touch.

From there, we headed to a nearby bar that only served to intensify the evening. One of the drinks: a shot that you had to take with the shot glass resting between the waitress' breasts.

Amazingly, we even got Miller, a spiritual man who rarely ran with us at night, to take one, though it didn't come without effort. WDAY sports director Stacey Anderson was the instigator, telling the waitress to make "that guy" take one. Scotty backpedaled until he ran into a wall, and the waitress who was much bigger than him won that battle.

A couple of hours later, Mike, Stacey and I were still on the premises – and we weren't in a mood to go home. That didn't happen for a while. Last call for us was at 6 a.m. and it was McFeely who brought the round to us.

"You know McFeely, I wasn't sure I liked you very much," Stacey said. "Now, I like you a lot."

We hailed a cab as the street cleaners were doing their job and got back to the airport hotel somewhere after 7 a.m. McFeely called the front desk for a 7:30 wakeup call. The response: Sir, it's 7:45.

"I went down to the lobby to get ready to go to the airport and I see Hallstrom," McFeely said. "The first thing he does is go, 'Are you OK?'"

"I'm doing great, how about you?" Mike said.

Mike stole a pillow from the hotel and pretty much ended up curled in the fetal position in the airplane aisle on the way home. The next day, at the weekly Monday Bohl press conference, we all thanked Taylor for scheduling the Nicholls State game.

"Why, did you like New Orleans?" was Taylor's general response.

***

Say this about our trips over the years: we have the process down to a science. Corliss has football timed to 6½ hours from the time we get to the stadium until we get back to the FBO to fly out. He grew up the same way I did as kids tagging along with our dads. His father, Ron Corliss, was the athletic business manager at NDSU for 17 years.

"I grew up as a locker room groupie," he said. "We went to everything, football, basketball, wrestling, track. Every night up there we would be doing something and I hung around by the locker room. Oh my god, I'm in the room with Bruce Grasamke. Look, there's Tim Mjos. Dad still reveres the names Mudra, Erhardt and Loftsgard. Those three bridged the gap from mediocrity to putting us on the map."

Mudra was the head football coach in the mid-1960s who started the tradition. Erhardt won national titles later in the decade. Loftsgard was the president who put emphasis on football from his office. Corliss knows his Bison history; he went to the Camellia Bowl in Sacramento, Calif., when he was 11 years old. Those were the college division days that morphed into Division II.

He was standing almost under the left goal post upright at Washington-Grizzly Stadium in 2003 when Montana kicker Chris Snyder was wide left with his game-winning field goal attempt. Corliss was holding the parabolic microphone for the radio broadcast. Anderson, shooting video highlights for WDAY-TV, was standing almost under the other upright.

"We looked at each other and our eyes got 'this' big," Corliss said. "We completely abandoned all journalistic ethics and started jumping around. Totally unprofessional, but it was such a moment. I watched it as it was coming toward the upright and then it just veered away. The refs looked at each other, and both gave the 'no good' signal. I'm like, holy shit, did I just see what I just saw? This program was one of the big boys on the Division I-AA block. … Yeah, over the years, I've been that camel with his nose under the tent watching this whole thing happening."

Ironically, it was the broadcasting debut for Hansen – who earlier that week as a fan was going to drive to Missoula.

"Then I get out the map and I'm like, Jesus, it's further to Missoula than it is to Buffalo, N.Y.," he said. "So I called Stacey Anderson and said, 'Hey Stacey, I know you get to fly out to those games, would there be any chance to catch a ride? I really want to go to the game.' He said, 'Oh no Phil, sorry, the flight is full and we have to take media and there is no room.' Well, I thought, at least I tried. Then he called me back two hours later and said, 'Hey Phil, would you like to go out to Montana?' I said, 'Yeah, but I thought the plane was full.' He said he wanted me to broadcast the game and at the time Mark Speral was doing the TV and he asked me to do the color for the radio. I said, 'Color? What's that?' But I said I can't get out there because you said the plane was full. He said don't worry about that, we'll fly you out there. So I said, 'So you do have a seat.' So that's what started it all."

Hansen became a fixture with the Bison media from that point on. NDSU loved having him in that position, not only because he was an 11-year NFL veteran and had the background to do the job but having one of its most visible and greatest players on board with the Division I transition. He also for a time did the Sunday morning TV coaches show.

"So that's what started it all," he said of the Montana game. "That was my first time. Yeah, that established the credibility for the football program or at least a starting point for Bison football at the Division I level."

Yes, Division I was a totally different animal. The King Air was never more useful than in 2006 when the Bison played a string of six games in seven weeks away from home in a season that saw NDSU travel 7,045 miles. This was no longer the North Central Conference when Corliss and I once did a story titled "The coffee shops of the NCC." It was a travel piece that identified the best coffee spot in each of the nine other NCC towns, to this day still one of my favorite stories and I don't know why.

In the Division I transition, you got games when you could and it just so happened that was a season when the Bison had to leave Fargo a lot.

"That was a ball buster," Corliss said. "You get to the point where everybody gets on the plane and everybody has their roles. We were so good at it."

We began the journey in Muncie, Ind., to cover the program's first FBS win – the 29-24 thriller over Ball State. Then it was on to Nacogdoches, Texas, for Stephen F. Austin, where we found out the best of plans don't always work out.

For starters, when I made hotel reservations earlier that summer, it was at the Comfort Suites and by the time we got there, it was sold and became the Nacogdoches Inn. One of our party opened his room to already find a roommate: a cockroach. Phil was so disgusted with the morning continental breakfast that he looked bleached white in the face on the way to the stadium.

That trip also provided a rare golf outing – one of two in the first 12 years of the DI experience. With plenty of time when we arrived early Friday afternoon, Steve Hallstrom and I decided to check out the local public golf course, one that I scoped on Google Earth a day earlier. It looked fine from a space camera, I told him. When we got there; not so much. It was dang near grown over, the worst course I have ever played but, oh well, it was still golf.

We flew back following the game, only to get ready the next Friday to head to Statesboro, Ga., and Georgia Southern. I couldn't wait. When it came to FCS or Division I-AA football, it didn't get any better than Georgia Southern. Stories on the GSU tradition flowed all week in our newspaper.

The school resurrected its program in 1981 after 41 years of dormancy and it did it right winning six I-AA national championships. So the conventional wisdom was a program in just its third year of a Division I schedule probably wasn't ready for the heavyweights of the division.

In The Forum's Game Day graphic, three out of five of us who picked the games on a weekly basis fell victim to the Georgia Southern tradition and picked the Eagles. That would have been me, McFeely and Hallstrom. In retrospect, we were clueless to how in disarray GSU really was that season.

It turned out to be the perfect year to play the Eagles in their stadium. Their new coach, Brian VanGorder, tried to shed the triple option that made that program so historic in favor of a multiple attack. It failed. It failed miserably. VanGorder was an NFL guy, coming from an assistant position with the Jacksonville Jaguars and for whatever reason went away from the tradition that Erk Russell established in Statesboro. The Bison defense had no trouble stopping a passing offense that was using option-type players in a 34-14 win.

"I look at North Dakota State, and that's where we're headed," VanGorder said. "They're big and they're strong and they're physical. We had a hard time with those guys today."

Those words would be echoed from several coaches in the years to come. NDSU was 11 of 14 on third-down conversions that day, an alarming statistic for a visiting team in the house that Erk built. Quarterbacks like Walker do that – burn you on third down.

Returning to Fargo, it was a breather of sorts for us with the one home game in the stretch: a homecoming game vs. Mississippi Valley. That was not the Jerry Rice Mississippi Valley and the final was predictable: 45-0, a game that was the back end of a home-and-home that saw NDSU travel to Itta Bena, Miss., the previous year. It was a small town of just over 2,000 people where we almost got beat up at a restaurant because Corliss took offense to some guy changing the channel on us from a Major League Baseball playoff game to a NASCAR event. Granted, it was very rude of the guy, but he didn't look like the type to mess with. McFeely told Corliss to shut his mouth before we all got killed.

The Mississippi Valley homecoming game done, all eyes were on the following week anyway: the first matchup at the University of Minnesota.

The final two of the road trip were back-to-back King Air flights out west, the first being a second straight year of traveling to Cedar City, Utah, and Southern Utah University. And for the second straight year, it was a beautiful weekend for weather in the Wasatch Mountains. The Bison took care of the Thunderbirds 31-7, putting the previous week's 10-9 tough loss at Minnesota behind them, flew back to Fargo only to get ready for the next week's trip to California Davis.

"I was concerned about that all week," Steffes said. "It was the opposite environment of the Metrodome, but we stressed all week that we're playing for each other. I think that's what we did today."

It was yet more evidence of Bohl's ability to get his team to buy into the business trip mentality. That was one of his strengths; the guy could just capture the spirit of Tom Osborne and parlay it into his players. That's a big reason why NDSU rarely lost a game away from Fargo.

It was that mentality that was a big reason for the historic comeback the next week at Davis. The thing about that; the biggest comeback in program history came on the last game of a seven-week, six-game road trip. You want to define mental toughness in building a dynasty? There's Example A right there.

The truth in the whole deal is NDSU returned from Davis 8-1 with the only loss to the Gophers by a point. Nationally, sports information directors and sportswriters and sportscasters were obviously troubled in how to pick NDSU. It was not eligible for the playoffs, and therefore clueless to how it would stack up with everybody else. The Bison were ranked sixth before the Davis game, and only went up from there.

The thing about the FCS and its national polls, with the two main ones being the FCS coaches poll and The Sports Network media poll, was the geographical setup of the division. The vast majority of schools are in the east, so there is a general tendency for eastern schools to get preferential poll treatment. Take 2014: NDSU was the three-time defending champ, opened the season with a 34-14 thrashing of Iowa State and there were still voters in the media poll who had to have had NDSU ranked fourth, fifth or sixth.

The beauty of the FCS is the champion is determined on the field in a 24-team playoff.

***

When Izzo arrived from the East Coast in 2006, and subsequently took over the marquee job at WDAY after Hallstrom left in 2010, things changed with Forum Communications. Steve was great, willing to experiment with the media blog and engage with the online audience, but Dom took it to new levels. The guy has an incredible work ethic, so much that his managers at WDAY were more apt to try and curtail his schedule more than encourage it.

Dom is a 2002 graduate of the State University of New York at Oswego. He never played sports growing up, but there is nobody more knowledgeable. He worked at WSTM in Syracuse, N.Y. for a couple of years, moved on to WNCE-TV in Glens Falls, N.Y., before taking the WDAY weekend job. The second week he was here, NDSU upset Ball State and Dom was trying to grasp how big of a story that really was. He had no clue.

He was a quick learner. When Hallstrom left for a private sector financial job in 2010, Izzo was immediately promoted.

"I'll never forget it, when I took over, the first thing I did was I called you," Dom said to me. "I had some of my own ideas that I thought could be good. I was kind of seeing where the medium was going, knowing that newspapers weren't dying but were less popular and people were more going to the internet. I wanted to pick up where Steve left off. I wanted to give them something unique and I thought with our partnership that was something we could really take advantage of. We just lost the radio contract (to Radio Fargo Moorhead) so I needed to make sure we were still viable and a presence. I knew you had radio experience so I thought people will watch this."

Dom's viability and "being a presence theory" turned into the first Media Blog pregame show in Lawrence, Kan., on Sept. 4, 2010, which aired on the WDAY.com and Inforum.com websites. "After that, I thought, you know what? We may have something here," Izzo said. "Then a couple of weeks later we did one in the old WDAY studio and I was hustling to get it online before the game started. I remember the response: people were saying keep it up, love to see it."

The tipping point of the Media Blog, however, came later in the year. If the general starting point of NDSU's Division I dynasty is considered to be the Montana game, the blast off point for the Media Blog came on Dec. 10, 2010. That's one day before NDSU was to play Eastern Washington in the FCS quarterfinals and Dom and I had an all-day travel schedule from Hector International in Fargo to Spokane, Wash., because our company plane wasn't available. The first stop was the Denver airport, where I tweeted something about the lack of good coffee in the terminal. About a minute later, former NDSU basketball coach Tim Miles replied to the tweet. He was several gates away waiting for a flight to the East Coast with his Nebraska basketball team, so he came over and we had a nice chat. Then, Dom and I headed to our gate, but before we got there, a guy stops us in the terminal hallway and says, "Hey, you're the guys from the Media Blog." He was a big Bison fan who lived in Alabama and watched us online. At that point, Dom was sold the Media Blog was another avenue to reach listeners or watchers and this thing was no longer just a couple yahoos talking on the web to just a few of us. We had an audience.

"I just thought this is something we need to continue," Izzo said. "We have to make this bigger. The people at The Forum were launching their own studio and I wanted to make sure the Media Blog was a big part of it."

Dom was ill with a cold/flu that Eastern Washington weekend, to the point where I thought he was going to pass out at any minute. Yet, there he was standing with me outside of Roos Field at 5:30 a.m. waiting for the EWU sports information director to open the front gate to let us in, so we could get into the press box to set up for our Saturday Morning Sports Show, which aired from 8-10 CST, but 6 a.m. Pacific. It was dark for most of our show from Cheney, although the glow from the red turf had an illuminating effect. After that, we did our Media Blog pregame show from atop the press box, covered the game, recorded the post-game show in the moonlight of Roos Field and drove back to Spokane.

Every trip, it seemed, had its moments. In 2011, we had Walker helping us on our Saturday Game Day section in the newspaper with a short "Saturday Morning Quarterback" column. He also came on a couple of road trips, including a 2011 game against Indiana State in Terre Haute, Ind., which had by far the worst facilities in the Missouri Valley. Memorial Stadium was built in the early 1920s and the venue had stands on just one side of the field. We covered the game, doing our pre-game online video and our post-game wrapup, the latter of which was done on the field with the stadium lights already turned off. It was Dom, Walker and me with only the light from Dom's camera illuminating us. The radio guys, Scott and Phil, were somewhere on the premises waiting for us to finish.

We filmed our post-game show and proceeded to the exit to find our rental cars, which were the only vehicles left in the parking lot. There was a slight problem, however: the gate was locked. The staff at ISU presumed we were gone – and you can't blame them because who in the Missouri Valley media tour stays around after a game in the dark? Yes, we do.

"We're always the last ones to leave," Corliss said. "The janitors are long gone. The work study kids have long cleaned up the stadium and the lights are out. The scoreboard is dark and there we are. After a long hard day, it's just neat to be done and fly home."

Not this time. The fences were old and high, about 10 feet, and were not safe to climb. We called the sports information director but he wasn't available. We called the Terre Haute police, but were told it would be at least an hour before they could get an officer there. We were locked in. Walker and Dom walked the entire premises, but there was no escape. We found a ladder near the ISU locker room building and thought about scaling that one-story structure, going up on the roof and down with the ladder on the other side. It was getting to that point of desperation.

That's when Walker pulled a "Cal Poly," miracle rally.

I don't know how he did it and I'm not sure I want to know, but he broke the lock on the front gate. All he would say several years later is, "it was just brute force from all those years of training with coach Kramer. I may have broken the lock, but I cannot confirm or deny that." We walked out, got in the two rental cars and drove to the airport to fly home.

Eric Peterson made his Media Blog debut almost by accident at the 2011 title game in Frisco when he stole my cowboy hat during a videotaping.

"You just knew right there that he had his own schtick," Dom said. "We had our own 'GameDay' sort of feel."

It was about that time when the Media Blog started to take off. The following season, The Forum made Peterson a regular in the coverage team and Big E was exactly what that online show needed: a personality that could play off of Dom and I.

By the 2013 season, my job responsibilities all kind of meshed into writing, video and radio. It sort of all became one gig – a long way from the first years of covering Division I football. The football program grew immensely from 2004 to 2014. So did the media coverage.

It all wasn't all pro-Division I, however. When word first surfaced that Joe Chapman wanted to move NDSU out of Division II, McFeely, for one, wasn't on board. In a 2002 column that preceded an expected positive recommendation from the consulting firm of Carr & Associates, McFeely took his stance.

"As much as it pains me to say this, NDSU has no business going Division I," he wrote. "It is painful because it is not often in North Dakota that somebody -- in this case school president Joe Chapman has the initiative to stand up and say, 'We should not confine ourselves to small-time thinking. Let's think big.' Instead, what too often passes for bold thinking are ideas like dropping North from Dakota so people from other parts of the United States will think we're a tropical paradise. The problem here is that there seems to be no compelling reason to upgrade to Division I."

Over 13 years later, Chapman could darn near recite the entire column. That was why the 2003 upset of Montana was so important, he said.

"Your colleague, McFeely, up until that game, he was having a hard time with this," Chapman said. "At that point, maybe he had to say there's something going on here. A lot of your colleagues were that way. You were there, you were crucial. You may not believe this but you were very important in this process."

Mike wasn't the only one. In the Twin Cities, Star-Tribune columnist Patrick Reusse nominated Chapman for his annual "Turkey of the Year" Thanksgiving Day column, writing: "The president of North Dakota State has been 100 percent behind the wacky plan to propel his school into Division I athletics. Meantime, the NDSU football team -- too mighty for its Division II rivals in Chapman's opinion -- finished 1-7 and last in the North Central Conference."

Reusse's award went to the Timberwolves braintrust of Kevin McHale and Flip Saunders for ill-advised personnel moves during that year, but the damage was done just reaching the nomination point.

"At that point, it was looking pretty bleak, it was not looking good," Chapman said.

It's a competitive business in Fargo, the media. The reporters from different outlets mostly get along, although there were moments. In 2004, before the convergence of WDAY and The Forum, WDAY's Hallstrom reported from an anonymous source that the Big Sky voted 8-0 against considering NDSU and

SDSU for league membership. It was a big scoop for Steve, if true. I was highly suspicious of the accuracy. I knew Montana State president Geoffrey Gamble was solidly in favor of Chapman's NDSU program and I couldn't imagine him voting no. The next morning, I called Taylor, who knew nothing about a vote. Big Sky commissioner Doug Fullerton said the same thing. So I called Steve and told him of the denials. He said his source came from the "presidential level" in the conference. "I am as confident about that as any other source on a story," he said.

***

Cancer struck the media fraternity when Scott Miller continually battled through ailments that started with melanoma in 2012. Sadly, we lost him in late February of 2016 at the young age of 57. My tweet that day:

"I don't really have the words other than one of the greatest guys ever. Put in a lot of miles with my friend Scotty. #myohmy."

He will go down as the only play-by-play announcer in radio history to see the team he works for win five straight national titles. The last one was hard, a Frisco day that he dang near had to save every ounce of his energy for the game against Jacksonville State.

This project has detailed several tough-guy stories of Bison football players, but sometimes I have to wonder if the toughest of them all was not a skinny redhead who called all of their games from the pressbox. He endured 17 surgeries – 17 surgeries without complaining to anybody. I saw him struggle to get up and down the concrete bleachers at old Coughlin-Alumni Stadium at South Dakota State, steps that I sometimes had a tough time dealing with healthy. Privately, Bison players and coaches did more for Scotty than anybody will probably ever know. Klieman and men's basketball coach Dave Richman drove him to his appointments on a pretty regular basis. One summer day, the Bison quarterbacks including Wentz showed up unannounced at Miller's south Fargo home and did all of his lawn care.

A couple of weeks after Frisco, his health started to deteriorate quickly. A week before he died, Dom, Eric Peterson, Mike, Stacey and I visited him at Sanford Health and his face lit up when Mike told him Eric was here to see him. "Even Big E?" he said with a smile.

Big E and Scotty spent many a night at Newman Outdoor Field covering the Fargo-Moorhead RedHawks. I never once heard Scotty call a Bison football game because we were always in the same press box, but he was so calming and professional with the Hawks. Scotty was a big-time talent in a medium-sized market. Back in the Division II NCC days, he was a recipient of the "Ed Kolpack Award" that went to the most deserving media member covering the league, a connection that I'll always cherish.

His passing resulted in an incredible number of tributes. His funeral was a Who's Who of athletics, with Craig Bohl coming back from Wyoming, Gene Taylor from Iowa, Bubba Schweigert from UND, Roger Thomas from the University of Mary in Bismarck and media cohorts from all over. Afterward, in the lobby of First Lutheran Church near downtown Fargo, Taylor and Bohl shook hands – the first time they had any sort of contact with each other since the 2013 coaching change fiasco. But perhaps the most fitting tribute came from an anonymous post on a Bison fan website that probably summed Scotty up best:

"Reflection on what Scott Miller meant to me: Like many Bison fans, I never got to meet Scott Miller. Yes, I saw him in person many times, but never had a conversation with him. From everything I have read, he was clearly a wonderful human being who touched the lives of many in more substantial ways than how he touched my life.

*Yet, what a legacy he has left in Bison broadcasting. The reality is he **DID** touch so many of our lives and I suspect even he did not fully realize this before his passing. I'd like just to tell my own story and how Scott touched my life. I am a lifelong Bison fan; the son of an alumni and having grown up the 1980s during the incredible run they had. I used to listen to every game in high school (prior to Scott). I then attended NDSU and closely followed each and every game.*

I admit, after graduation from NDSU, and undergoing more post graduate training in the Twin Cities, I did not follow NDSU as closely for a few years. I maybe streamed one-two games in 4 years, and traveled up to the UND game each year. I would not even have known who Scott Miller was at that time even though he was working games. But like many things associated with NDSU, everything changed for me when they went Division 1.

At the same time of the move up, I moved to Duluth, MN. Streaming was no longer a new thing, and NDSU even started tinkering with video streaming around that time. The Division 1 move completely changed my apathetic attitude like I suspect it did many others. I so wanted to see them succeed as I thought the move was so long overdue. I started streaming games more regularly. Of course the voice I heard was Scott Miller. 2006 was a year that will stand out as a watershed moment for many Bison fans; it is also the year that reverted me to the complete crazy fan of my youth, including college. I, like many, travelled to Minneapolis hoping to have a good time, pretty excited the Bison were getting a chance to play the Gophers. But everything changed for me that day. Suddenly, I started to fully understand what was possible despite the loss. I realized NDSU was on the cusp of dominance once again. I watched or listened to basically every single Bison game starting at that time.

So there I was, in an unfinished room in the basement every Saturday streaming every game. My kids were too little to appreciate football, and my wife was not interested. So I was by myself, or so I thought. In retrospect, Scott Miller was with me.

My most vivid memory was listening to the 2007 Sam Houston State game completely despaired that NDSU seemed to be destined to defeat. Then, two of the most improbably plays in Bison history happened, and NDSU wins. The joy of the moment literally came through the computer speakers. And who was it that described the scene? Scott Miller.

My point is Scott Miller was there for all of us who could not be at every game. His voice was flawless; his excitement real, his delivery, perfect. He was the friend who took us to the game when we could not be there.

So, all of you business folks who were on the road, so you could not get to every game; all of you North Dakotans who could not watch the games before the TV days; all of you transplants in other states who started following the Bison more closely due to streaming and the D1 move; all of you younger fans who have watched the numerous You Tube clips NDSU has put out with Scott's voice; all of you farmers who were busy bringing in the harvest listening to the Bison; when you get home tonight, raise a toast to the memory of Scott Miller. Ask your spouse, kids and other family to say prayers for the family of Scott Miller for comfort and support. Say a prayer for all those associated with NDSU who are hurting due to his passing. And finally, say a prayer of Thanksgiving to the Lord for giving us Scott Miller.

Scott, I hope you know how you touched all of our lives for the better."

IX. Season on the brink

The 2009 calendar year started with the departure of the two Bison coordinators: defensive coordinator Willie Mack Garza, who took a position at the University of New Mexico and before he got there got a position at Tennessee, and offensive coordinator Pat Perles, who ended up with the Kansas City Chiefs after initially getting a position at Ball State.

It was not an amicable separation between Perles and Bohl, who thought Perles was negotiating for another position behind his back. Perles said he wasn't looking for another job, but ran into Stan Parrish, the head coach at Ball State, at a suite at the Motor City Bowl in Detroit, an event founded and operated by George Perles, Pat's father.

Parrish asked Pat Perles if he wanted to have lunch the next day.

"He said if lunch goes good, I'll bring you in to Ball State and interview you," Perles said. "At lunch, he offered me the job. I didn't accept it, said I need to talk to my head coach. I think as I step away from it now, Craig and I both handled it incorrectly. I have no hard feelings; I have way too many good memories hanging around Craig."

Perles had been with Bohl from the beginning of his NDSU tenure and was instrumental in developing the physical West Coast offensive line mentality. It was also about that time, in January of '09, when the program decided not to renew defensive assistant Kyle Nystrom's contract. Nystrom did not go softly. I ran into him a few days after the news hit and he was still livid at the head coach for not being considered for the defensive coordinator position. Not only was he not considered, but Bohl let him go. Bohl was looking for better recruiters and evaluators and he was not happy with the way the program was going. He thought his staff got complacent after the successive 10-1 seasons, the last in 2007.

NDSU had some talent returning in 2008, but the chemistry within the team took a hit. There are those inside the program who think players were more worried about pro scouts and getting into post-season all-star games than the Bison regular season. There were complaints about the shoes or football gloves not being good enough.

Privately, Bohl told a few people that he thought his program had lost its competitive edge. He felt like players had selfish agendas. He felt like too many players had a sense of entitlement. The strong cohesiveness of the '06 and '07 teams started to falter in '08, Bohl told a friend.

In the Missouri Valley, Northern Iowa was getting the better recruits and Bohl was tired of watching the Midwest FCS recruiting train end up in Cedar Falls, Iowa. But as disappointing as '08 was, the next 15 months were worse.

The '09 staff was finally completed in mid-February when Bohl hired Mike Breske as the defensive coordinator. At the time, it looked like a good hire; Breske was Joe Glenn's main man for back-to-back Division II titles at Northern Colorado and a Division I-AA championship at Montana. He became available that year after Glenn was fired at Wyoming. Breske would only last one year and that was probably for the best because there appeared to be some tug-of-war between Bohl's beloved Tampa 2 and some 3-4 looks that Breske brought to the table.

"I think we got away from the philosophy of the cover 2 a bit and tried more matchup stuff," Tim Polasek said. "And there was no doubt about some of that off the field stuff. No distraction is a good distraction. That was hard to overcome. … In 2009, the togetherness wasn't as good and we lost sight a bit in the pride of the program. Most certainly, it wasn't that coach Bohl did something different."

Six days after Breske was hired, backup quarterback Troy Jackson pleaded guilty to a marijuana charge and that was just the start of NDSU's problems. Bohl suspended him for two games. Perhaps in retrospect, the head coach may have wanted to clean house right then and there.

The following week, defensive end Garrett Johnson was arrested for DUI and minor in possession. That wouldn't be the last time Johnson would make the news for something other than football, but as the spring thaw was starting to hit the Red River Valley, another reality started to hit the local residents: the river was about to flood to historical levels.

Spring football started in late March, but the schedule was erratic at best. Bison players and coaches spent the week of March 24 helping sandbag. There's nothing like a group of big, strong, in-shape football guys showing up at a house to throw some bags, kind of like the cavalry coming to the rescue.

The late snowmelt rendered NDSU's grass practice fields unusable anyway and the start of spring ball was delayed until the beginning of April. A new Sprinturf surface was supposed to be finished by the spring, but construction delays only made Bohl want to crawl into a hole even further. He may have put on his strong face to the public, but inside he was churning.

Head coaches are creatures of routine. When something like a flood interrupts the schedule, paranoia creeps in. I bet in retrospect Bohl knew 2009 was going to be a tough year even in April, when the Bison were fighting a flood rather than competing against each other on the practice field. NDSU, by the way, lost running back Tyler Roehl, receiver Kole Heckendorf, linebacker Ramon Humber and safety Nick Schommer – all of whom signed an NFL contract of some sort.

"All football teams need to practice, but this football team needs to practice more than any other we've had here since I've been the head coach," Bohl said.

NDSU finally did field its first practice on April 4 – in the Sports Bubble indoor driving range on the south side of Fargo. I'm not sure what they got done in a space that at its biggest is 50 yards long by 50 yards wide, but it couldn't have been very productive. The Fargodome was still not operable because it was Sandbag Central to fill thousands of sandbags to fight the flood. A $400,000 cleanup was to take awhile.

And the drama was far from over. Less than two weeks later, backup quarterback Jose Mohler and standout kickoff returner/receiver Shamen Washington were each picked up for DUI about a half hour apart early on a Sunday morning. It was the third DUI for a Bison player. Understandably, the Bison athletic director was reaching the end of his patience.

"Three in the last three months," Gene Taylor said. "That indicates to me the message is not being listened to. Somebody in that football team is not getting the message and we need to find out the root of the problem and deliver a different message."

McFeely, who earlier wrote that Bohl did the right thing in not booting Troy Jackson off the team, called for the head coach to "drop the hammer." Bohl's deterrents were not working, he wrote.

Two days later, Jackson was dismissed from the team and Johnson, Mohler and Washington were suspended indefinitely. Bohl said Jackson's departure was unrelated to his marijuana charge.

"They need to get their personal lives in order," Bohl said in a news release.

If Taylor was adamant about the football players not getting the message, his words weren't resonating. In May, starting receiver Jordan Schultenover was dismissed from the team in what later would be uncovered as charges for drug possession and the intent to deliver.

My source in the police department said Schultenover's apartment was the subject of a stakeout and when undercover officers got in the elevator to go to their top-floor apartment near campus, they could smell marijuana. A police drug dog was going crazy. Schultenover didn't do much to hide his affection for narcotics on social media, either. His public MySpace page included an animated video on how to roll a marijuana cigarette.

In one section on his MySpace page, which was last updated in 2007, Schultenover listed his general interests as "girls, parties, blowin' drow, drinking, playing football, sports, girls, music." "Blowin' drow" is a slang term for smoking hydroponic marijuana, a weed grown indoors using a system of tubes, filters and fertilizers, according to Urban Dictionary online site. What struck me was nobody alerted any administrator or coach on his MySpace page despite it being public and online for a significant amount of time. A photo on the page showed a male with a marijuana-looking cigarette in his mouth. In another section under "Jordan's Details," he listed "yes/yes" after the following: "Smoke/Drink:"

All of this caught the coaching staff totally off guard. It was not the image that he portrayed around the players and coaches and not once did they suspect that he was part of the marijuana scene. There were no obvious signs like carrying a lot of cash or driving a nice car; Bohl said it was almost the opposite, with Schultenover driving an old beater car.

A search warrant filed in Cass County District Court showed investigators found drug paraphernalia "designed for using, packaging, marketing, receiving, selling and growing" a controlled substance for use and delivery at Schultenover's apartment in north Fargo. Documents show investigators also believe Schultenover was bringing "large quantities" of marijuana with the intent to sell.

Schultenover was first suspected of illegal activity in February when a confidential informant told authorities that Schultenover was bringing marijuana from the Minneapolis area to Fargo. Schultenover is from the Twin Cities suburb of Minnetonka. On April 29, documents showed investigators brought a police dog trained in finding controlled substances to Schultenover's apartment complex at 1919 North University Drive.

The dog led them to Schultenover's place, where investigators found bank ledgers, account books and directions for using a controlled substance. Fargo police records showed an inventory of evidence obtained during a search of Schultenover's apartment included marijuana pipes, digital scale, plastic bottles with marijuana residue and baggies.

In June, promising Central Florida transfer receiver Sidney Haynes was booted from the team before playing a down. In July, backup linebacker Blake Sczepanski was arrested for DUI and was suspended indefinitely. He later transferred.

You don't think the folks in power were paying attention? As part of Joe Chapman's State of the University address later that fall, he announced a $50,000 campaign to change the culture of drinking. It was obvious within the football team that the culture needed to be changed. Every time Bohl saw a police car around the Fargodome, he wondered if it was a problem he would have to deal with.

One reason for all of this: Taylor, in retrospect, said he thought the coaching staff got lazy with recruiting after the consecutive 10-1 seasons in 2006 and 2007.

"Some of them weren't recruiting as hard," Taylor said. "The kids we were recruiting; the coaches weren't doing their homework grabbing kids that they probably weren't as detailed as they needed to be. And that's what Craig said; the fact we were not doing our homework – finding that kid who is going to go out and outwork somebody as opposed to just taking the first one that comes along. To his credit, Craig reshuffled the deck and said we need to get back to work."

I also thought Craig made a philosophical mistake by going two years without recruiting a quarterback and it was costly. There was no FCS-capable player to backup starter Nick Mertens, so to protect Mertens from getting hurt, the playbook was shrunk to avoid him from running the ball and risking injury. The problem: Mertens was an average passer at best and his strength was running the ball.

It was a rough offseason, but hope sprang anew in the beginning of August when fall camp started. After a disappointing 6-5 season in 2008, the plan was to find a new beginning.

There was an air of uncertainty in fall camp with eight NFL prospects from the previous season gone. An unproven team would find out where it was at right away with the opener at Iowa State. Running back Pat Paschall had 146 yards and there were some glimpses of excellence, but in the end, the Cyclones were too much in a 34-17 win. A couple of key turnovers that would plague this team all season surfaced early, especially when Mertens fumbled inside the ISU 1 and the Cyclones recovered in the end zone. They drove 80 yards the other way and instead of a 7-7 game, the Bison were down 14-0. ISU controlled the second half and the 17-point defeat was one of the very rare times when a Bohl-coached Bison team was out of it in the fourth quarter.

The rebound game was supposed to come the following week at Sam Houston State, but in another precursor to the season, the Bison failed to make the right plays in the fourth quarter. When it came to a shootout, you probably didn't want to mess with a Texas team. The 48-45 loss was the worst defensive performance in the Division I era and the 48 points were the most NDSU had given up since a 49-42 loss to Nebraska-Omaha in that miserable 2002 season. Perhaps even worse, the Bison gave up a school-record 482 passing yards breaking the old mark of 442 that Minnesota State-Mankato put on the Bison in 1997.

I wrote a column the following Monday that read in part:

"Ladies and gentleman, the swagger has left the Fargodome. And no matter what happens in North Dakota State's season opener against Wagner College on Saturday, it still won't be there on Sunday morning. Because, well, it's Wagner.

Swagger can only be earned. It was earned in 2006 and 2007 with 10-1 seasons. Last year you say? Despite a 6-5 record, the swagger was still there because of injuries and players with pro potential.

That team still looked good walking off the bus.

But it's lost now, vanished by Sam Houston State quarterback Blake Joseph putting record numbers against the Bison defense on Saturday in a 48-45 win. The Bearkats passed for 480 yards and had 620 total yards. No opposing quarterback in Bison past – not Jim Hart, Don Horn, Ken O'Brien, Steve Mariucci, Todd Bouman or Rhett Bomar – put up that kind of yardage.

The home opener will be all fine and dandy because the Bison have built a fan-friendly atmosphere. As for swagger? It can only be earned back in two weeks when the Bison travel to Southern Illinois. It takes a quality win or two to restore the roar. NDSU wrestling coach Bucky Maughan, the Philosopher of Winning, says tradition doesn't win you a match. Beating your opponent to a pulp does. With apologies to Smith Barney, swagger is accumulated the old fashion way. You earn it."

Well, the swagger was not restored two weeks later against Southern Illinois. That was the beginning of five straight losses including Illinois State scoring with 1:24 remaining to win 27-24 at the Fargodome. The Bison rebounded driving to the Redbirds' 9-yard line on a 24-yard run by Mertens, but a personal foul penalty on the play nullified that and the Bison ran out of steam.

NDSU dropped to 1-5 for the first time since 1975 in a home loss to Northern Iowa, a defeat that was a broken record in that the Panthers were the better team in the final quarter. Perhaps the bigger news the following Monday was Paschall getting suspended by the Missouri Valley. Paschall threw a punch, after UNI linebacker L.J Fort rode him all the way to the dome sideline wall.

An interception return for a touchdown by South Dakota State helped drop the Bison to 1-6. By the fifth straight loss, a 21-17 home loss to Missouri State, players were pointing fingers at each other. One unconfirmed report, although it was probably true, had a player or players stealing stuff from other players in the locker room. It was not a good scene.

"The whole year was kind of a low point," defensive tackle Matthew Gratzek said. "That wasn't the Bison defense that we all took pride in."

Although he wouldn't come out and directly say it, Gratzek wasn't a fan of Breske. When asked about the 2010 turnaround, he pointed to new defensive coordinator Scott Hazeltine changing the culture of the players. "It was a lot different than we had with Breske," he said. "You just wanted to play harder for them."

At this point, I got the assignment from my editors to write an analysis on what happened to this team. I did something similar in 2002 when NDSU went 2-8 and a day later I saw Babich in the Bison Sports Arena foyer. I was expecting a verbal beatdown from the coach but instead, he paused, looked down and said, "I can't deny it. I can't deny anything you wrote."

The losing streak finally ended in an ugly 14-7 win at Western Illinois, a game in which the Bison got a gift via a late penalty from the Leathernecks that kept a game-winning drive alive. The season ended almost predictably, however, at home against Youngstown State. The Penguins scored on a five-yard pass with 22 seconds remaining to win 39-35, leaving NDSU's home record at 1-4 – the worst since 1962.

As if 2009 needed anymore explanation, a Best Buy theft ring that was eventually busted in April of 2010 included two Bison players: Johnson and recruit Greg Reid. Johnson was actually arrested while attending a Bison baseball game at Newman Outdoor Field and was taken out of the stadium in handcuffs with fans watching. Although those two were never factors in the rise of the success, it was the publicity that the "Best Buy scandal" drew that was potentially more damaging than anything.

It was juicy and here's how it worked: Two of the 12 who were charged worked at the store as security guards and they simply let the other 10 selectively put items on a cart and walk out of the store. In one day, seven televisions were stolen and taken to the home of one of the security guards, Adetimisola Ogundipe, who was known in the circle as "Best Buy Jr." Ogundipe was no stranger to Bison players – he practiced with the team for a few days before disappearing.

Bohl cooperated with the police investigation and helped police have access to the players.

Johnson was promptly booted off the team. His role in the theft was somewhat of a shock to some Bison coaches, mainly because he came from a pretty well-off family and probably wasn't desperate for money or electronics. Privately, Bohl was shocked that Johnson would even need a big screen TV. After his DUI charge the previous summer, Johnson looked Kevin Schnepf straight in the eye when Schnepf asked him about it for a preseason story in August and Johnson said, "After going through all the police and school officials, it's just not worth it. I have a full ride and they could throw everything out the window. It has been a real eye opener."

He was a starter in the 2009 season and was second on the team in quarterback sacks. So even before the 2010 season really got going, NDSU had this public embarrassment to deal with.

Schnepf, as the sports editor and columnist, finally reached a saturation point with a column titled: "With NDSU football, when is enough, enough?" He questioned Bohl's recruiting.

"After kicking two players off his team last week – bringing that number to six in the last 12 months – some are wondering what kind of players Bohl is bringing into his program," Schnepf wrote. "Some are asking when is enough, enough – especially after last week's dismissal of Garrett Johnson and Greg Reid, who were charged with being involved in the mind-boggling theft ring at Fargo' Best Buy. Bohl will probably be the first to tell you that dealing with such scrutiny comes with the territory. That's why, as they say, he gets paid the big bucks (more than $180,000 a year).

"So with the six players who were kicked off this past year for either stealing, drinking while driving or smoking – and even intending to sell – marijuana, is Bohl letting too much go?

"'No. Absolutely not,' says Bohl's boss, athletic director Gene Taylor. 'That's what's frustrating ... people think he is. He's not doing things that would raise a red flag with me.'

"Fair enough. Bohl, like all college football coaches, oversees nearly 100 players. That's nearly an impossible babysitting task. He and his staff were shocked when Johnson who vowed he would never get in trouble again after last year's alcohol violations, was charged with a Class C felony in the Best Buy case. Equally as shocking was standout wide receiver Jordan Schultenover, who last year was charged with possession of marijuana and intent to distribute.

"Like Taylor said, some people 'just don't get it' and some are 'going to get into trouble.' Taylor also said with high school recruits committing to colleges earlier, it reduces the time coaches have to really get to know them. And if they don't take them early, other schools will.

"'As much as you would like to recruit choir boys, you've got to win football games,' Taylor said. 'You are going to recruit kids who live on edge ... and that's in every sport. If you want competitive, hard-nosed athletes, some of those kids will push the envelope. Some of those kids are the kids you really have to monitor.'"

Johnson pleaded guilty to felony theft and was sentenced to 18 months of unsupervised probation. He transferred to Minnesota-Duluth, but ran into a felony charge of criminal damage to property and never played.

Amid all of the negative publicity, the Bison surprisingly were racking up verbal commitments, nine at a point in the 2009 season when things were going south, including running back Ryan Smith, defensive back Marcus Williams and defensive lineman Mike Hardie. Nobody knew it at the time, of course, but these were the guys that would quickly change NDSU's course of history.

That had to be one of the best recruiting jobs ever by Bohl and his staff. After going 3-8, there were those who were questioning Bohl's job security and it was a question that Taylor took more than once.

"He was safe," Taylor said several years later. "Now if the following season turned into something like 4-7, then he and I both knew something was going to have to happen the next year. I probably would have taken grief for another year and I think he had two years left on his contract. The (2010) year started out a little rough (NDSU beat FBS Kansas but got rocked the following week by Northern Iowa), but then they got in the playoffs."

The Forum asked the athletic director during media day that christened the 2010 season. His simple reply was "Craig Bohl is not on the hot seat."

Bohl, of course, got a similar question.

"That doesn't sit well with me either," he said of 3-8. "I can tell you this, I came here to win a national championship ... this program deserves it. When you talk about pressure, I look at myself in the mirror and ask, 'Are we getting better or are we getting worse?' If we're getting better … you know what … I'm going to be fine with that. I will be real fine with that. If we are not getting better, I will struggle with that. So when you talk about pressure and stuff like that, you can throw that out the window. That doesn't faze me. That's like water on a duck's back. That doesn't bother me at all."

A few years later, not long after being named head coach, Chris Klieman called Pat Simmers and asked him to meet over a beer. Klieman wanted to tap into Simmers' extensive experience as a former Bison player, assistant coach and current administrator. Simmers said the subject was winning and what would happen if Klieman didn't win.

"I told him, they talk about having to win at North Dakota State and I don't agree with that," Simmers said. "You have got to represent us well. You have got to play hard, not give a game away, go to class and you have to stay relatively out of trouble for a college kid. If you do that, you'll be 8-3. You have some injuries you'll be 6-4, 7-5, but you'll never be bad. Our people can handle losing. Someday, you're not going to win in the last 30 seconds (2014 national title game) but it's not about that. It's about representing us. The thing I saw in the 3-8 season is players quitting in the third quarter. We can take losing, but we can't take quitting."

Not everybody was like that. Some of the younger players who came in as true freshmen in 2009 already had an idea of what they were not going to do. Some of the older players, like Gratzek, wanted no part of the players who weren't all on board. "We needed a different atmosphere, no more mudslinging," he said. "It was kind of like everybody needed to step up to the plate. We discussed as a defense that things needed to change and it was not acceptable."

Looking back, Jim Kramer said the coaches didn't really see the negative flags and that the off-season as far as work habits was shaping up to be like the others.

"We didn't see some of that stuff until later, just because as coaches you're not going to see that," he said. "Guys weren't letting us know about it either. I don't know if there were red flags more so that year than others. Sometimes we questioned guys' commitment during that year."

The biggest problem, Kramer said, was players not policing other players.

"That's what you try to get each group to do," he said. "This is your team, you guys police the team. You talk about college athletics and it's up to the poor head coach to babysit 18- to 22-year-olds. No, you have an assistant babysitter with the upper classmen. Now, the upperclassmen grow apart from underclassmen so you have to develop leadership with each class along with each team. That's one thing we learned from that season. There were a lot of good individuals maybe in that losing year but those individuals weren't having a positive influence on each other. Those individuals knew what was going on and they weren't policing the team. I remember Cole Jirik coming to me once and said so-and-so was doing this, how do we address it? He wasn't ratting anybody out; he was taking care of his teammates. He was taking care of the team."

X. Gateway to the dynasty

Joe Chapman loved the Big Sky Conference. A former administrator at Montana State, he figured that would be the home of NDSU when the Bison got into the heart of their Division I reclassification and beyond. When you think of North Dakota, Chapman once told me, you think of the western part of the United States. It's only natural, he figured, the Big Sky would eventually take the Bison.

Since taking the NDSU job in 2000, Chapman did a lot of his own research on how to get the Bison into the Big Sky and a president he relied on the most was from his own school: Montana State's Geoffrey Gamble.

"He wanted us really bad," Chapman said.

Terry Wanless, however, was on the other side of the spectrum. The Sacramento State athletic director, and a former A.D. at UND, said geography was the main reason he was opposed to expansion to the Midwest.

"I have a great personal stake in this in a roundabout way," he said. "But at the same point, my first responsibility is to this institution. And for the betterment of our program, putting them on the schedule doesn't make sense."

Still, Gamble got NDSU and SDSU on the Big Sky Council of Presidents meeting agenda in January of 2003. A month earlier, both schools sent the league office letters saying they would like to apply for membership. A special expansion meeting was set for Feb. 20 at an airport hotel in Salt Lake City.

But it would turn out to be the first in a line of conference membership disappointments for both schools. There were more thumbs down than thumbs up. Gamble, the chairman of the Council of Presidents, told me he sensed hesitation in the room. Schools needed a two-thirds majority to gain acceptance, meaning six of the eight Big Sky schools would have to vote yes.

"If a vote were taken today, I don't think it would have gone favorably," Gamble said.

The issue surfaced again a year later, only this time with Northern Colorado and possibly Southern Utah in the mix. Chapman and Taylor continued their public confidence, saying until NDSU hears a "no," it is still a serious contender for membership. In December, UND joined the discussion parade when officials indicated they were interested in Big Sky membership if they decided to reclassify to Division I.

The matter got serious about a year later. At the Big Sky Council of Presidents meeting in December of 2004, at the Hilton Salt Lake City hotel near the Salt Lake airport, NDSU, South Dakota State, Southern Utah and Northern Colorado were on the agenda for expansion and hoping to get a league invite. The presidents only chose to accept Northern Colorado.

It was the second time in 10 months NDSU had an expansion dalliance with the Big Sky, but this one, for whatever reason, was said to be showing promise.

"What hurt them is the same thing that's always hurt them," said Big Sky commissioner Doug Fullerton. "It's a long way from a lot of our schools."

The Big Sky council evaluated the schools based on a set of criteria that included academic quality, athletic competitiveness, commitment to gender equity, commitment to student-athlete success, and geography in regards to cost of travel and travel time, according to the league office. I was told there was no way Montana was going to let Southern Utah in because of the academic issue. There are those who to this day believe Montana president George Dennison stonewalled NDSU because he didn't want Montana's status as football kingpin in the league diminished.

In a 2015 interview, Chapman said, "I don't want to dis people who didn't want it to happen. Geoff indicated there were some stumbling blocks he had to deal with. But George was very important in the process. When I first became president, he was one of the first people I visited with for my vision with NDSU and how important the athletic piece was."

At any rate, Taylor was home in his kitchen when his cell phone rang. It was Chapman. His wife Cathy was out of town in Alabama and Gene had already made arrangements for somebody else to take care of his two children when news came that the Big Sky was going to accept NDSU. In essence, he was preparing for a victory party.

What ensued turned out to be the low point in his NDSU athletic director tenure.

"You're never going to believe this crap," Chapman told him.

"What?" Taylor replied.

"They just took Northern Colorado," Chapman said.

Taylor was stunned, paused and didn't say anything. He slowly fell to a squat, and then ultimately sat on the kitchen floor. There was still silence.

"I just sat there and thought, "What the hell just happened?"" he said.

Chapman told Taylor he had to come to the Bison Sports Arena and face the music. Dave Wahlberg, then the NDSU communications director, phoned Taylor and told him to "put his happy face on."

"This is devastating," Taylor told Wahlberg. "How are we going to tell our coaches that we didn't get this done?"

When Taylor appeared in front of the local media later that day, he looked like he just lost his last friend. His face was red. Beat red. He looked like an administrator who was back to square one and that wasn't a place Chapman expected the Bison to be.

"I'll never forget McFeely's article the next day," Taylor said. "It said Gene Taylor looked like he got hit in the head with a pillow case full of quarters and that's just how I felt. What are we going to do? I tried to put on a happy face but I just couldn't. After that day, I thought, what are we going to do now? Was it time to panic?"

If you're going to make a difference in Division I-AA, the Great West Football Conference was not the place to do it. So even though the Bison had that league, there was still a sense of homelessness. The Great West did not have automatic qualifier status to the I-AA playoffs because it didn't have enough teams with NDSU, SDSU, Cal Poly, UC Davis and Southern Utah. So for the most part, those programs were operating as independents in football with the nugget of playing for a conference title that really meant nothing except to the players and coaches.

The biggest problem with a five-team league is finding seven non-conference opponents. The Southland Conference was in a similar boat, so that is why the Bison ended up with so many Southland teams over the Division I years. The Great West served its purpose for football, but NDSU always had an eye on finding something with an AQ. The break came in the fall of 2006 when Western Kentucky of the Gateway Football Conference (now the Missouri Valley Football Conference) started getting serious about moving to FBS and the Sun Belt Conference. The imminent departure of WKU meant the Gateway would be down to seven members. A week before the WKU Board of Regents were scheduled to vote on the FBS issue, the Gateway asked NDSU and SDSU for institutional profiles, generally regarded as the first step to expansion. A few months earlier, NDSU and SDSU were accepted into the Mid-Continent Conference for most of its other sports – so the Midwest league footprint was starting to take shape.

Unbeknownst to almost everybody was that on the day NDSU announced it was accepted into the Mid-Continent Conference (August 31, 2006), Taylor went back to his office after the press conference at the Alumni Center. There, he received a call from Gateway Football Conference commissioner Patty Viverito – the same commissioner who said, politely, that NDSU would never find a league home. Taylor would occasionally run into Viverito at NCAA conventions or national athletic director meetings and the response from one party to the other was the same: there was no room for NDSU in the Gateway.

Taylor said when he first answered the call, he paused and there was silence.

"I know I'm eating a little crow here," Viverito said. "Would you consider coming to the Gateway?"

Just like that, NDSU essentially was on its way to finding a football home the same day it aligned with the Mid-Con for most of its other sports. What a day. Earlier at the press conference at the Alumni Center, Taylor stepped to the podium, paused and cried before saying a word. Perhaps the emotion of those years of trying to get into the Big Sky hit him.

"They're going to start calling me Dick Vermeil," Taylor said, in reference to the former NFL coach known for shedding tears.

Taylor kept the call from Viverito under wraps for a few months. In January, Chapman was invited to the Gateway Conference winter meeting in St. Louis. The league publically said it was going to address expansion at its February meeting of league presidents even though Viverito phoned Taylor much earlier saying it wanted to start those wheels in motion. But there was still work to do because not everybody in the Gateway wanted NDSU or SDSU.

"There were people who didn't want us in the Big Sky for the same reason people didn't want us in the Gateway. They could see a train coming," Chapman said.

Talk of NDSU and SDSU's inclusion, however, was put on hold. The league officials decided they needed more information about the schools, but promised they'd address the topic directly in a March conference call.

"The presidents requested additional information from both institutions," said Gateway associate commissioner Mike Kern.

Taylor said that was better than if the presidents waited until their June meeting. Taylor and Chapman said they were pleased with their presentation before representatives from the seven league schools. Taylor said there were no questions that surprised him. Chapman and SDSU president David Chicoine each gave an opening statement at about 12:30 p.m. They were out of the Renaissance Hotel conference room by 1:15.

Taylor said he fielded questions related to finances, travel, Title IX, competitiveness and commitment to the league. Chapman said he addressed the similar size of NDSU in relation to the seven Gateway teams, the school's commitment to its student-athletes, NDSU's alumni footprint in the Midwest and the experience of opponents playing in the Fargodome. Both Chapman and Taylor said getting a read on feedback from the group was tough.

"They were a poker-faced group," Taylor said. "Some heads were nodding, but I don't know if they felt one way or the other. You couldn't necessarily tell how they were leaning."

Said Chapman: "They didn't ask a whole lot of questions."

Behind the scenes, Chapman said Chicoine, who just assumed the office in January taking over for Peggy Miller, kept the NDSU-SDSU Division I bond together. Chapman said the Gateway approached Chicoine and asked him if the league wanted to take just one school, would that be OK with you?

It could have been a historical moment in the NDSU-SDSU brotherhood in joining Division I. Remember, it was NDSU that started the process and SDSU wasn't far behind. Now, SDSU could have put NDSU in a huge hole by accepting league membership without NDSU – if that indeed was a possibility.

But Chapman said Chicoine stuck to the brotherhood.

"He didn't hesitate saying we're going together or not at all," Chapman said.

Why just SDSU? Chapman said one of the Gateway coaches put out an email to the rest of the league coaches with an attached picture of the Fargodome and wrote something to the effect: "Would you want to recruit against this?"

SDSU's stadium, Coughlin-Alumni, was not very nice. The Jacks had a long way to go in the facilities race and Gateway coaches probably figured they wouldn't be a title threat like NDSU.

"Both of us or neither of us: that was a pretty bold statement to make," Taylor said several years later.

On the way back from the meeting, the university-owned Cheyenne twin engine turbo prop private plane carrying Taylor and Chapman had to make an emergency landing in Kirksville, Mo., when a heating pipe problem caused the plane to lose cabin pressure at 22,000 feet. The plane eventually returned to Fargo traveling at 7,000 feet as a precautionary measure.

A month later, NDSU was finally flying with a legitimate Division I-AA league. The league voted in favor of NDSU and SDSU during a March 7 teleconference at the low, low cost of a $250,000 entry fee paid over a three-year period. Taylor couldn't write the check fast enough.

McFeely wrote a beauty in the next day's Forum, putting a wrap on NDSU's conference-seeking woes over a three-year period, when he started his column:

"The most amazing thing happened Wednesday at the press conference announcing North Dakota State's union with the Gateway Football Conference. Joe Chapman, Gene Taylor and Craig Bohl stood in unison, turned toward Ogden, Utah, and raised their middle fingers.

Or not.

But it would've made a great photo opportunity. It also would've been perfectly appropriate, if the NDSU president, athletic director and football coach felt like doling out a little what-do-you-think-of-us-now smack talk. Ogden is the home of the Big Sky Conference, the geographically arrogant arrangement of schools that two years ago turned up its nose at NDSU and South Dakota State so it could add the major media market of Denver to its lineup.

One problem. The University of Northern Colorado is located in Greeley, which doesn't look or smell anything like Denver and doesn't get covered by the big TV stations or newspapers unless, say, a backup punter for the Bears stabs the starter in the leg. You couldn't blame the Bison honchos if they had their noses turned up this time, sniffing the air for a pleasing scent, since NDSU is coming out of its four-year conference odyssey smelling like a rose.

Big Sky? They don't need no stinking Big Sky. NDSU did better."

In the Gateway, the Bison were in a league where most resided in the central time zone. It was home to forceful football members like Northern Iowa, Youngstown State and Southern Illinois. It set the table for NDSU's FCS dynasty because five titles never happens if the Bison were still in the Great West Football Conference. It never happens if the Bison don't have the Gateway (Missouri Valley) to recruit to. The fans don't sell out the Fargodome because Cal Poly or UC Davis are coming to town for a league game.

Taylor said in retrospect getting into the Gateway was big for keeping Bohl from looking elsewhere more seriously.

"The Great West was OK but Craig was really pushing for the Big Sky," Taylor said. "With the Missouri Valley (Gateway), even though we got it handed to us for a couple of years, it was critical to him."

NDSU dived into its first year in the Gateway in 2008 as the pre-season favorites to win the league. Obviously, that didn't sit well with the established big brothers of the league, most notably Northern Iowa, SIU and Youngstown. UNI felt especially jilted because a new school was admitted into the conference and was immediately anointed the favorite. Case in point: NDSU didn't ask for the pre-season ranking, but the Bison paid for not coming in with a more incognito look to it.

It particularly pissed Northern Iowa off.

It was something Chris Klieman will never forget. Before he was the Bison head coach, he was a long-time assistant with UNI. In 2007, the Panthers went undefeated in the league but that was also the season NDSU went unbeaten until the final game against SDSU.

"We heard all the whispers," Klieman said. "In 2007, we had run the table but people were saying it was tainted because North Dakota State was going undefeated. Low and behold, South Dakota State beat them."

But that NDSU 10-1 record was enough to make the Bison tops in the poll – and every other league team used that as motivation.

"Absolutely," Klieman said. "To think a program that hasn't played in the Gateway yet could come in and be ranked No. 1. You have to prove yourself in this league first and I didn't think people in the Gateway had a lot of respect for the Great West as far as the week to week competition. In the Gateway you have to go through the gauntlet of all these teams and I think it proved out that year."

The Bison went 4-4 in their first Missouri Valley season including 1-3 against ranked league foes. The one victory was a 35-27 homecoming win over Southern Illinois, whose head coach Dale Lennon was returning to coach in his home state for the first time since leaving UND. It was a stirring comeback with the Salukis leading 20-7 at halftime, but NDSU scored three fourth-quarter touchdowns.

There was to be no magic at Youngstown State (32-24 loss), at home against Western Illinois (27-22 defeat) and at Northern Iowa (23-13 loss).

UNI was waiting for the Bison like a piranha waiting for a bloody fish. When the Panthers take the field at the UNI-Dome, they stand behind a garage door located on one end of the field and when the door goes up, they run onto the field to the roar of their fans.

"I remember that garage door going up," Tim Polasek said. "I'm standing next to coach Bohl and he looked at me and said, hope you guys have our guys coached up. When that door came up, you know what it felt like? A true home field, just like what people must feel when they come here. I felt like, holy shit, here we go. They weren't intimidated. I think they wore black and purple that day. UNI … they were a good football team."

That Bison game, however, caught Klieman's attention and it wasn't anything NDSU did on the field. It was all the Bison fans that made the trip to Cedar Falls. Klieman knew about the Bison tradition because his head coach at UNI when he was a player was Ardell Wiegandt, a former NDSU defensive coordinator from 1969-73.

"I was really surprised at how many people they brought and that was a sign of things to come for me," Klieman said. "I kept that in my memory bank for a long time."

The loss left NDSU 3-4 overall with plenty of questions. Running back Tyler Roehl had a 40-yard run on NDSU's first play of the game and then the Panthers held the Bison to just 59 yards on 30 attempts the rest of the way.

I'll never forget that post-game press conference. NDSU was first and it brought in a couple of players along with Bohl. Then it was UNI and the first guy in the room was defensive tackle James Ruffin, all 6-foot-4 and 270 pounds of him. My lord he looked big, certainly the guy NDSU didn't have. Right then, and there, it was obvious to me that if the Bison were to ever compete for a conference crown in the Missouri Valley, they needed to recruit the James Ruffin's of the world.

Bohl knew it too.

He not only eventually succeeded in outrecruiting the Panthers, he was able to tap into the UNI staff, too. It started with Klieman, who not only saw how well the Bison fans traveled to Cedar Falls in 2008, but saw the Fargodome atmosphere in '09 and the NDSU road show returning to UNI in 2010. He was in his comfort zone in Cedar Falls, with his parents and brother close by. It was his alma mater. But he also knew that if he wanted to grow as a coach, he needed to go somewhere else.

"I saw they had an opening and I was intrigued," Klieman said. "In 2010, after they beat KU, they brought a huge crowd to the UNI-Dome and I thought, wow, this program really loves football. I also vividly remember in 2010 UNI making the playoffs when we got beat by Lehigh at home. I bet we had 4,000 people on a Thanksgiving Day weekend game and I thought (the NDSU job) is something I have to at least look into."

Klieman knew Bison offensive coordinator Brent Vigen and called him. NDSU returned the interest because it was intrigued with how long Klieman was in the league. NDSU defensive coordinator Scottie Hazelton later called Klieman a couple of times in December and January and Bohl appeared to be settled on hiring Klieman. It wasn't going to be official until February, however, because recruiting was in full swing and coaching changes can negatively interfere with signing players.

Bohl flew Chris and his wife, Rhonda, to Fargo a couple of days after signing day.

"I had kind of been offered the job before but he wanted to make sure it was the right fit," Chris said. "We both knew for me to grow professionally I had to take the chance."

Klieman wasn't officially hired until March 8 to replace Brian Ward as the defensive backs coach, who left for a defensive coordinator position at Drake. Two weeks earlier, Bohl acknowledged that he interviewed Klieman thanks to social media. In one of the first times I used a Twitter reference in one of my stories, UNI players were putting it out there that they were going to lose Klieman. Defensive back Garrett Scott said on his Twitter account "our db coach just left us." Varmah Sonie, another defensive back, tweeted "imma miss my coach."

The general backlash of a hometown guy like Klieman leaving to a rival school was tough, he said. He said the UNI assistants were happy for him and were respectful of the process. Some fans weren't as understanding.

"It was hard for people to understand why I was going to leave my alma mater and go to a rival school to be a position coach from being a defensive coordinator," Klieman said. "That didn't bother me. For me, it was a chance in this business of better networking and I needed to know 10 more coaches as opposed to status quo. The hardest thing was talking to my parents and my brother but they understood why."

NDSU paid its coaches more, too, with Klieman starting at $75,000. As for the timing of him taking the position: priceless.

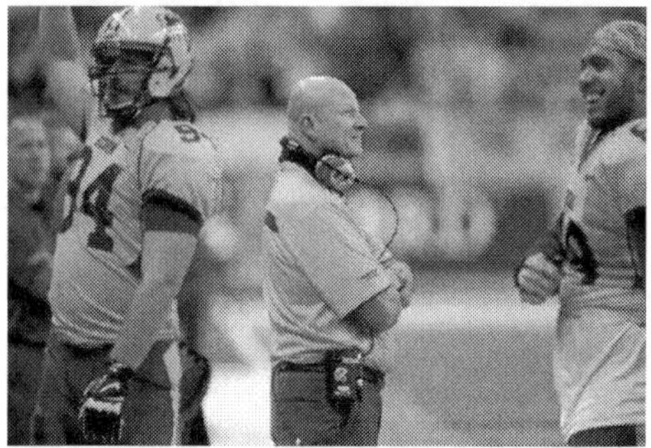

Above, the Fargodome: one of the toughest home field advantages in college football. Craig Bohl, middle, started the dynasty with three straight titles. Tyler Roehl runs in 44-14 rout of defending MAC champion Central Michigan in 2007.

The Bison were known for their rallies, above R.J. Urzendowski's TD beats SDSU in the playoffs. Travis Beck returns a key interception in the 2011 title vs. Sam Houston. Kyle Emanuel and the defense were stout in the five titles.

Craig Bohl leaves a tense team meeting after resigning in 2013. Chris Klieman, shown here on ESPN's "College GameDay" with Sam Ponder, took over. Strength coach Jim Kramer, upper right, is often referred to as the MVP of the dynasty.

The media guys doing our Media Blog video pre-game show during a playoff game in December, with Big E declaring it ugly sweater vest night in front of graduated quarterback Brock Jensen. There was plenty to cover, including a handful of celebrations in Frisco, Texas.

XI. Signing day secrets

The best thing that ever happened to the North Dakota State recruiting footprint came on Jan. 15, 2007. That's when the University of Minnesota hired a tight ends coach from the Denver Broncos named Tim Brewster, who signed a five-year contract for $400,000 a year with a package that put it well over $1 million. If NDSU had an unlimited pocket book, it would have paid Brewster's salary – it would even have doubled it – if the Gophers would have guaranteed that Brewster would be their coach for life.

It would have virtually assured the Bison would have first pick of some of the best football prospects in the Twin Cities and the state of Minnesota, because Brewster evidently didn't have much of an interest in those kids.

I'll make this short and to the point: the biggest reason NDSU began a run of five straight FCS titles was because the Minnesota Gophers, and to a lesser extent, the University of North Dakota, were not much competition in the recruiting game. In the case of the Gophers, it was because Brewster thought he could attract five-star recruits from any big city in America. In the case of UND, it was just completing a five-year reclassification under a head coach, Chris Mussman, who proved to be not much competition in landing North Dakota and Minnesota high school players. The transition wasn't kind to UND, the result of the school not hopping on board when NDSU and SDSU made the move in 2003. Those behind the scenes at the UND football program, namely former head coach Dale Lennon, were pushing to join the Bison. By not doing so, then President Charles Kupchella and athletic director Roger Thomas probably set the UND football program back about 10 years.

It wasn't the rosiest of starts for the NDSU administration, either. Chapman vividly remembered the first story in The Forum on the thought of moving athletics to Division I, written by veteran reporter Pat Springer.

"Just the negativity he brought to the story, he basically thought I was an idiot," Chapman said. "But I'm like, 'We're already a major institution here. This is about a singular institution with enormous potential.'"

Chapman may have started on an island but slowly people started to join him. I thought one of the biggest factors came when some of the biggest stars of the Division II era, namely Phil Hansen and Jeff Bentrim, publicly voiced their approval. They didn't ask for it, but they took a leadership role in a sense and their support essentially said this: don't worry about our glory days, it's time to make a change.

Hansen and Bentrim were recruited to the North Central Conference; the move up was a different animal in competition but the Bison still maintained they were going to mainly recruit North Dakota, Minnesota and Wisconsin.

If that was the case, and if NDSU was ever to compete in the Valley, it needed to start out-recruiting Northern Iowa, especially for the Twin Cities recruits. That's exactly what happened in the recruiting class of 2009 when the Bison signed defensive end Cole Jirik from Northfield, Minn., and defensive tackle Leevon Perry from Saint Agnes High School in St. Paul, the start of a trend of getting the best kids out of the Twin Cities.

NDSU really hit the Minneapolis-St. Paul jackpot the following year with running back John Crockett from Totino-Grace, linebackers Carlton Littlejohn from Minneapolis North and Grant Olson from Wayzata, wide receiver and the state's Mr. Football Zach Vraa from Rosemount and offensive lineman Billy Turner from Mounds View High School.

The fact the Gophers didn't want those players was an incredible oversight that was part of the reason Brewster failed at Minnesota. Why Brewster only offered Turner a preferred walkon opportunity had to be the biggest recruiting gaffe of the decade. Turner had a Minnesota Vikings pedigree with his father, Maurice Turner, having spent four years in the NFL including with the Vikings as a running back. His older brother, Maurice Turner Jr., was a standout receiver at Northern Iowa. His stepbrother, Bryan Kehl, the son of Maurice Turner, was a fourth round draft choice of the New York Giants and played for four NFL teams.

And Brewster only offered Billy Turner a walkon? The Bison said "Merry Christmas and thank you very much." UNI didn't get him either despite having a Turner in the program.

I recall Bohl telling a story of watching film in the coaches office at Wayzata High School and paying specific attention to a pair of linebackers. One was about 6-foot-3 and 240 pounds and the other was 6-1 and about 215. The major schools were all after the 6-3, 240 guy and Bohl said he understood why: the guy had size and speed.

But the more Bohl sat in the office and the more he watched tape, the more he noticed the 6-1, 215 guy making more plays. He was hoping the majors would stay on the 6-3, 240 guy and away from the 6-1, 215 guy. That latter happened to be Grant Olson. That was the guy Bohl wanted. Minnesota offered him a walkon opportunity but NDSU put the all-out scholarship sell on Olson and he accepted. If Jerry Kill, Brewster's successor, were on the job in 2009 and 2010, no way he would let Olson, Turner, Vraa, Jirik, Perry and possibly Littlejohn get away.

But by and large, NDSU had to find a way to beat UNI on the recruiting trail – something that was obvious in 2008 when the Panthers physically schooled the Bison. The Bison signed 19 high school seniors and two junior college players and added three walkons. In all, the '09 class was the largest in Bohl's tenure to that date. It was also large in stature – eight were at least 6-foot-4 and 215, including several skill players were at least 200 pounds. It was a necessary step in the Missouri Valley and NDSU discovered first hand in its first year in the league that it was a physical league.

"I think in the league we saw not only excellent skill players but you better be strong up front," Bohl said.

The bar for that, Bohl said, was set by UNI. The Panthers had a formula that has made them a perennial FCS playoff contender. NDSU, which was playoff-eligible for the first time in 2008, wanted to emulate that status. But first, the Bison needed to get the players.

"Our first time through the Missouri Valley, we learned how the league operates and the level of competition," Bohl said.

On the recruiting field that year, NDSU competed primarily against league schools UNI, Illinois State and Western Illinois. At the Division I FBS level, it went up against Mid-American Conference schools like Western Michigan, Central Michigan and Eastern Michigan. And in the case of defensive end Justin Juckem from Chilton, Wis., the Bison out-recruited Washington State of the then-Pac-10 Conference.

The list included three from North Dakota: Fargo South linebacker Brandon Jemison, Hillsboro fullback Andrew Grothmann and North Sargent defensive end Ryan Drevlow. Two others walked on: Fargo Shanley linebacker Logan Hushka and South defensive end Danny Luecke. The class included five defensive ends. That wasn't part of the initial plan -- Bohl said he originally wanted two -- but expanded it when other players were too good to pass up.

"Some of those guys traditionally grow into inside guys," he said.

One guy who didn't was Jirik, who not only was an athletically-gifted defensive end for his size but one of the mentally toughest you'll ever want to know. Moreover, he sacrificed a shot at an NFL career to play his senior season in 2013, the team that went unbeaten.

He tore the labrum on his left shoulder during the ESPN "College GameDay" game against Delaware State, coming around the edge of the line of scrimmage and getting hit while reaching for the ball. The next few days, after talking it over with his parents, trainers and a team doctor, he opted against surgery and decided to play the rest of the season with one healthy arm. They told him he couldn't hurt it any worse, so he kept himself in the starting lineup. But two weeks later against Northern Iowa, he tore the labrum in his right shoulder.

"After that, I'm like, I don't know how I can play – no shoulders, no arms," Jirik said.

Most football players would have called it quits and it would have been an easy decision. Not Cole. He talked his situation over, again, with the medical personnel. Once again, they told him he couldn't hurt it any worse – a tear is a tear. He also had this dilemma: if he got surgery that week, he would probably be ready for NDSU's Pro Day in March when NFL scouts come to NDSU to test Bison prospects. It was the ultimate inner battle of individual vs. team. He and his father, Pete Jirik, talked a lot about it and Cole kept coming back to this thought: he's already invested four years with most of the 26 seniors on the team and now was not the time to leave them.

"I had played with my 'brothers' for so many years, I didn't think it was fair to them not to finish it out with them," Cole said. "I didn't want to let anybody down."

But the pain was bordering on unbearable, to the point that sleeping hurt. He would often wake up in the middle of the night in pain. When driving his car, it felt like somebody was stabbing him every time he took a right turn. And this is a guy who stepped on the field every Saturday and battled against 300-pound offensive linemen?

"As the season went on, you got used to the pain a little bit," Jirik said.

NDSU had pretty good depth on the defensive line, so he was afforded the luxury of not playing every down. But you would see it every once in a while; Jirik getting off the turf very slowly and walking to the sideline.

"Sometimes when I would get hit my arm would go numb," he said. "I would get to the sideline but there's nothing anybody could really do. I'd maybe pop an Advil to take the pain away, or at least some of it. I just took a couple of plays off, hope the adrenalin would kick in again and get back in there. Once I got on the field, I thought about it a lot less."

Jirik's story, although extreme, was not unique to those title teams. That 2013 team had a beat-up defensive line, mainly from playing so many games over a four-year period. Starting in 2010, the seniors on the 2013 team played 59 games and were 52-7. Starting in 2011, the seniors on the 2014 team played 61 games and were 58-3. That was the infamous class that had more titles, four, than losses, three.

Two played all 61 games: defensive end Kyle Emanuel and safety Christian Dudzik with Dudzik starting all 61. Although not found in any record book, the 61 games played is the most by any FCS player in a subdivision that began in 1978. Littlejohn is next with 59 career games. Safe to say, it wasn't easy for any of them.

In 2014, Dudzik sprained his shoulder against Northern Iowa and it barely healed the rest of the season. In practice, without the aid of pain killers, he couldn't use his left arm at all. Like Jirik, his pro stock was dropping because he had a tough time showing his physicality of tackling during games. "But I was a senior captain," Dudzik said, "and I took that role more seriously than any other. I felt personally responsible for having our team prepared to win and I felt I was a vital part to that so at no point did I consider removing myself from practice or games to ease my pain. The goal of winning another national championship always came first for me and that mentality was easy because I felt all my brothers had it, too."

Emanuel was another recruiting find from small-town Schuyler, Neb. Once again, the Bison staff was surprised a Big Ten school didn't offer, in this case Nebraska. He was a model player and a model student, regularly attending bible session meetings at St. Paul's Catholic Newman Center and a member of Blue Key Honor Society.

He originally was slotted to be a middle linebacker, but one day in practice the Bison were short on defensive ends and he was asked to join that group. He never left and in 2014 became the school's first Buck Buchanan Award winner, which goes to the best defensive player in the FCS. He became NDSU's first major award winner since quarterback Chris Simdorn won the Division II Harlon Hill Award in 1990.

He led the FCS in quarterback sacks with 19.5. In eight games against ranked opponents that year, he had 47 tackles with 16.5 going for lost yardage, 10 sacks and nine QB hurries.

A fifth-round draft pick of the San Diego Chargers in the 2015 draft, he finished ninth in FCS history and fourth in Missouri Valley history with 35.5 sacks. And this was while rotating in and out the first three years to accommodate NDSU's impressive depth. There were games when he would play just 25 to 30 snaps.

On the flipside, he was probably remained healthier than most of his linemates – like Jirik.

"You're hurt but you're not injured," Jirik said. "You find a way to get out there."

He did have the surgery after the win over Towson in Frisco, first on one shoulder and then when that was healed enough he had surgery on the other. Jirik gave the NFL dream a shot the following year by training for a 2014 Pro Day, but a training camp shot didn't materialize. He probably lost his chance by not choosing surgery during the 2013 season.

"Maybe I would have went to camp and got cut, maybe I would have went to camp and earned a spot," he said. "I like to believe I had the talent to play at that level."

***

The Gophers' 2010 recruiting class had a total of 74 stars in the Rivals.com rating system. Only three of the 25 players were from the Twin Cities with Brewster taking kids from all over the map, from Pennsylvania to Maryland to Florida to Texas to Missouri to Ohio – pretty much everywhere but his own backyard. NDSU reveled in that philosophy and several of those players were playing in Frisco early in January for four straight years while the Gophers were starting off-season winter workouts.

Nobody really kept track of FCS recruiting rankings but if NDSU's 2010 class had more than 10 combined Rivals.com stars, that would have been a shock. Crockett was the most sought-after but his academic problems kept the Big 10 schools away.

Crockett was a testament to the savvy recruiting abilities of the Bohl staff. The Bison were well aware of his learning deficiencies and were willing to wait and help him get academically eligible – if he was willing to put in the time. It was a marriage of patience and effort that paid off handsomely for all parties involved.

Crockett's progress at NDSU was a special part of the Bison's ascent to Division I power. One of the most personable players of his era on the roster, he had a tough upbringing in Minneapolis. For a couple of years in high school, in fact, he was homeless.

What helped him the most was probably AAU basketball when his Twin Cities team would travel during the summer and spend many weekends in hotels. It was a chance for him to take the clothes out of his bag – who knows, maybe they were all the clothes he had to his name at that point – and put them in the hotel room drawer. It was a period in his life when he didn't have a drawer to put stuff in very often.

"Just to see what it would be like to be in a home for a bit," he said.

That was one of those interviews where you leave thankful of your upbringing – here was a kid who didn't take putting clothes in a drawer for granted. The journey hit Crockett emotionally in the post-game press conference following his last home regular season game against Youngstown State. It was "Senior Day" and Crockett had trouble finding the words when asked to reflect on his Bison career. He talked about his life, all that he went through to just be able to put on a Bison uniform. For perhaps the first time in his five years in college, he was speechless. You couldn't blame him.

"I could not be prouder. I've told people it's a miracle," said Jeff Ferguson, his high school coach at Totino-Grace in the Twin Cities. "He had ambition and hunger. He just didn't have a road map."

As a high school kid, the road map went all over the Twin Cities, at times finding a place to sleep wherever he could find it. Some people call it couch surfing, staying at different friends' house for a little bit at a time. It's a definition of being homeless, although not in the sensationalized sleeping-on-a-park-bench view of it since there were always people willing to help. Crockett said he got very good at going into somebody's kitchen in the morning and saying thanks and we'll see you later. He said he can't thank "the village" enough for helping him when his mother, Jackie Martin, went through some tough times. And they were tough.

She was hospitalized for about two months after she said she suffered a mental breakdown that came out of nowhere. Her son thinks it was brought on by stress. They were always together growing up, mother and son. A woman of faith in a middle-class neighborhood, her son was never exposed to alcohol or drugs in the home. She worked hard to get him in good schools, and she always surrounded herself with successful people. He's always had that personality, she said, ever since he was a baby. He was given the nickname "Taz" in high school, in reference to the Looney Tunes cartoon character "Tasmanian Devil." Crockett said that Taz attitude was essential while his mom was struggling. She eventually recovered and enjoyed following his career in college.

"I have an amazing mother and she gave me everything possible I ever wanted and needed," he said. "Just at that time it was something she couldn't control. She being able to fight through that – that's what keeps you fighting. Everybody has a story. I tell kids all the time. These (Bison) rookies – they want to complain, they want to whine about missing home. I tell them it's all about how you create your own story. It's either you fail at the end or you prevail."

He obviously prevailed. Those two years he spent getting academically eligible was the result of several factors that added up at Totino-Grace. Everybody, especially Ferguson, did the best they could. Crockett says he didn't take care of business, but business was hard. There were times, Ferguson said, when Crockett's clothes would be at one house and his homework at another. Combine that with an Attention Deficit Hyperactivity Disorder condition that was diagnosed in junior high, and the situation got complicated.

"'Where's my homework?' takes on a whole new meaning when you're sleeping in multiple homes during the week," Ferguson said. "He was really, really frustrating and really, really uplifting at the same time. He touched my heart in a special way and I was committed to helping him."

It was a hot-cold relationship, Ferguson said. He remembers a conversation, fondly now, when Crockett told his coach in figurative terms, "I want to kill you and you want to kill me, and I think you're winning."

"We were the odd couple," Ferguson said. "I'm a white guy with two parents who never had it tough. And here's him, where it was hard enough to get his homework done when you don't know where your stuff was last night."

An all-state running back who helped Totino-Grace to a state championship, Crockett was recruited by most Big Ten schools – until they saw his transcript, anyway. So he took a different path, heading to Fargo. He wasn't alone.

The Twin Cities was just the start of the '09 and '10 classes. The 2009 class was really the beginning of it all with the first big get when NDSU out-recruited major FBS schools for Juckem from Chilton, Wis., who had offers from Pittsburgh and Washington State.

At 6-5 and 245 who was a member of his high school team's record-breaking 1,600-meter relay team, Juckem had that look of being special. He was very good on the 2011 team but by the time NDSU reached Frisco in 2012, his surgery-scarred knees had enough. The Bison signed one player out of Illinois, Ojuri, who turned into a top 10 rusher in school history, and one player out of Nebraska, fullback Garrett Bruhn.

So, from the 2009 class, these players were major contributors to the run of titles: Drevlow, Grothmann, Gimmestad, Jirik, Perry, Kevin Vaadeland, Bruhn and Ojuri. Safety Bobby Ollman from Mequon, Wis., had some big games and junior college cornerback Josh Gatlin turned into a starter his last year.

The gem in the class, however, came from a small school in Wisconsin. Brock Jensen led Waupaca High School to an unbeaten season and a Division III state championship. He was by no means hidden away – Wisconsin Sports Net ranked him the second-best quarterback prospect in the state, but not many others thought so. Only Division II Minnesota-Duluth and NDSU offered him.

But the re-emphasis of the Bison coaching staff of looking beyond a player's talent level and getting to know his character, academics and leadership paid off with Jensen. It paid off with a lot of guys.

***

It was also during this period of time when the Bison coaching staff started to stabilize. Bohl was constantly replacing somebody on his staff starting in 2004 with offensive coordinator Tim Albin (Ohio University), defensive coordinator Jimmy Burrow (Ohio University) and defensive line coach Nelson Barnes (Oklahoma State).

"Coaches came and went but what I thought you had were two guys who were constant in Gene and Craig," Pat Perles said. "Gene had the general vision and the direction he wanted the program to go. Craig also had a vision of what each team could do based on the talent and he did a great job of showing that vision to us coaches."

After the 2004 assistants left, the departure role call went like this:

In 2005, defensive coordinator Casey Bradley (Tampa Bay Buccaneers).

In 2006, running backs coach Steve Laqua (Fargo Shanley High School) and defensive line coach Todd Wash (Tampa Bay).

In 2007, wide receivers coach Reggie Moore (UCLA).

In 2008, linebackers coach Kyle Nystrom (fired, later Central Michigan), Perles (Kansas City Chiefs) and defensive coordinator Willie Mack Garza (Tennessee).

In 2009, defensive coordinator Breske (Washington State), linebackers coach Charlie Camp (Akron) and wide receivers coach Terrence Samuel (Central Michigan).

In 2010, defensive backs coach Brian Ward (Western Illinois).

In 2011, defensive coordinator Hazelton (USC).

In 2012, running backs coach Polasek (Northern Illinois).

And, of course, 2013 when most of the staff went to Wyoming.

After a while, Bohl figured out that hiring guys who were at one time at some sort of FBS program and were looking for a ticket to get their coaching career going again wasn't very good for consistency. When Division I coaches are on the move, they move fast.

So Bohl made a philosophical change after the 2009 season: he started to look for Midwest guys who were on their way up. Look at his 2004 staff: Barnes came from the Nebraska staff in 2003 that was fired and Albin and Burrow knew Bohl from the Nebraska days. A lot of these guys never lasted more than two or three years at NDSU and then it was on to a bigger school. Moore was working as a firefighter in Houston when Bohl called. Reggie was a big name as a receiver at UCLA and was a big reason the Bison reached into the Houston area for recruits for a good seven to eight years. Those Texas kids were mostly misses, but the ones that hit were bullseyes, specifically receiver Warren Holloway and running back D.J. McNorton.

Moore was great. The day before he left for an assistant position at UCLA in January of 2008, he said something to the effect: "Look out for Warren, that kid is going to be special." He was; Holloway was the go-to receiver in the first FCS national title team in 2011.

Holloway also had one of my favorite nicknames: "The Old Car," so given to him by Bohl for his troublesome knees – ailments that he somehow overcame to catch 77 passes for 1,003 yards in the '11 season. That playoff run produced one of my favorite stories, too, when Randy and Trudi Smith of Wahpeton took him in for Christmas since his hometown of Houston was too far of a trip to go home for a few days. NDSU had defeated Georgia Southern 35-7 in the FCS semifinals on Dec. 17. The team practiced until the following Wednesday before being dismissed until Monday night.

"I told him after Thanksgiving if we make the national championship, you're probably not going to be able to go home so you're welcome to stay with us," Ryan Smith said. "He said he would like to spend it with a teammate and we had a lot of fun."

"They even got me a couple of presents," Holloway said with a smile.

For Holloway, another present: returning close to his home in Frisco, Texas.

XII. Frisco

If you thought there was growth in western North Dakota during these title years because of the oil boom, you should have gone to the north suburbs of Dallas. Everything was new, with the exception of the water tower in Frisco that stands out almost as a historic monument to a city that was once a zit on the prairie. No longer. Located just off the Dallas Parkway Tollway, the powers that be in Division I FCS football decided they had enough of Chattanooga, Tenn., and took up Frisco's offer of a three-year contract starting with the 2010 title game. It pitted Eastern Washington vs. Delaware and the attendance was not a resounding success, to say the least. Pizza Hut Park, as the stadium was known then, looked about half full with 13,027 fans.

It was a great game, with Eastern Washington making the big play at the end to win 20-19. Eastern was the same team that eliminated NDSU that year in the famous 38-31 overtime win on the red turf in Cheney, Wash. Dom, Eric and I are steadfast in our belief that if NDSU would have run D.J. McNorton on a third-and-two late in the fourth quarter at the Eastern 34-yard line, instead of a slow developing quarterback bootleg with Jensen that went for no gain, the Bison would have been playing Delaware for the title instead of Eastern. The semifinal opponent would have been Villanova, which would have been at the Fargodome and the Bison had the team to match up with 'Nova, and then some. It would have been the Blue Hens' third straight road game and we just don't think they would have made it past Fargo, after traveling to Stephen F. Austin (Texas) and Appalachian State (N.C.) the previous two weeks.

As it was, the Bison punted – it was questionable if that was the right call being so deep in Eagles territory. The way McNorton was running and the way NDSU's offensive line was playing in the second half, the theory is Eastern would not have been able to stop McNorton on two tries with two yards to go. But Eastern, taking over at its own 10-yard line with 2:29 left in the game, drove 90 yards in 13 plays to tie the game and send it into overtime. It was packed with drama with Eastern converting a fourth-and-3 and a fourth-and-10 to keep the drive alive.

It was a tough loss for the visitors, with the now-infamous failure of the booth replay official to figure out that Jensen was down before he fumbled at the 1-yard line in overtime. Instead, the call on the field stood and the Eagles were off to the semifinals.

NDSU's experience with Frisco would have to wait another year.

But what an experience. When the Bison stomped Georgia Southern 35-7 in the 2011 semifinals at Gate City Bank Field at the Fargodome, it was helter skelter for their fan base to do two things: 1. Figure out the ticket situation. 2. Figure out how to get to Frisco.

The ticket fiasco caused Gene Taylor massive headaches and probably a sleepless night or two. The problem was in the allotment: NDSU and Sam Houston State were each granted about 4,000 tickets and the paranoia for Bison fans was there was nothing left after that. Pizza Hut Park capacity was 21,500 but many of those were divvied by the local tournament committee to local groups because Frisco and the NCAA did not want another half-empty stadium in front of the ESPN cameras. They had no idea what NDSU had to offer in terms of fans willing to travel.

NDSU has a priority points system that rewards its fans, both in longevity and financial gifts. If you were a season ticket holder since the 70s and were a regular Team Makers donor, no problem, you had tickets to Frisco.

If you had end zone seats since 2010, you had a problem. And the biggest problem in it all was those who didn't qualify for the Bison 4,000 allotment were fearful of not getting a ticket at all. It was stressful. Eric Peterson did the story and at one point asked Taylor if Forum photographer Dave Samson could take a photo of one of the tickets. Taylor was on the verge of losing his temper, probably from all of the hassle with the situation.

The guestimate for the number of Bison fans in the 2011 game was somewhere around 15,000 and there were generally accurate reports that hundreds of fans left for Texas without a ticket. To this day, I have yet to hear of a fan who didn't find a ticket for one of the five straight title games. There were tickets, you just had to look; whether it was StubHub, local Frisco fans who had them but had no interest to go to the game or the Bison message board fan site.

The Marriott hotel in Plano, however, was caught blindsided. That was the locale for the Friday night pep fest, an event put on by the Bison Alumni Association. The ballroom had space for about 5,000 people and I'm certain the Marriott folks figured a school located in remote, old North Dakota would not bring near that many people. It turned into a fiasco, despite the warnings from the Alumni Association and a hotel in Minneapolis. When the Bison played the Gophers, The Depot convention center hosted the NDSU pre-game tailgate party in 2011 and the Bison fans damn near drank them out of beer. The Depot folks and the folks at the Bison tailgating location on the Minnesota state fairgrounds compared NDSU fans to those from Wisconsin. Both can drink beer and alcohol like it's water.

The fairgrounds reported more cars for the NDSU game than the previous Wisconsin game. The Depot general manager reported more alcohol sales for the Bison-Gopher game than any Badgers-Gopher game. And in the spirit of communication for hotel convention management, somebody from The Depot actually called the Marriott in Plano and said essentially this: Do not underestimate these people; they can put the drinks down faster than you'll probably realize.

The Marriott didn't listen. The pep fest was jammed almost before it started. The Bison fans drank them out of beer before 10 p.m., causing the Marriott to dial 9-1-1 to other Marriotts in the Dallas area asking for kegs. It reminded me of the scene in the movie "Back to School" when police cars came screaming to a party thrown by Thornton Mellon, played by Rodney Dangerfield, and delivered beer.

"When we opened the doors of the Marriott, it was like, holy smokes, where did all these people come from?" said Jim Miller, who then was the executive director of the NDSU Development Foundation. "The way ticket sales went, it went so fast. We didn't envision people would go through StubHub and all those other locations to get tickets. I was surprised that first night the whole thing didn't get shut down. I did talk to a police officer the next day and I just said I was curious if there was any trouble last night. He said I had one report of four guys singing the Bison fight song and we just quieted them down. Other than that, there was no trouble."

We were at the Marriott covering the madness and by around 9 p.m., I saw a Bison fan paying another Bison fan $100 for a 12-pack of beer. I ran into Rocky Hager in the hotel lobby, and he couldn't believe the following. Rocky flew in from the East Coast for the game and was constantly thanked by former Bison players and long-time fans for being there. Rocky would cry at a Folgers commercial and he didn't leave Frisco without a few tears that weekend, either.

Frisco was perhaps the fastest-growing city in the country at the time. When we got there in 2011, the story was the city had just finished building 56 public schools since 2000. Fifty-six.

A migration of corporations setting up shop in the area was given as the main reason. Over the course of five years, NDSU fans came to know the area well.

"Just the sea of Bison fans in the bowl," Phil Hansen said. "It's not even fair almost from a fan's perspective. That's probably the single thing that stands out; the way the Bison traveled. And consistently traveled. They did it all five of those years and you marveled at how much better they got at it. You would see the opponent's two sections and you would see Bison fans in the front row. They would stick out like a sore thumb and you wonder how in the heck they got those tickets."

There were five title games between 2011 and 2015, and this is how all five played out:

2011: NDSU 17, Sam Houston State 6

One of the most touching moments before the game was even played was turned in by Hansen, who led a fundraising effort of 26 former players and boosters to get every player who was a member of the NDSU freshman class of 2003 to come to the Bison's first FCS title game appearance. Those 13 players spent all five years of their NDSU career in a Division I reclassification and got most of their travel expenses and hotel paid for.

They were all at the Friday practice where the Bison coaching staff and players addressed the alums.

"You look at all these guys out here," said Chad Pundsack, while surveying a throng of former players of all ages. "The reason I came to North Dakota State was to be in the playoffs and have a chance at a national championship. This is a way to thank them for their time in doing what they did."

What they did was bite the bullet of having no chance at the playoffs, all the while raising NDSU's level of play to where it was able to compete for a national title by the time the Bison were eligible in the 2008 season. It took until the 2011 season to do it.

The question everybody covering the game had no concrete answer for was simple: how many Bison fans actually got into the game? How many went into Sam Houston's website and ordered tickets through the Bearkats?

Quite a few because in the time from when we arrived in Frisco on Wednesday until Friday night, there were not very many people walking around Plano or Frisco wearing orange. Of the sold-out stadium, probably 80 percent were NDSU fans.

"I knew it was going to be big, but until walking into the stadium and seeing all that green and gold, it was nuts," Miller said. "We thought going to Alabama for the Division II championships was a big deal. We thought it was a big deal when we took two charter planes to Florence. But my god, that was crazy in Frisco. The way Frisco reacted after that first game, I don't think they knew what to expect."

The Bearkats came into the game unbeaten and ranked No. 1 in the FCS behind record-setting running back Tim Flanders. NDSU had McNorton in the backfield, who was returning to his home state to play in his final college game. It was also a chance for McNorton, from the Houston suburb of Channelview, to fulfill a promise he made to his late mother. The only game Tonya McNorton saw her son play in college was in 2009 when the Bison played at Sam Houston, of all teams. NDSU lost and she died less than a year later from cancer.

"We lost that game and now I have a chance to make up for it," he said. "That feels really good."

Not surprisingly, McNorton made a difference. So did the punter. For four years, Matt Voigtlander was a backup running back who showed some flashes of fine play. He also showed some flashes of not playing, so with the graduation of John Prelvitz the previous year, Voigtlander took up the coaches' offer of concentrating on punting full time.

He had a great season, and a great title game moment. The Bison special teams came up with a momentum-shifting play early in the second half, running a fake punt on its first drive of the third quarter. Voigtlander rushed for 27 yards on a fourth-and-4 play from NDSU's 34-yard line and reached the Bearkat 39 on a play designed by Tim Polasek that was based on how the Bearkats lined up in punt defense.

"It was wide open, my eyes were wide open," Voigtlander said.

On the next play, Jensen dumped a middle screen pass to McNorton and McNorton did the rest, weaving through the Bearkats defense for a touchdown and a 10-6 lead with 12:47 to play in the third quarter.

"We work all the time on sudden change," said Sam Houston State head coach Willie Fritz. "It was a good play call, running a little middle screen to the back and caught us in a zone. It was the right call at the right time."

The second "play of the game" came in the fourth quarter and was turned in by linebacker Travis Beck, who picked off a Brian Bell pass with about nine minutes left in the fourth quarter and returned it 63 yards to the Bearkat 1-yard line. Jensen scored from there and NDSU had a coveted two-possession lead. Beck was gassed when Bell went back to pass and his job was to disguise the coverage. When Bell threw it right to him, he took off running, got a great block from Christian Dudzik and remembers Jirik almost passing him down the right sideline. His legs went heavy. Once he got inside the 10-yard line, Bell made a diving tackle attempt at his knees and Beck said he should have "jumped and landed on my feet, but I tucked and rolled. I didn't want to pop out my shoulder."

That play was a big reason Beck was named the game's Most Valuable Player. While accepting it on what is now a familiar stage at the Frisco stadium, North Dakota Gov. John Hoeven, standing about 10 yards away, marveled at a North Dakota kid being named MVP in a title game. Up in a suite somewhere, Pat Simmers said he cried.

"You just don't know if you can do it," Simmers said. "Maybe that old North Dakota sentiment settles back in. Just to see all that work come to fruition. The Upper Midwest kids. Tough kids. Not necessarily the fastest or the biggest but they're the toughest. I cried because I've been there; it was the same feeling in 1983 when we got there."

What sold Bison assistant coach Brent Vigen in offering Beck during the recruiting process was when Vigen drove to Munich to watch him play a basketball game. What he saw was an athlete. Bohl also flew his single-engine plane to watch Beck play a basketball game at Park River, N.D., a game where Beck noticed the head coach probably only watched a half because fans were wanting to talk Bison football.

UND came in late in the recruiting process and Beck said a UND assistant wanted him to hold off on committing to NDSU. He committed anyway.

His hometown is listed as Munich, but that's not really accurate. It was Calio, which in the last census had a population of 22. It does have the Calio Bar, and if you look out the window of the place, you can see the Beck farm in the distance about a mile away. The town lists its most famous native as Eldon Bernard Schuster, an Oxford-educated clergyman who reached the status of bishop in Great Falls, Mont. How Travis went from an area where for several years there was no high school football to the FCS title stage in Frisco was a fascinating story in itself. He had uncles and cousins who won boys and girls North Dakota Class B state basketball championships and played college basketball and baseball. It would take a master's thesis to sort it all out, but know this: The names Beck and Wirth are to athletics what farming is to the economy in that part of the state. Travis' father Gary and mother, Lynette Wirth, both played basketball and ran track in high school. His brother, Riley, played baseball at UND.

Travis figured baseball would be his sport of excellence. In one sense, he was lucky to have played football. It wasn't a priority in Munich. The school allied with Border Central and Starkweather for football in a cooperative for a while in the 1980s. When that split, Border Central went to Langdon and Starkweather went with Cando, leaving Munich with nothing. Munich probably could have allied with Langdon, but the two schools were fierce rivals. Those feelings finally caved later in the decade and Munich kids, what few there were, were allowed to play football at Langdon. For Travis, that would mean driving about 30 miles one way to practice.

Travis already knew a bunch of Langdon kids from playing with them in youth hockey – the only Beck/Wirth grandchild to take up that sport. Those friends convinced him to try football in junior high.

"It's just a basketball and baseball area when I grew up," said Justin Fletschock, also a former star Munich athlete. "No one was desperate to get football, but looking back and thinking about it, there were a lot of kids who would have excelled at it."

Several years later, it was Travis Beck who broke the mold.

He may have been the MVP of the 2011 title game, but his career wasn't all roses. In the summer of 2013, he was the subject of a much-publicized assault charge, the result of an incident after bar hopping in downtown Fargo. What followed was a tug-of-war between me, the beat writer, and the editors of The Forum. They won.

There will always be disagreements in journalism on how to play a story, whether it's front page, sports front page or somewhere inside. It's the nature of the business; there is this imaginary line called fairness and the goal is to get as close to it as possible. Because we are human, we all don't see it the same and that's what happened here – and it's not uncommon in the business. What I took from my reporting of the incident that day was it was a bar fight. Two guys. Drinking. Bar fight. I lobbied that it was a story for the front sports page to Kevin Schnepf.

The final decision by editor Matt Von Pinnon was the front page of the newspaper with the headline "NDSU star charged with felony assault." Moreover, to add a further dagger to my viewpoint, The Forum online folks chose to run much of the police car camera showing a drunken Beck jabbering about the incident. It was obtained through an open records request to the Fargo Police Department.

There were a few instances in the tape that I thought were relevant to the story and were fair game to use online: a piece where Beck said the other man in the fight, Matthew Aanenson, was egging him on, and a short blurb where Beck thought his career was over because of potential disciplinary action. He already had a minor in possession charge from a previous off-season incident.

I thought running the entire squad car episode was piling on, and not fair, and the result of inexperienced video guys who probably didn't think things through – or maybe didn't have the journalism training to think like a reporter. Later the next night, I got a call at home from Lynette Beck, Travis' mother. She was disgusted, and for the most part I couldn't blame her. For a good part of what had to be a half-hour conversation, I took her through the decision making process of the editors. At one point, she said she wished the family never heard of Bison football.

Video from a nearby business later surfaced that Beck may have been acting in self-defense, which led the State's Attorney's office to drop the more serious charge. Beck eventually pleaded guilty to resisting arrest charges, although even with that his attorney, Bruce Quick, argued Beck was merely walking away from officers after getting hit in the head twice.

Beck said watching video of the incident with Quick in the attorney's office was interesting in that he didn't remember much about it.

"I basically said, Bruce, it doesn't matter what you say in a statement, I don't remember it," he said. "It was embarrassing but it happened."

It was a tough time in the kid's life. He was probably drinking too much. There were times when he stayed in the homes of Bohl and linebackers coach Steve Stanard.

"The fight was a culmination in what I was doing," Beck said.

Was Travis wrong in following Aanenson into the alley? Yes. Was he wrong in throwing a punch, rather than walking away? Yes. But was it worthy of the front page of The Forum and the subsequent embarrassing online video footage? No.

The concern of the Beck family at the time was that incident was going to define his career. As it turns out, it did not. Quick, a very good and well-respected attorney in Fargo, was masterful in taking over the case and putting a quick end to it by negotiating a plea of the reduced charge and putting it out there that Beck accepted responsibility for his actions.

What defined Beck's career was an outside linebacker who was so freakishly athletic that he could stuff the run and cover a wide receiver on back-to-back plays. He was also one tough dude, often playing through dislocated shoulder pain, especially during his junior season. Despite that, he played every down of that season. Yes, every down at a physical and explosive position.

***

It was a cold winter day in 2015, more than a year after his career was done, when Travis Beck sat down at Atomic Coffee in downtown Fargo and reflected on a career that had its share of ups and downs. He seemed content, and did not seem bitter at anything that transpired in his playing days.

He called the Bison coaches "incredible" and said no team worked harder in the FCS than his team. He harbored no anxiety with any of the media reporting. He said the toughest running back he ever tackled was Indiana State's Shakir Bell, who he called "heavy" every time he hit him. He said former Bison fullback Lee Vandal was the hardest worker in practice, a trait that was an awakening of sorts for Beck when he was a true freshman. One of the most amazing feats he ever saw was linebacker Carlton Littlejohn doing a 360-degree dunk with a basketball. "I've seen a lot of 360s but that was better than anyone," he said. He said the 2010 Eastern Washington overtime playoff loss started the dynasty because the players figured if the Eagles can win an FCS title, so can they. NDSU had several star linebackers in the Division I era but if given the choice of starting three of them, I would put Beck as the starter at his outside position.

What defined Beck's career was a small-town kid who was a title game MVP. A shy kid with those outside his inner circle, it took him awhile before he was OK in talking with the media. He did some immature things but so did I in college, although I was not a star athlete who got his name on a police report. During the 2014 title game weekend, when Beck's season was already over because of a torn Achilles tendon, Eric Peterson did a story on the linebacker not being able to be on the field for his final game. My name came up during the interview and Peterson immediately thought this to himself: Oh no, here we go with the bar fight story again.

No, that was not it. Travis told Big E his hometown was Munich, not Calio, that I had in a big game day cover story during the 2012 season. "I told Kolpack that," he told Eric.

Well, OK Travis, I'm still a believer that your farm is closer to Calio, but if you prefer Munich, then Munich it shall be. I truly believe the Achilles injury prevented him from an NFL career; I think he was that good and the reason was he was good enough to tackle a guy like UNI and NFL running back David Johnson one-on-one and good enough to cover receivers and tight ends in the flat on passing routes. Nobody was better than Beck at being multi-dimensional in those two areas. All he needed was to sign a free agent contract and get into an NFL camp and like the Bison coaches saw in 2010, an NFL coach would have immediately taken notice of the speed, explosiveness and toughness.

Once, during a game against Illinois State in 2013, the same game where Grant Olson tore his ACL, his shoulder popped out when tackling Redbirds star running back Marshaun Coprich. He asked Drevlow to pop it back in.

"I'm not going to touch it," Drevlow told him.

"Just hit my arm a little bit," Beck said.

Think about it: Beck is shouting at his teammate to knock his shoulder back into place between plays, which tells you something about the sheer courage of these guys not wanting to come off the field even for a play. Beck tried unsuccessfully to do it himself. Not wanting to go to the training staff and therefore risk not playing the rest of the game, he pleaded for defensive tackle Brian Schaetz to pop it back in, who promptly did his best amateur trainer impersonation. It worked. Did it hurt? That's not a question you asked these players.

"It was just a different mindset," Beck said. "Then I went a couple of weeks without it popping out, but Friday night before a game, it came out while I was sleeping. I woke up and said this is just ridiculous. You get used to it. The first time it happens you go right to your knees and all you can think about is the pain, but you get used to it."

2012: NDSU 39, Sam Houston State 13

The first order of business was obvious: how was the NDSU Alumni Association going to avoid the Friday night pep fest overload of the previous year? Well, rent out a minor league baseball park, of course. NDSU moved its event to Dr. Pepper Ballpark, home of the Frisco Roughriders Class AA baseball team. The crowd was capped at 8,000 at $10 ticket and the soiree sold out. The Roughriders staffed it with 300 employees.

The ballpark organizers promised they wouldn't run out of beer. Well, although not totally, they did come up short again. People were seen leaving the stadium saying there was no more Bud Light.

"If you would have told me two weeks ago that 8,000 people would show up here for this, I would have been skeptical," said Scott Sonju, the Roughriders' president. "This is impressive."

What was even more impressive? NDSU's performance in the repeat title match with Sam Houston with an estimated 14,000 Bison fans filling Toyota Stadium. Like the previous year, some fans went on the Sam Houston website and joined the school's booster club for $50 to get in line for the Bearkats' allotment to the game.

It was 10-10 at halftime when the Bison put together one of their patented second half beatdowns that would repeatedly mark the five-title dynasty.

After being off early in the game, Jensen was fantastic finishing 9 of 16 and engineering a potent running game that ran for 300 yards. He was named the game's MVP, but the real MVP in my mind? Offensive coordinator Vigen. Once the subject of "fire Vigen" banter on the Bison football fan website, he showed his growth. It was the same Brent Vigen who in 2002 was dang near begging Bohl for a job after Bob Babich left.

A few plays were genius, such as a fleaflicker to receiver Zach Vraa that led to NDSU taking a 25-10 lead and a 31-yard "jump pass" from Crockett to Vaadeland, where Crockett took a handoff with an apparent run up the middle, stopped, jumped and threw a pass to a wide open Vaadeland. Jensen scored from the 1 on the drive and it was 32-13 early in the fourth quarter.

The Bison defense, meanwhile, picked off four Sam Houston passes, two by cornerback Marcus Williams. The big pick was by Littlejohn, whose interception on Sam Houston's first possession of the second half led to NDSU's go-ahead touchdown. Flanders, the all-American running back, was held to 53 yards on 19 carries.

"This is the best defense we've played this season, and I'm comparing that to Texas A&M and Baylor," Bearkats coach Willie Fritz said.

It was a defense that played with Olson, even though it looked doubtful because of an appendectomy. Olson's own account of the ordeal started with a trip to a walk-in clinic the previous Sunday, where he received some antibiotics to address the pain. He returned to the hospital the following day, as scheduled, to get a CT scan. The radiologist who performed the procedure came out to the lobby where Olson was waiting and told him a surgeon was called and he needed to get to the emergency room immediately. But because Olson was already feeling better from the walk-in clinic antibiotics, he said doctors decided against surgery. He said one of the doctors believed the problem was a combination of a few factors that included a strained groin injury from the Georgia Southern semifinal game and the flu.

"He's been through a lot this past week," Jensen said. "For him to go through everything and tough it out, to play in that game and give it all for us and his teammates says lot about him as a person."

After the game, a fan's near-miss with losing his wallet said a lot about some unknown good Samaritan. While running onto the field with his sons Adam and Nick, Jim Laschkewitsch of Fargo lost his money and credit cards – something he realized later at a restaurant. Not large on confidence that it would be found, he went back to the stadium to check it out anyway.

"I made it back to the stadium in about 30 minutes through the massive traffic jam," Jim said. "At the stadium, I found an older gentleman locking up all the gates and he directed me to the security office. Their first search came back empty-handed, but they agreed to look one more place."

It turns out somebody turned in the wallet with every penny and cards intact. "There has to be some Bison fan out there who deserves our thanks," said Jim, a 1988 NDSU graduate.

Hearing stories like that only reinforced the Fargo-nice opinion of Bison athletic director Matt Larsen, who took over for Taylor in the fall of 2014.

Larsen was the associate athletic director at Stony Brook University (N.Y.) when the Seawolves lost a close 34-27 second round playoff game at Sam Houston in 2011. Before the title game, by the way, a member of the Bison football staff reached out to Stony Brook and inquired on how the Seawolves almost pulled off the upset in Huntsville, Texas. That week also turned out to be Larsen's first glimpse into his future – his initial experience with the Bison Frisco frenzy.

"I thought for sure going down there that Sam Houston was going to pack the stadium," Larsen said. "Again, not knowing about North Dakota State that first year and all of those things. I was blown away, not only walking into the stadium but walking around town. We were staying at a hotel about handful of miles away and the entire hotel was Bison fans. And that was my first introduction to what North Dakota State was all about. Everywhere you went, they were all over the place. I mean, some of these people -- we have some people that have money -- but there are people who don't have money.

"This is their savings. Their vacation is not going to Hawaii, it's not to going to Florida; they're going to Frisco. And they're spending a lot of money and in some cases a lot of money they don't have. To me, that just speaks to the importance of it. So it's pretty special, when you look up there and you see all the fans and all the tradition."

2013: NDSU 35, Towson 7

The story leading up to the game, of course, was Bohl coaching in the playoffs despite already accepting the head coaching position at the University of Wyoming. It was the end of a long month. There are those that believe the three coaches that stayed – Chris Klieman, Conor Riley and Nick Goeser – could have coached this team through the playoffs. They were that loaded.

The Tigers were no match for the best team ever in the FCS. Youngstown, Georgia Southern and Appalachian State all fielded great teams in their run of titles, but none of them matched the offensive firepower, the defensive toughness and the special teams ability of NDSU. That 2013 team had it all. They became the third FCS team to finish a season unbeaten at 15-0. They were rarely challenged all season, with the exception a 24-23 win at home against Northern Iowa.

Weakness? No such thing.

Even a torn ACL couldn't keep Olson out of this title game, either. His season, and Hall of Fame-type career, appeared over earlier in the season when he went down against Illinois State. Although certainly not at full strength, his presence in uniform was more of a marvel than anything else. He wasn't expected to play much, certainly not in passing situations, but the mental toughness was duly noted and he actually was the second Bison player to appear in a title game with a torn ACL. Defensive end Jeremy Gordon was the other.

"Who the hell does that?" Mike Hardie asked.

By now, NDSU had the Frisco routine down to a science. The Bison players knew their way around town. They knew the exact time a Frisco greeting party would meet them at the team hotel. They knew the ins and outs of the press conferences, closed practices and open practices.

"You certainly can't get complacent or take something for granted," Bohl said, "but our guys are in a routine – everything from the equipment to the surroundings, and that certainly helps. Players usually function better in a routine. You take them out of a routine and sometimes that can cause problems."

Since 1992, the town went from 6,000 residents to a major suburb of 140,000. Frisco Mayor Maher Maso said the FCS title game had a yearly $3 million impact on his city. I bet $2.8 million of that came from Bison fans.

Many of them risked their tickets and flights on this team, booking them well in advance – some in the spring and summer. They were that confident. Those that drove vehicles knew the route. Whenever anybody stopped for gas or food between North Dakota and Texas, there was a very good chance of some green and yellow familiarity. By now, it was a staple that somebody would strap an NDSU flag to the Texas state line sign.

By now, the Third Base bar in Frisco was an NDSU fan staple. About every 20 minutes, the Fargodome Bison entrance with "Thunderstruck" by ACDC played on every TV. By now, every bartender and wait staff wore some sort of Bison T-shirt or jersey. The owner of Third Base even joined NDSU Team Makers booster club, mainly because the best days of business in the history of his bar were when NDSU was in town. The experienced bartenders and waitresses were given a choice: Work New Year's Eve or FCS title weekend. The ones who wanted to make more tips chose the FCS weekend.

The fans drank a lot and partied a lot, but there were very few complaints, if any, to the Frisco or Plano police. "These people are the nicest drunks I've ever seen," one Plano bartender said.

Once again, the Friday pep fest at the local ballpark sold out the 10,000 tickets, prompting some to put messages on Twitter asking if anybody was willing to scalp their ticket. The Fargo band 32 Below played.

"I am continually amazed at the passion of this fan base," Scott Burchett, vice president of the Frisco Roughriders baseball team, told The Forum's Schnepf. Burchett had a pretty good idea that all these Bison fans would be invading his park again this year. After he and some of his staff watched the Bison claim a semifinal win over New Hampshire on ESPN2, they immediately started selling pep fest tickets online. It was quite a change from the previous year, when Burchett and his staff had an eight-day notice to host the pep fest. They were much more prepared for the 10,000 fans compared to the 8,000 fans who showed up last year.

"Bud Lite and Windsor … we ordered much more of that this year," Burchett said, referring to the two most popular adult beverages consumed by Bison fans.

By Saturday, attention turned to the swan song of 26 seniors and most of the coaching staff, who earlier in the playoffs announced they were moving on to Wyoming, most notable Bohl. In retrospect, Towson didn't have much of a chance.

Jensen's 48th win as a starting quarterback against the Tigers was a masterpiece. He completed 13 of 18 passes for 135 yards and a touchdown to earn MVP honors and also rushed for 20 yards and a touchdown on three carries in his final college game. Jensen's nine-yard touchdown run gave NDSU a 28-7 lead with 9:09 remaining in the third quarter.

"That is something I will remember my whole life," said Jensen. "We've got something special here at NDSU. It gets better every time I think you win it."

The Bison seized control in the final five minutes of the second quarter with the game tied at 7-7. Towson kicker D.J. Soven lined up for a 41-yard field-goal attempt with a chance to give the Tigers their first lead. However, NDSU junior Colten Heagle sliced through the line of scrimmage and blocked the kick.

Kyle Emanuel scooped up the loose ball and returned it 59 yards to the Towson 5-yard line. On the next play, Ryan Smith scored on a jet sweep, giving the Bison a 14-7 lead with 4:43 to play in the half.

"We noticed on film they weren't a very disciplined unit on their field-goal team," Heagle said. "I saw the gap and I hit it. It was so fast I didn't even know what to do."

The win moved NDSU's three-year record to 43-2. It was the eighth time in more than 100 years of college football that a team three-peated. Carroll College (Mont.) did it at the lowest level of college football (NAIA) in 2005. Three teams did it at the NCAA Division III level – Augustana of Illinois in 1986, Mount Union of Ohio in 1998 and Wisconsin-Whitewater in 2011. North Alabama did it at the Division II level in 1995. The only major-college team was, ironically the Minnesota Gophers who won their third in a row in 1936. Moreover, NDSU became the 31st three-peater in the history of major sports – which included professional sports of football, baseball, basketball, hockey and NASCAR plus the college sports of football and Division I basketball.

Toward the end, both Bohl and Klieman got the old Gatorade ice bucket bath from players, a sign that perhaps some of them were "Bohl guys" and some were "Klieman guys" in the few weeks following the Wyoming announcement. A few players, one source told me, were bitching at each other saying dumping water on Klieman was disrespectful to Bohl. "You also had assistant coaches fighting with each other during the game," he said. "The national championship week, that was the worst. It shows how much some took going to Frisco for granted. Teams get there like once in school history and here's the NDSU Bison there for the third straight year and they're all fighting each other. They wanted to play the game and go home."

Dom Izzo said in watching the replay of the game that the body language of some of the coaches and players was interesting, especially when Klieman got an ice bucket bath.

"Craig had no reaction on TV, you could see it," Izzo said. "It was really weird – I remember we never saw Craig and Chris together that three weeks. I remember Chris talking to select members of the staff. I remember talking to Steve Stanard the night before the championship with Tyler Roehl and Riley, but there was no interaction. We heard rumblings about how things had gotten awkward and weird."

2014: NDSU 29, Illinois State 27

The definition of a winner was probably best exemplified the week of the championship game when senior receiver Trevor Gebhart was asked about his string of title game appearances – seven including three in high school and four in college (not counting his redshirt freshman season). At Sioux Falls

Washington High School, his team made the South Dakota Class AA title game three straight seasons.

The week was a culmination of a smooth rookie year as the head coach for Klieman, although he found out early that being in charge has its tough moments. It was at Hope Congregational Church in early August in Granville, N.D., where Klieman pledged to Michelle Bacon, mother of true freshman offensive tackle Luke Bacon, that the Bison team will be there for her son. It came before the mother of all nightmares: The funeral for her 21-year-old daughter. Luke Bacon was part of Klieman's first recruiting class, and never was that more evident than when the head coach attended the funeral of Kaitlyn Bacon, Luke's only sibling. One of the first people Klieman saw was Luke's mother.

"My mom grabs him by the coat and says, 'He's all I got. You better take care of him,'" Luke said.

NDSU was only four days into fall practice when Luke got the call from his father, Ryan, around 5 in the morning. At first he thought it was his alarm, so he silenced his phone. Then it rang again. Kaitlyn was killed in a motorcycle accident late that night in Minot, N.D. She was the passenger on a bike that was traveling at a high rate of speed when it left the road, according to police.

When it came to being away from home for the first time in his life, he was in the right place at the right time. It wasn't long before Bison players were there for support, and they rarely left his side. Some of them probably didn't know who this kid was from small town Towner-Granville-Upham High School in north central North Dakota. Bacon's first call that morning was to Klieman at 5:30. "He probably thought I was calling to quit or something," he said. Klieman said a few days later he was happy he could be there for the Bacon family. On the flipside, the Bacon family was grateful for football.

In early January, Luke took the first plane ride of his life – to Frisco for NDSU's fourth consecutive appearance in a title game. This one wasn't expected on the same level as the prior year and the matchup was intriguing to say the least: it was not only the FCS title but a showdown of two Missouri Valley teams who didn't play each other in the regular season because the league has 10 teams and eight conference games.

Illinois State got a nice off-season acquisition in quarterback Tre Roberson, who transferred from Indiana and it didn't take long before head coach Brock Spack named him the starter. NDSU got a nice acquisition in the 2011 recruiting class in Carson Wentz. At almost 6-foot-6 and 231 pounds, he was quite the find for the Bison on a couple of fronts: One, he had a scholarship offer from FBS Central Michigan and, two, he had a cannon of a right arm, a 4.0 grade point average and leadership abilities – he was named a Bison team captain as a junior.

How do you maintain an FCS title streak? You sign guys like Wentz to a letter of intent and then have them wait their turn. He redshirted his first season and then spent the next two seasons as the top backup to Jensen. It was worth the wait for both he and the team. When Wentz was going through his NFL Draft experience, a popular question from the rest of the country was why did this guy only start for two years? Because he was behind a guy, Jensen, who was 31-1 in those two years.

Wentz got better as the season wore on, and was close to sensational in the playoffs. He led a Jensen-like drive in the final minutes to beat SDSU in the second round, leading the Bison 76 yards in eight plays in just 2:18, culminating with a 12-yard beauty to R.J. Urzendowski with just 54 seconds to play.

It was that moment, that place in time, when the new athletic director in town realized the football program he was in charge of was a different place. Larsen was a three-year starter at wide receiver and an assistant coach at Stony Brook and before moving into management, where he became the senior associate director of athletics. His duties included overseeing the football program, and he was well-versed in the FCS and the quality of programs across the country.

"South Dakota State goes down and scores late and I swear to god there were 19,000 people in that stadium that thought we were going to lose the game," Larsen said. "There were 19,000 no-doubt-about-its. The place was deflated. I was down on the sideline, I looked down and I see our players and I see our coaches and just the look on their faces and the way they carried themselves. Every single person genuinely believed we were going to win that game. I think that's the difference. That's the difference. I've been around plenty of programs, where you have talent, where you have buy in, but the unified belief that we were going to win, and do those things – I've never seen it exist like it exists here. And our seniors do a great job of when the new freshmen come in of teaching them that. And hopefully they don't have to teach a ton. If you look at the recruiting class this year (2015) and the kids that are being recruited, they are being recruited from winning programs. Very rarely do you see us taking a kid from the 1-10 program. We're recruiting kids from winning programs."

Wentz was a winner. The next week, he was 11 of 17 and two touchdowns in a 39-32 barnburner quarterfinal win over Coastal Carolina. He was 13 of 19 with a touchdown in a 35-3 demolition of Sam Houston in the semifinals. All three games were typical frenzied playoff-type loudfests at a sold out Fargodome.

The title game was about as good as it gets for drama.

The last drive was videogame worthy. When Roberson scored from 58 yards out with 1:38 remaining, you got the feeling that fate eventually tilts against a team trying to win four straight titles. It's almost an impossible thing to do at any college level. That's when Wentz gathered the troops.

Not far away, Larsen vividly remembers Wentz grabbing his helmet and just having "that look" on his face. He did it earlier in the playoffs against SDSU, but this had more riding on it.

"Once Carson speaks up, we all become unified, and we know good things are coming," Vraa said.

Crockett said it's his job to support Wentz, although he admitted to giving a few words of advice after Roberson's score. Up in the coaches' booth, Polasek and quarterbacks coach Randy Hedberg charted a couple of plays that they liked, but Polasek said, by and large, it was Wentz who called the game-winning drive.

"We prepared for that moment so many times," Polasek said. "We challenged him in (fall) camp, 'Change the damn play once in awhile, see it through your eyes, get us in something better.' The kid was underappreciated in our conference, but hopefully the country saw what he could do."

Not far away, Klieman kept his distance, not wanting to interrupt Wentz talking with Hedberg.

"I was just watching him and there was no panic in his eyes," Klieman said. "He actually seemed kind of excited for the opportunity and I knew what was going through his mind: this is why we do this every week on Monday."

Still, it didn't look good when the Bison were called for illegal motion, forcing a first-and-15 situation from their own 17-yard line. But on the next play, Wentz threw a strike to Urzendowski over the middle for 32 yards to near midfield. A 13-yarder to Urzendowski on the next play reached the ISU 38 with 1:10 left.

You could sense the change of momentum in the stands.

"I really believe this: we don't have the numbers of an Alabama, but pound for pound, we have the best fan base in the country," Larsen said. "And not a lot of people know about it, which is OK. It's OK. When people ask why you guys are so successful, it's those things – the intangibles that people for years have been trying to do but they can't. It's what makes us different."

The next two plays were incompletions. On third down, with the Redbirds blitzing from all angles, Wentz lofted a pass to the left sideline that Urzendowski, a true freshman, made an adjustment on like a senior and the 33-yarder reached the 5. It was the same play the two used to beat SDSU in the second round – a fade to the left sideline.

There was still work to do with 57 seconds left. NDSU called timeout. That was about the only time Klieman vocally got involved with anybody on the offense, taking Urzendowski aside and talking to him about one of the potential plays the offensive staff was thinking of running. Near the sideline, Wentz put on a headset to talk directly to Polasek in the booth. They decided on two plays, with Wentz being given the final decision on what to go with by calling it at the line of scrimmage.

"A relationship like that is so nice, and so special for the coach to have confidence in me to almost choose what play," Wentz said.

The play is something NDSU did with Jensen; put the ball in the QB's hands. With the Bison lining up, Polasek saw the defensive alignment of ISU and told Klieman over the headset that it was going to be a touchdown before the play even started. Wentz took the snap, went around left tackle and scored easily.

"We had them outnumbered on one side," Klieman said a few months later. "We had two slot receivers and they had three defensive backs over there. They were three-on-two so we knew the short run play away from the slot was the way to go. We always know from a defensive standpoint that if you do that, the only person they can't account for truly is the quarterback. I think Carson was giddy when he saw it; he couldn't get the snap fast enough. We did a nice job at the point of attack, to get him on the edge. I thought the linebacker took a good angle but I didn't think he could tackle him."

He didn't.

There were 37 seconds left. "It really comes down to just a lot of preparation and then our tradition of looking at the guy next to you and saying he's going to get his job done," Wentz said. "I'm going to get my job done. It's just a lot of trust in your brothers."

Linebacker Esley Thorton, who like Wentz came to NDSU as a quarterback but was beaten out by Wentz during spring ball a couple of years earlier, picked off a Roberson pass to seal it. It was yet another defeat for those who said NDSU's move to Division I would be the end of in-state players.

A full scholarship player from Dickinson, Beach, Cavalier, Wahpeton, Fargo or any other city or town? Forget it; go to Division II schools like Minnesota State Moorhead or St. Cloud State. The Bison coaches were going to spend all of January recruiting in Minnesota, Wisconsin or Texas, or so the theory went.

The MVP in the win over the Redbirds was Wentz from Bismarck Century. Thorton was from Bismarck High School. It was an irony of sorts that Thorton's last career play was picking off a pass from a quarterback, the very position that got him to NDSU.

"Coming in, my goals were to be a four-year starting quarterback and probably doing what Carson was doing today," Thorton said. "But to end it like this – I couldn't have ever imagined playing linebacker, first of all. But to seal the deal with an interception like that, it was very rewarding."

It had to be rewarding to the framers of the Bison Division I constitution that players from North Dakota continually made a difference in building the best dynasty FCS football has ever seen. Beck was dominant in 2011. In 2013, Ryan Smith from Wahpeton scored a touchdown against Towson University. Beck led the team in tackles. In 2012 and 2013 title games, Drevlow from Gwinner was a major force in the middle. In 2013, Luecke from Fargo South, a walkon who overcame two ACL surgeries, made life miserable for Towson running back Terrance West by helping clog the middle.

In the 2014 postgame news conference, Wentz paid tribute to growing up in Bismarck and seeing the program grow from Division II to Division I. Twelve years after the Division I announcement, you could have made the case that NDSU moving up a level actually kept the top in-state kids from leaving the state. If the Bison were still in Division II, no way Wentz doesn't go to Northern Iowa, Central Michigan or some other Division I program. After winning state titles in basketball and football with the Demons, no way Thorton doesn't follow a similar route. I still believe Thorton would have been a multi-year starter at quarterback at most FCS schools other than NDSU, but it so happened he was beaten out by, first, Jensen – the winningest QB in FCS history – and then Wentz in a battle for the backup job behind Jensen.

But of all the stories surrounding that game, I thought the most heartwarming was Hedberg, the veteran Bison assistant coach who finally got to coach in a championship game. As history goes, there were not many football minds from the state of North Dakota who had the credentials of Hedberg. There are not many who could say they started the first game of their NFL rookie season, at quarterback no less.

His NFL career went from 1977 until 1980 starting with Tampa Bay and ending with Oakland and Green Bay. What followed was a coaching career that by now was on its fourth decade. There were some stellar teams in those years, from the University of North Dakota to Southern Illinois.

"He's been coaching for what, 30 years, and this is his first time ever?" said NDSU running back John Crockett. "People don't understand, we've been spoiled. Bison fans have been spoiled. The state of North Dakota has been spoiled. It never really happens like this. This is really a great thing that is happening. Win, lose or draw, people have to understand this has been an amazing run."

Hedberg understood. He left SIU a year prior to join Klieman's staff at NDSU. A native of Parshall, he wanted to return to the state. He was the head coach at Minot State from 1982-89 and an assistant at UND from 1996-98.

"I think all of these coaches are enjoying this," Wentz said. "It was a little bit of a difficult road to get here this year, there were a lot of doubters and those type of things, so it's been a lot of fun for everyone involved."

Hedberg and Wentz were linked as coach-player on a one-to-one basis probably more than any other assistant-to-player on the team. In a lot of ways, they seem alike, such as in stature — both have ideal quarterback height — and in mentality. Both take a calm, cool approach to football. A big reason Wentz was the No. 2 overall pick in the 2016 NFL Draft? Hedberg.

2015: NDSU 37, Jacksonville State 10

Wentz was the fashionable story and nobody had an issue with that. But the real story of the game was what the Bison defense did to a Jacksonville offense that came in scoring against everybody. They shut down a potent Jacksonville offense that averaged 53.7 points in its first three playoff games. The Gamecocks were limited to a season-low 204 yards and 10 points. In their four playoff games, NDSU limited its opponents to an average of nine points and 216 yards. All four Bison playoff opponents finished with a season low in total yards.

Jacksonville didn't match the Bison in anything in the first half. It was 24-0 before the Gamecocks started doing anything of consequence with one of the biggest plays a diving interception by Bison linebacker Nick DeLuca at the JSU 28-yard line. Four plays later, Wentz scored from 11 yards out, diving to the corner pylon in the last five yards, and it was 17-0.

It was a pretty impressive performance for Wentz considering he hadn't played since mid-season. He first came before the cameras in Frisco on Friday wearing plastic-rimmed glasses that made him look more like the 4.0 student he was than a quarterback. One day later, he showed the rest of the FCS why Twitter was enthralled with his NFL prospects. He had the first-game jitters, he said, and that was evident in the minutes leading up to kickoff. He was jumping around. Sprinting. But then again, this was it for a fifth-year guy whose senior season was cut in half with a broken bone in his wrist.

It wasn't the greatest of games statistically, completing 16 of 29 passes with one touchdown and two interceptions. But the mere presence of the 6-foot-6, 232-pound two-year captain was worth more than that, and that was a big reason the Bison will forever be a historic part of this college football question: Which team became the first to win five straight national titles in the modern era? He was named the game's Most Valuable Player, not so much with his timely completions, but also for leading the Bison in rushing with 79 yards on eight carries. His 11-yard touchdown run was a thing of athletic beauty, beating a smaller and more seemingly quicker Gamecocks defender to the corner pylon.

It came one series after Wentz threw an 8-yard dart for a touchdown to tight end Andrew Bonnet. It was a culmination of a performance that probably started the day after he found out he was injured. There was no feeling sorry for himself; on the contrary actually. He was the first guy to start coaching backup Easton Stick as the starting guy.

The injury was a bugger. The should-he-play-or-should-he-sit game wasn't truly resolved for offensive coordinator Tim Polasek until Wednesday. Until then, Polasek still had at least a couple of series for Stick in the game plan. "He said, 'Coach, call it like you need to call it," Polasek said, referring to not limiting the playbook for Wentz. "When he looked at me with conviction and said, 'Coach, call it all,' I knew it."

He called it all, and Polasek coached it all, although he paused to catch himself at one point during the game. This was his last time calling plays for one of the greatest quarterbacks in Bison history after all.

"He got back and a couple of throws that weren't great, and I said, 'Carson, we're expecting more out of you,' " Polasek said. "I just thought maybe it's one of those moments I should just enjoy of being around him. When you're calling plays for Carson, he's not going to put you in a bad situation."

One of the most heroic performances by a Bison quarterback was when Brock Jensen was so sick during the Georgia Southern playoff game in 2013 that he needed intravenous-fluid therapy. Wentz's performance was heroic in the sense the general came back after an extended absence to lead the troops.

XIII. ESPN and the Bizon

The street sign on the corner of Broadway and Third Avenue North in downtown Fargo has BISON BLVD on the avenue side and ESPN WAY on the Broadway side. It's a corner that will live in infamy in NDSU football – and FCS football for that matter.

I'm still not sure what was more impressive: winning five straight FCS championships or the fact ESPN's coveted "College GameDay" pregame show came to Fargo two years in a row. Not only that, the connection the show made with the NDSU program and the fans in general were something nobody saw coming. Certainly, Gene Taylor was as blown away as anybody.

The first connection came the previous week when Troy Goergen, the NDSU associate athletic director for marketing, walked into Taylor's office with a survey from ESPN. It was the first hint that NDSU was in the mix to host.

"Get out, are you serious?" Taylor said.

Goergen had a way of finding out how serious. A friend of his, John Althoff, worked for State Farm, which is a major corporate sponsor of the "GameDay" basketball pre-game show. Althoff knew how to contact a bus driver for the ESPN "GameDay" crew and usually when a city is in the mix to host, it's the driver's job to have a route ready to go. In this case, the crew was at Texas A&M the previous weekend.

"Bus driver Bob," Taylor said. "Sure enough, Bob calls me back and sure enough, Bob has a map of how to get here."

I found out about the announcement on a Saturday night when the Bison were idle. I ran into a guy who knew someone who knew something, so I tweeted the possibility of the show coming to Fargo. The next morning, the announcement was made. The Bison football folks were in marketing heaven. You couldn't buy this exposure. Seriously, Lee, Kirk, Chris, Desmond and the crew in Fargo?

That would be Lee Corso, Kirk Herbstreit, Chris Fowler and Desmond Howard. If college football is a rock concert, then those guys are the rock stars. Combined with David Pollack and Samantha Ponder and reporter Tom Rinaldi, NDSU was going big time the following week. I bet back in Colorado Joe Chapman fell off his rocker.

"I was just so proud," he said.

It's easy to see why the show has longevity; the cast of characters are genuine. On the Thursday before the 2013 show, my wife Ruby and I went to Mezzaluna restaurant one block off Broadway at happy hour time. It just so happened several folks from the "GameDay" show reserved a small upper level of the place for dinner – among them Herbstreit and Lee Fitting, the show's producer.

Jim Werre, the restaurant owner, saw me and quickly introduced me to both Herbstreit and Fitting. Instead of just saying hello and moving on, Herbstreit wanted to know more about the NDSU upset over Kansas State a couple of weeks prior. He wanted to know about the last drive when NDSU went 80 yards in 18 plays to win the game 24-21.

That's a good reporter. That's a guy doing his homework. The two thought nothing of having their photo taken with the local folks.

A day later, the local media had an informal presser of sorts with Fitting, Herbstreit and Fowler at the subsidiary venue of the Fargo Theatre. Again, they stressed the importance of their chemistry, both on air and off air. They do it, they said, because they have a love for college football. One question that was asked a couple of times: Why are you here? Why are you in Fargo?

Because they're story tellers and Fitting recognized that not every good story is in Athens, Ga., Tuscaloosa, Ala., or Eugene, Ore. They did a show right in the middle of the FCS dynasty and you sensed they knew that perhaps there were a couple of more titles to come.

What developed was a love affair the network had with NDSU. In subsequent shows, "GameDay" routinely had some Bison (or Bizzzon as they liked to say) reference to it. If there was a chance to pick an NDSU game in the prediction segment that closed the show, they did it.

NDSU was to play Delaware State that week and Bohl did the right thing by acknowledging the importance of the show all the while getting his team ready for the game. He took his players to the set on Friday to perhaps get the aura out of their system. On Saturday, in the locker room two hours before kickoff, the massive fan excitement of the "College Game Day" experience had not filtered to the team.

"You could hear a pin drop," videographer Kasey Byers said. "I put a camera in their face and they didn't care. They were so locked in and every guy was just zoned in. None of those kids got to enjoy 'Game Day' because it was a military-style type of operation."

Being 100 percent locked in wouldn't have mattered against Delaware State anyway and here's the first reason: the night before the game, a high school classmate of mine from Fargo South, Mark Halliday, was staying at the Holiday Inn in Fargo where the Hornets were staying and saw them hanging out in the pool and the sauna. College football players getting ready for a game in a pool and sauna? You don't let PeeWee hockey players do that.

Mark saw one of them in an elevator and asked him that same question. The response: we're going to get killed anyway so what's the difference?

The final was 51-0.

Anyway, the show was a smashing success with fans filling Broadway and its surrounding streets. The weather was almost perfect, a little cool to start, but sunny and light winds. There were those within NDSU that were paranoid of that fact; of the stereotype of Fargo weather being somewhat parallel to that of the Arctic Circle.

Bohl was fantastic, as you would expect in that setting, although sitting in the ESPN trailer prior to his interview with Ponder, he felt a sudden shot of nervousness – especially after seeing on a video screen in the bus the aerial shot of downtown Fargo in the show opening. That was rare for the veteran coach.

Phil Hansen was the guest picker and represented his school well in the final segment – as you would expect.

Not all was rosy within my company, however, and it turned into a media in-house scrum in the aftermath of the show. It was an amazing climax to the show when Corso, in his prediction segment, walked out of the Fargo Theatre with a live baby bison. The timing by the ESPN folks was impeccable, and the little "Corso," as he was named, behaved just fine.

Amidst the fanfare, the Fargo Police were ready to take action in case "Corso" got out of hand and included in the discussion with the ESPN folks was whether firearms could be used.

"No," said Fargo Police Ltd. Joel Vettel, "but I'll shoot you if that happens."

Ultimately, the group decided that the only course of action if "Corso" got angry was to tackle him. Vettel, a former standout NDSU wrestler, probably would have been first in. As it was, nothing happened.

It wasn't long before Christopher Gabriel, who hosted a radio show on WDAY-AM, trotted out his own website photos and cell phone video of "Corso" in the Fargo Theatre waiting for his grand entrance. Gabriel had an inside source who got him behind the scenes of the show. The problem was he chose not to share that information with anybody in the company; rather he wanted the "exclusive" to himself on his own website. Once Forum editor Matt Von Pinnon got wind of the photos, he wanted to put them out on the Forum website. Gabriel shot back, saying he wanted full credit for the photos and a say in what was being said about them.

I was not happy. Here was a great "in" to the pinnacle of the show and he chose to orphan his own cohorts. It would have made even a better story to the lead story of WDAY 6 p.m. news that day but Gabriel kept it to his own website, essentially saying his radio show brand was more important than the company as a whole. I would have done a column just on the flavor of the baby bison in the theatre. It would have made great company synergy.

"I was definitely perturbed on that," Izzo said. "Christopher had video of Corso inside the Fargo Theater. I had heard rumors of it, I asked for it, but he wanted all sorts of lavish things beside the credit for the video. We weren't going to do that. He worked for 970 and inside our umbrella, or so we thought. Get some synergy, that was our big word and we did not get that. I was not thrilled with that."

I felt bad for Dom, the TV sports director. He started his day at 5 a.m. when we did a Media Blog pregame "College GameDay" internet show from a parking lot next to the "GameDay" bus with Dom, Eric Peterson and I. It aired on the website about 20 minutes later. We covered the event; me from a top floor balcony condo owned by Pam Paseka above Broadway overlooking the set. The thousands of fans all over downtown, the residents, were tremendous and the ESPN brass knew it. They were on to something. People were on every square inch of balcony space and even on rooftops giving the setting a Wrigley Field feel.

"It was a perfect fall day in Fargo," Izzo said. "The sun came up that morning, there wasn't a cloud in the sky and no wind. We were up on the rooftops for a good part of the show and it was unreal the energy of the people there."

Chris Fowler, not long after the show, tweeted : "… one of our favorite @CollegeGameDay ever! Bye-Zun fans are incredible. Love to do it again!"

About the only thing missing for Dom was the inside access Gabriel could have provided, but didn't. ESPN, however, was ecstatic. The viewers paid attention because the show had the sixth-best ratings among all 15 "GameDay" shows that season, which translated to 1.8 million viewers for the Fargo show. It was the biggest television event to ever hit Fargo and probably the biggest viewer event associated with the town since the movie "Fargo" came out a decade earlier. Fitting tweeted a photo of him holding a glass of beer at a Fargo bar not long after show's conclusion, a signal that the entire production went off with his approval.

I was shocked. I thought Fargo changed when it built the Fargodome that opened in 1993. It really changed when I saw Mick Jagger walk on stage on the dome on Feb. 17, 1999. As a resident of Fargo, that's probably when I canceled my flight from going nowhere. The plan was to come back here, cover college football, and then move on to cover some program like Nebraska. As it turned out, it all happened before my very eyes. Right place. Right time. The big acts that came through were pretty regular in the years since. What a stroke of luck and a lot of credit goes to building the dome.

It was the brainchild of Bob "Goose" Johnson, the longtime superintendent of the Fargo Parks. Goose was a good friend of my father and a regular in dad's "Poker Club" that met once a month. I can only imagine what was talked about as the cards were being dealt. I would guess one popular topic was the future of Fargo, however, and "the dome we need to build." Mom was adamant about staying out of the way, but I was the elementary-aged kid at the top of the stairs wondering what they were talking about. Decades later, I have a pretty good idea.

Never doubt a dreamer. As Steve Jobs once said, "the people crazy enough to think they can change the world are the ones that do." Well, Goose was crazy enough to think he could change Fargo. Guess what? It changed. Sadly, Goose never lived to see the fruits of Division I football it but without visionaries like him, ESPN never sees the light of Fargo day.

Goose died in 2002, before the Bison ever set foot in Division I. He was the superintendent of the Fargo Parks for 26 years, but somehow took that position and had a pulse on the city and its growth. In his obituary, he was known as "The Father of the Fargodome."

In a Forum editorial before the first title game, editorial page editor Jack Zaleski called it like it was: Before there was Bohl, there was Goose. In part, it read:

"A case can be made that many others can claim credit for the team's success, not the least of whom is coach Craig Bohl. He and his staff brought coaching and recruiting to new levels. They built a great program and a great 2011 team. But before Bohl, there was Johnson and his dream of the Fargodome. And before NDSU got serious about transitioning from Division II status to Division I, there was the dynamic campus leadership of Chapman.

In the late 1980s, Johnson was relentless in pursuing his dream of a multipurpose dome-like building for Fargo. He not only generated enthusiasm for the project, as only "Goose" could do, but he also solidified support among the community's movers and shakers. Despite naysayers and a small, vocal band of organized opponents, a special city sales tax measure passed easily, and the Fargodome rose on the NDSU campus."

When Goose had his vision, I doubt he had a Division I dynasty in mind. Nobody did. Nobody ever figured "College GameDay" would come to Fargo.

And, to top it off, the show came back for a second straight year. How rare was that? At that point in the history of "GameDay," there were three Big Ten schools that had yet to host the show including the University of Minnesota. The others were Indiana and Illinois. Only once did the show go to the FBS Mid-American Conference and that was to Bowling Green in 2003. Only Air Force and Boise State of the Mountain West had the boys on campus and no Sun Belt, Conference USA or Big East school was part of the clique., although in the case of the latter, Houston of the American Conference (formerly Big East) hosted in 2011.

In the Pac-12 Conference, neither California or Washington State had yet to be included and WSU took exception. Yes, the flag. The Wazzu flag was on a 10-year run when it made its first stop in Fargo in 2013.

The tradition went back to 2003 when the school started a campaign to get "GameDay" to come to Pullman, Wash., and as part of that quest was to have the Cougar flag present at every show until they landed the show. As of the conclusion of the 2015 season, it had yet to happen.

It's an exercise in cooperation and communication to get a flag at each "GameDay" site, usually done through the WSU alumni throughout the country. In Fargo, I knew exactly who to turn to: Pam Miller. The wife of Jim Miller was never shy talking about her Wazzu pride.

The ESPN folks love the flag and one crew member on Friday actually told Pam the best place on Broadway to position the flag for the cameras. The first Fargo show was the 135th straight show for the flag.

But who would have thought the Wazzu flag would be back on Broadway in 2014? It wasn't as much of a shock, mainly because of the Twitter love affair between Fitting, Fowler and Bison fans who frequently hashtagged "GameDay." NDSU became a regular mention on the show the rest of 2013 and the beginning of 2014.

But before the show returned to Fargo, ESPN made life tough on Klieman when Fowler tweeted the NDSU and Weber State game may have "GameDay implications." Fitting got right to the point tweeting later Saturday morning: "If @NDSUfootball wins today, @CollegeGameDay to Fargo next week."

The Bison had a night game at Weber State (Utah) yet to play, meaning the players and coaches had that win-or-no-ESPN hanging over them. I posed the question to Klieman two hours before the game and he downplayed it, like you would expect.

It wasn't the best of performances, but the Bison overcame two early interceptions and beat the Wildcats 24-7, thus cementing the unforeseen: two years in a row for "GameDay."

"To think two years in a row, I don't know what to say," Kyle Emanuel said. "It's unreal. It's more than a dream come true."

Unlike the previous year, there was no real debate by Bison fans on the location of the show. When ESPN first announced it was going to Broadway, many fans thought NDSU's popular tailgating area would be best. The problem is the backdrop: there is nothing new about fans tailgating and the Fargodome from the outside doesn't cry "college football stadium" because it's one big, enclosed brick building.

Plus, Fitting is very good at his job. Like a good movie director, he knows what looks good in a camera shot and what looks average.

"ESPN made it clear that they had a great experience last year in downtown Fargo and they wanted to go back there," said NDSU interim athletic director Prakash Mathew.

The second year was even better. There were more people jammed downtown and the students got in prime position even earlier – like 4 or 5 a.m. With the crisp, booming ESPN sound system, a DJ was flipping records turning Broadway into something of a college dance party for students from 5 a.m. until the 8 a.m. start of the show. Dom and I did our "Kolpack & Izzo" radio show from the rooftop of Chad Stark's condo overlooking Broadway, only doing it two hours earlier from 7-9 a.m. to accommodate the show hours. It will forever go down as one of my favorite K&I shows, with WDAY TV sports reporter Jody Norstedt doing live remotes with fans on Broadway.

Fargo Police estimated the crowd at 9,000. Like the previous year, there were no reports of arrests or complaints of bad behavior to police. It didn't matter that the opponent was the University of The Incarnate Word (Texas) – the opponent really doesn't matter to ESPN because it's all about the scene, not the game.

"The energy, the enthusiasm, the pictures – it was better than the first time, which I never would have imagined," Fitting said. "There was not a better scene, I don't think, in the history of 'College GameDay' than what we had today."

The weather was a little cooler than the previous year, but nothing anybody couldn't handle. It followed essentially the same format as the previous year, including another appearance by "Corso" the buffalo to close the prediction segment. Only this time, "Corso" was a little bigger.

Lee Corso walked to a nearby animal trailer to introduce his namesake this time. It was the first national television foray for new head coach Klieman, who like Bohl the previous year was smooth in his live interview on the set. Before going on the set with Ponder, however, he felt like a kid doing his first presentation in a Speech 108 class.

"I was nervous because I hadn't coached a football game yet in the Fargodome," he said, "and I'm sitting in the production truck being almost whisked to the stage. My gosh, it was surreal. I'm going on 'College GameDay' because we had a great game at Iowa State and I haven't coached a game in Fargo yet. Just the whole moment of being on national TV. Now, I was more nervous about coaching my first game in the Fargodome as the head coach then going on live. But the 'GameDay' people were so accommodating, so professional and it was neat because I had my whole family back there – my wife, my kids and my parents."

The day before, on Friday, Klieman brought the Bison players to the set to take pictures and check out the scene like they did the previous year. This time, Fowler sought Klieman out of the Bison contingent and told him why the show returned for a second straight year.

"We're back here because of you guys," Fowler told Klieman. "We're back here from the football side of things, what you were able to do the last three years and how impressive this is for an FCS school."

As for the guest picker, it wasn't as much of a slam dunk as the previous year when most everybody guessed it would be Hansen. I do know the ESPN folks contacted actor Josh Duhamel, a North Dakota native from Minot who took an interest in his home state's sports teams. Duhamel also had relatives in the Fargo area and has a parent with a cabin in the Detroit Lakes area. Duhamel, however, was booked and couldn't do it but you have to admire his humbleness. A few years earlier, his wife Fergie and her band "The Black Eyed Peas" played a fundraiser in Minot for victims of a devastating flood.

Actor Billy Bob Thorton, who played Lorne Malvo in the television version of "Fargo," was also unavailable, so the ESPN crew went for the local sports star. Jensen, one year removed from his playing days, showed up on the set with his three national title rings and his four years of dealing with the media. Earlier in the show, Jensen unveiled a huge three-peat banner from the roof of an adjacent building.

"I was in the mix with Billy Bob Thorton, Josh Duhamel and Miss North Dakota," Jensen said, the latter referring to Miss USA runnerup and Fargo native Audra Mari. "I'm thinking I don't have a chance to be in this deal. Luckily, a football background actually mattered."

Jensen got the call from somebody from ESPN on Thursday asking if he would be the guest picker. One of the first people to congratulate him was Ponder, who sent him a private Twitter message saying as much. Ponder and Jensen followed each other on Twitter, which is the only way two people can privately send messages through that avenue.

Like Klieman, Jensen got to hang inside the ESPN bus. He talked a bit with Corso, who was wearing a buffalo fur coat he wore to open the show. Corso actually borrowed it from Jay Stibbe, an NDSU graduate and Fargo resident who offered it to an ESPN crewmember while hanging around the set on Friday.

"He spent a lot of time drinking his coffee and he was just a really nice guy," Jensen said.

Former Bison quarterback Arden Beachy was also in the bus, somehow, Jensen said. Howard had a great personality. Jensen wished he could have talked with Herbstreit more since he was a quarterback back in the day at Ohio State.

"Those guys have the best job in America," Jensen said.

For an FCS school, it was the best experience in America.

VIX. The Laramie project

Craig Bohl came to North Dakota State from the University of Nebraska and was named the Bison head coach on Feb. 28, 2003 at a packed press conference at the new NDSU Alumni Center. He was 44 years old that day and in taking the job he diverted his career path from being a career assistant at the power school level in favor of a university that was about to make the Division I move. He also had an opportunity to be the defensive coordinator at Stanford, but decided he no longer wanted to be an assistant.

It was a risk.

It was a risk several didn't want to take, including former Northern Iowa and Kansas head coach Terry Allen, who appeared to be the No. 1 target of Gene Taylor and Joe Chapman. They had lunch in Alexandria, Minn., to discuss the position, but Allen said no. But Bohl took it on. He saw the facility. He saw the potential that perhaps nobody else did. He must have taken a big pay cut from possibly being the Stanford defensive coordinator to a head job that paid him $113,000 that first season. He was leveraging years of being mentored by Tom Osborne and decided now was the time to put it into action.

Before that action started, it was a stressful time for athletic director Taylor, who by the end of it all encountered health problems. In emails obtained by Forum reporter Mike Nowatzki and editor Lou Ziegler, the coaching hire situation played out at a frantic pace.

Taylor spent a good part of February in Tucson, Ariz., discussing and interviewing head coach candidates and it was obvious the pressures on Taylor grew as the month was winding down. On Tuesday, Feb. 18, Taylor started interviewing the finalists, using the Radisson Hotel City Center Tucson as a bunker for conducting the last days of his search. Working out of the Manzanita Room, Taylor scheduled interviews for six coaches, with some of them virtually crossing paths on the highway, coming from and going to the airport. Pat Simmers accompanied Taylor to Arizona and shuttled most of the candidates to and from the airport. Piecing together comments in emails obtained by The Forum from a North Dakota Open Records request and adding to that information from interviews, it became clear how Bohl got the head coaching job. But even in the final hours of Taylor's search, Bohl's hiring was no sure thing.

The records obtained by The Forum show Taylor relentlessly tried to hire a coach in February – the same month NDSU expected a critical indication if it would win in its attempts to join the Big Sky Conference. Although Taylor said the two issues weren't related, he rushed to find a coach. One top candidate,

Fresno State University assistant Dennis Wagner, told Taylor "I've got spring ball starting, and my coach needs to figure out who he's going to hire in place of me, and I need an answer from you and I'm not getting one and I can't leave my coach hanging."

Taylor went to Arizona every year about that time for an annual fundraising trip, but this one had more intensity to it. He gave up family vacation time to pack five long interviews into three short days in Tucson. Simmers said they tied the coaching search on the backside of the fundraising events on purpose, flying candidates into Tucson.

On the first day, at 11:25 that night, Simmers picked up Western Michigan quarterbacks coach Dan Enos at the Tucson airport. Taylor did all of this on the cheap, too -- as he would for several nights in Arizona, he drove 90 minutes to spend the night at his brother Kenny's house in Elfrida, Ariz.

The following day, Taylor was back at the Radisson in Tucson, where he interviewed Enos from 8:30 a.m. to 11:30 a.m. Afterward, Taylor drove Enos to the airport. As Enos was going to the airport, Wagner was coming from it after Simmers greeted his 11:07 a.m. arrival. Taylor returned from the airport to have lunch with Wagner at the hotel, and interviewed him between 1 to 4 p.m. Simmers returned Wagner to the airport for a 6:39 p.m. flight. At 11:25 p.m. he picked up Bohl at the airport and took him to the hotel.

Next up was Gus Bradley, who literally crossed paths with Bohl at the airport when Simmers picked up Bradley from an 11:54 a.m. flight while Taylor dropped Bohl off for his departure. The schedule was so hectic, Taylor didn't even have time to escort Bohl into the airport terminal. And Simmers had to duck out of the morning Bohl interview to pick up Bradley.

"It wasn't the most friendly thing," Taylor said.

In fact, Bohl nearly missed his flight when Taylor dropped him off at the airport 15 minutes before departure, according to reporting by The Forum.

"No one was at the ticket counter and I had to get up to the gate, so I had to do some fast talking to get past the counter," Bohl said. "So that at least showed him I had some resourcefulness."

Bradley, the acting Bison head coach after Babich left, was interviewed from 2 to 5 p.m. by Taylor. Later that night, Simmers was at the airport, this time to pick up Allen. Rather than drive back to Elfrida, Taylor decided to spend the night in Tucson, "because my wife was getting worried that I was going to fall asleep and crash," he said.

Simmers was back at the airport the following morning so Bradley could catch an 8:05 flight. Allen departed at 1 p.m. after a three-hour interview with Taylor.

Taylor returned to Fargo two days later, the search still in a tizzy. This time, it was a Bison legend who got into the mix: Rocky Hager, who led the Bison to a pair of Division II national titles in 1988 and 1990. Taylor drove the almost four hours to the Minneapolis-St. Paul International Airport to talk to Hager, the tight ends coach and recruiting coordinator at Temple University. The interview took about three hours.

"We had talked after the Tucson interviews and knew pretty clearly … what our group was, and we said OK, we've got Rocky on Monday, let's see where he fits in," Taylor told Forum reporter Nowatzki. "And he didn't rise, at that point, to the top of the group."

Also in the mix was Hedberg, at the time the St. Cloud State head coach who later accepted an assistant position with Klieman in the 2014 title season. Taylor said he and Hedberg had two hours of "great conversation" over water at a Holiday Inn in St. Cloud, but Hedberg did not make the final list of candidates.

It was a long day for Taylor, who arrived back in Fargo at 2 a.m. only having to be in Alexandria, Minn., the next morning for a 9 a.m. interview with Allen. For this meeting, Chapman was along at an Alexandria restaurant. Also having breakfast there: Tom Reif, the father of Molly Vigen, the wife of Bison assistant coach Brent Vigen. Tom Reif contacted me about his sighting and I broke the story the next day that Taylor and Chapman were meeting with Allen.

Allen was the leading candidate, but ultimately rejected the NDSU pursuit and pulled out of the search a day later, saying he didn't want to go through a Division I reclassification. With Allen out of the picture, it was down to Bohl and Bradley, and Taylor talked to both the next morning.

"It was a committee of two," Simmers said of he and Taylor. "I remember this distinctly: after we're all done, we would sit down and have a couple of beers after interviewing each candidate. We both ranked them. He was scared to death but we both had the same rank. Gene said, thanks, I was scared what you were going to put down there."

They both had Bohl ranked over Bradley, although both had Bradley No. 2 with some serious reservations.

"Casey obviously sure wasn't going to let us down," Simmers said. "Would he have brought the same strength out of the gate? Probably wouldn't have had the same connections. Craig had an aggressive personality that made some difference. He pressed and pressed and pressed and made stuff happen. Gus is an old Bison who will get it done no matter what. Would the transition have gone as well with Gus? Probably because Gus is good, too. Would Gus have pressed the envelope? I don't know."

Simmers and Taylor both felt Bohl had better connections across the country in terms of getting some junior college players who could make an immediate difference. With the final year of a Division II schedule in 2003, the Bison needed some bigger and quicker players, especially in the defensive line.

Simmers said he did not want to turn NDSU into a JC school but at that time, the program had a need for some immediate help.

"I had some questions of Gus on his presentation at his interview out in Arizona, and then Craig wanted to talk to Joe as well about the Division I move," Taylor said.

Bohl phoned Taylor on a Thursday morning and said he was still interested in the job. Taylor spent the morning weighing his decision. Would it be Bohl, an assistant with years of experience at one of the nation's most prestigious D-I programs and a year as an assistant, in 1984, at NDSU or Bradley, a Bison fan favorite known for his dedication to the program and popularity among players? After lunch, Taylor called Bohl and offered him the job. Unknown to Taylor, Bohl had a major decision of his own to make: He had just been offered the assistant head coaching position at Stanford, and in fact was at the airport in Palo Alto, Calif., when Taylor reached him by cell phone. Taylor knew he had to make another quick sell because Stanford was also going to offer Bohl's children tuition breaks at a Pac-10 Conference institution.

But Bohl did an abrupt turnaround and after returning to Lincoln, Neb., he consulted with his two daughters. He'd made up his mind. Around 5 p.m., Bohl accepted Taylor's offer. Taylor sat down with Bradley to break the news and then spent the evening trying to get Bohl to Fargo for Friday's news conference.

Bohl arrived at Hector International Airport at 10:07 a.m. and had a final interview at 10:30 with the search committee at the Alumni Center. He then met with football players at the Bison Sports Arena, had lunch at Bennigan's Grill & Tavern and met with Chapman and his cabinet before the 4 p.m. news conference.

Years later, Taylor said the only reason Bohl got the job over Bradley was because of his Division I experience.

"As hard as it was to look him in the eye knowing he's going to be a great coach," Taylor said, "it was just a fact that Craig had been in so many Division I programs."

Ironically, 10 years after the move was made, Bradley, the head coach of the NFL's Jacksonville Jaguars, said he agreed with Taylor's decision and backed up what Simmers said: that Bohl was the guy to press change within the university.

"Looking back, I think it teaches a lot about humility," Bradley said.

Bradley had just walked into the NDSU football team meeting room in the Fargodome for the first time. When he left in 2005, the coaches still gathered in the cramped offices of the Bison Sports Arena and the team met in a large, sterile, tile-floor, vacant-looking classroom in the BSA.

"I look at this team meeting room now, and some of the additions to the dome and what's taken place on this campus specifically for football and what Craig Bohl spearheaded," Bradley said. "He had a vision. He felt very strongly about that vision and people bought into it and lot of changes took place. I think that was one of the great hires North Dakota State made because I don't know if those changes would have been made as fast without Craig Bohl."

At the time, however, there was immense pressure on Taylor in what turned out to be one of the most important hires in Bison football history. Hager had a "Bring Home Rocky" website. It was obvious to close friends that Taylor was showing signs of stress. Two weeks after the coaching decision, Taylor experienced symptoms of dehydration and was treated at a hospital in Brookings, S.D., where he was watching NDSU in the North Central Conference women's basketball tournament.

"I didn't think I was stressed, honestly, I thought I was flying through it," Taylor said. "Everything was over at that point but I think my body had just had enough. I didn't realize it while going through it at the time."

I'll never forget after that first press conference. Afterward, Bohl got some media types together and said something to this effect: "Guys, here are the rules."

He had just weathered a media heat storm in Lincoln the previous couple of years. His trust for writers and broadcasters was obviously at a low point. Cornhusker fans were pointing the finger at him as one of the reasons for the demise of the program. When it came to the national spotlight, the NDSU job was like being in the witness protection program. Not many in the college football world outside of North Dakota and Minnesota knew much about North Dakota State. Yes, it used to be a Division II power, but those years were getting further and further behind. The last title was 1990 and here was Bohl 13 years later taking over a program that made the Division II semifinals once in 2000, but that was about the highlight.

Nobody thought any head coach could do much with a program about to start a five-year Division I reclassification. Bohl's first year was still going to be a Division II season in 2003 and how anybody thought he could recruit players to a school that was ineligible for post-season competition until 2008 was beyond crazy.

Tim Miles freely talked about how coaches in Division I transitions got fired nearly 100 percent of the time. When Miles accepted the Bison position, NDSU was still solidly in Division II with not much mention of a Division I transition and he wasn't jumping for joy when the Division I move was announced.

Yet, Bohl took the challenge.

It took only two games for Bison fans to think maybe he wasn't that crazy after all.

Sept. 6, 2003, Missoula, Mont.

What a way to introduce yourself. That was the second step to the FCS dynasty as we know it; with the first being the Division I announcement. I ran into Bohl outside the Bison Sports Arena the week of the game and told him how heavy of a favorite Montana was. He put his finger to his mouth, as to say "shhhhh." He didn't want his players to know.

I picked 42-7. The Forum/WDAY team of Steve Hallstrom, Phil Hansen and Mike McFeely had similar scores.

Making the win all the more remarkable? The Bison team plane was diverted to Helena, Mont., because of smoke from forest fires in the Missoula area. Then, the team bus from Helena broke down and the Bison didn't reach their hotel in Missoula until around 10 p.m. the night before the game. They missed their walkthrough practice at Washington-Grizzly Stadium. So what happened? They get up and shock the Division I-AA world. The last couple of minutes of that game were played on the stadium video board at Montana's rival, Montana State, which was hosting a game of its own.

The upset aside, perhaps the biggest nugget Bohl took from the game was NDSU's travel routine. It never changed after that Montana game and it was as if Bohl stumbled on something he liked by accident. NDSU never conducted a Friday practice at an opposing stadium under Bohl.

"It just so happened it started by a fluke," said offensive coordinator Vigen. "I remember vividly we are not going to the stadium. 'How are we going to do this?'"

Generally, in every road game since that Missoula weekend, the Bison practiced at home on Friday and then flew to their destination, going against the grain of most teams practicing Friday at the opposing stadium.

There were a couple of reasons for Bohl's road routine: One, several FCS stadiums are not located near an airport or team hotel, so therefore Bohl eliminated that hassle of bussing somewhere on Friday after flying in. He simplified it. Practice in Fargo early Friday afternoon, hop on a plane and get to the team hotel usually late in the afternoon. Have dinner. Meetings. Go to bed. Get up and play a game. It was a business trip mentality that never wavered in his 11 years as the head coach.

The offensive and defensive linemen don't need to see the stadium; they put their hand in the grass or turf and hit another guy in the trenches. The quarterbacks, receivers and running backs see enough of the opposing stadium on film, so it's not as if they need to get acclimated to a place.

"It wasn't a huge deal what stadium we were playing in," Cole Jirik said. "It's still 100 yards long, and it's just a football field to us. We liked the routine we were in here. We would do our walk-through, hop on a bus, fly out, go eat some food and watch film."

Not only was NDSU's 33-game FCS record winning streak an amazing feat, perhaps even more striking were the 22 straight wins away from home that ended in 2014 at Northern Iowa, a streak that consisted of 1,142 days. From a quarterfinal loss at Eastern Washington in the 2010 playoffs, nobody beat the Bison away from the Fargodome.

It had a lot to do with Bohl, and his ability to keep his team focused on the road. Credit the routine. Bohl built a masterful program because he was a very good CEO. I bet he could run any top corporation in America and make it profitable because his organizational skills were second to none.

It's just too bad it ended the way it did.

***

The Bison were in the process of steamrolling through the 2013 playoffs when long-speculated rumors of other schools coming after the highly-successful head coach came to fruition. The image is one that will never be forgotten. It was outside the Bison locker room at Toyota Stadium in Frisco two days before the 2012 title game against Towson. It was a day when the team practice is closed, so talking to players for me or Izzo was off limits.

That left any sound to finding a coach or two. We were standing between the stadium and Bison busses when Bohl was walking toward us while Klieman was walking the opposite way. They passed each other – Bohl looking south and Klieman looking north. We were not experts in body language but that was the definition of tension. That moment was the culmination of a month of behind-the-scenes anxiety where nobody went unscathed – head coach, assistants or athletic director. "Stressful is not the word; I would say awkward," Klieman said over two years later.

It started the week of the NDSU and Furman second round playoff game at the Fargodome. Bohl told Taylor that he was going to fly to Minneapolis on Thursday to interview with officials from the University of Wyoming. Taylor and Bohl had coffee every Friday morning during the football season so when they met, Taylor asked Bohl how the interview went.

"Gene," Bohl told Taylor, "it went really well."

At that point, Taylor surmised that if Bohl got the offer, he was gone. Taylor knew NDSU would not be able to match Wyoming financially so he didn't even bring it up.

"What are you going to do?" Taylor asked Bohl.

Bohl said he was going to make a decision sometime on Friday and then let Taylor know.

"On Friday, I could tell something was up because during the walkthrough, you could just tell there was some tension with the coaches," Taylor said.

After practice, Taylor approached Bohl.

"What are you doing?" he asked him.

"Well, I got the offer and I'm going to let them know sometime tomorrow," Bohl said, according to Taylor.

"OK," Taylor replied, "What are you thinking?"

"Gene I just need to think about it." Bohl said.

After practice, Taylor noticed the two coordinators, Klieman and Vigen, hanging around wanting to talk to him. Taylor told them something to the effect: "Guys, let's just wait, you have a game to coach."

The Bison easily disposed of Furman 38-7, and that's when things really got interesting. Izzo remembers speaking to Taylor right after the game "and he had an odd look on his face," Dom said. "It certainly looked like he wasn't excited to just win a playoff game. He looked sullen. He looked upset. I only remember that after the news came out – it didn't strike me as different then."

Well, Taylor had a lot on his mind other than a playoff victory. Afterward, Bohl summoned Taylor to his office on the second floor of the Fargodome. Present were Bohl's parents, Phil and Roberta Bohl, his wife Leia, family friend Lance Wolf and Cathy Taylor, Gene's wife.

Bohl told Gene that he accepted Wyoming's offer.

"I said, OK, let's go figure this out," Taylor said. "We went down to a conference room and I said, 'OK, how are you going to tell your team?' He said he wasn't going to tell them tonight and he said he didn't think they would find out, but he was going to call them together the first thing in the morning."

"Can you trust the folks in Wyoming?" Taylor asked Bohl.

Bohl said yes.

"Are you sure you don't want to do something tonight?" Taylor asked Bohl.

The central figures in the decision left the dome and the Taylors went home, where they were hosting a few people.

"And the next thing you know my phone starts blowing up and at that point, it was too late," Taylor said.

Taylor contacted Bohl and asked if he still wanted to do an announcement that night.

"Craig said no, they were probably out and doing whatever," Taylor said.

Why did Taylor's phone blow up? Because word started to leak. The Forum team finished its game coverage around 8 p.m. and a few of us headed over to Labby's Grill & Bar for some post-game eats and drinks. I was about two sips into a beer when a text message appeared that rumor had it Bohl was headed for Wyoming.

Wyoming?

That was our first thought. Wyoming? Laramie? Would Craig want to coach in Laramie? We shrugged it off as another in the long line of coaching gossip. Wyoming seemed like a lateral move albeit an FBS program and no way, we thought, would Bohl settle for anything other than a career jump. Then another message from a trusted source followed that. Whoa, cowboy.

A few minutes later, Bruce Feldman, the senior writer for CBSSports.com, posted on the CBS website that he had confirmed reports through an anonymous source that, indeed, NDSU head coach Craig Bohl was going to be the next head coach in Wyoming. "Wyoming will announce North Dakota State's Craig Bohl Sunday as its new head football coach, a source told CBS Sports" is all the story read.

Back to work we went. Dom had just finished putting the Media Blog post-game show on line and was two minutes from leaving the WDAY building when he saw the tweet. He immediately called me "and everything went into a tailspin after that."

The more I thought about it, the more it didn't surprise me. Bohl had a photo of a horse back trip he took with his family in Wyoming on his desk in the Bison football offices and at times talked about how he liked the expansive outdoors of the state.

Players began texting each other. Brock Jensen was at a hotel lobby across the street from the Fargodome with members of his family when news first hit him.

"I'm watching the news and here's this 'breaking news' that coach Bohl has accepted the job at the University of Wyoming," Jensen said. "I'm like, are you kidding? Very shocking and rightfully so because we're right in the middle of the playoffs. We're on an undefeated run going for an undefeated season and now we have this to deal with."

It was that moment -- those tweets and text messages -- where some inside the program say was the cause of the entire strife of that playoff run. It all could have been avoided if Bohl would have put out an announcement after the game that he got the Wyoming job and then held a press conference the next morning. The fact the players heard the news on their smartphones never did sit well with many of them. Remember, Bohl was an old-school coach who wasn't on Twitter and didn't get much into the social media. I'm not sure he knew how fast news could spread through those avenues.

I would bet if Bohl sought the advice of sports information director for football Ryan Perreault or NDSU director of marketing and promotions Justin

Swanson about the social media aspect of a coaching change they would have told him to not wait a minute. I would have told him not to wait a second. One program insider told me "that if the team was told before they found out on Twitter, I think none of this would have ever happened. None of it. If the team found out before someone else told them, this would never have happened. There would have been no resentment among the coaches and there wouldn't have been a problem between Gene and coach Bohl. It would have been a smooth bon voyage. That Twitter incident changed everything. It was as if no one knew what to do from PR to Gene to everybody. Do we have a team meeting? Or not. Do we have a press conference? Or not. What do we tell the players? What do we not tell the players? It was like no one knew what to do. Neither of those guys are technological guys and neither of them thought about the repercussions of having something on Twitter. Lo and behold, that one tweet by Bruce Feldman … you could say Bruce Feldman caused all the problems at NDSU. His one tweet set off a chain reaction that was never recovered from."

I filed a story citing the CBS source, which in all probability came from a leak in the Wyoming camp. Taylor said he's pretty certain it came from somebody with Wyoming and it may have had something to do with the scheduling of a press conference. That certainly wasn't what Bohl – who according to later reports intended to tell his players Sunday morning – would have wanted. As it was, that Sunday morning was unforgettable.

***

When it comes to high profile coaching changes like this one, there are go-to reporting methods like checking the local private airplane traffic on the flight aware website. It showed one flight plan from the Fargo Jet Center to Cheyenne, Wyo., which wasn't the true blue smoking gun we were looking for, but close enough.

So Dom, photographer Dave Samson and I drove to the Jet Center parking lot at 7 Sunday morning and kept a low profile in Samson's car. Samson had his mega camera lens that can snap a photo of a zit on a person's face from the other end of a football field.

"We had no idea what was going on, we had no idea if he was flying to Laramie Sunday morning to accept the job, but we had to be there to stake it out," Dom said.

We went early because we knew of a team meeting that was scheduled for 10 a.m. at the football team room. So we bagged the surveillance and headed over to the dome.

The dome is normally closed on Sundays, but a local church was using it for its service so while the Bison players were coming into the facility one-by-one, they did so among a large group of worshippers. The last one to enter was Bohl, dressed in a suit and tie. He briskly walked by Dom and I, not acknowledging our presence, and closed the door behind him. About 20 minutes later, only Bohl emerged from the room. Again, his pace was quick. And as Dom said, "we got the infamous Heisman that said guys I'm not going to talk to you now."

He straightened his left hand toward us and damn near shouted his no comment, walked quickly into the Bison locker room and presumably left the dome for his Sunday morning TV show. That's it.

I was offended. Still, there was nothing confirmed at this point from NDSU that Bohl was leaving until his only interview that morning with Nicole Johnson of Valley News Live.

"Guys like Jeff Kolpack and Dom Izzo have given their whole time the last 10 years and the person who gets to sit down with him is Nicole Johnson," said Kasey Byers. "Are you shitting me? I heard that and I'm going what is going on here? Nicole effing Johnson – she's not even a sports person. She's the last person to talk to him before he left, how does that make you feel?"

In retrospect, I really didn't expect Bohl to comment considering there had yet to be a formal announcement from Wyoming. But the manner in which he bolted by us was offensive. This is a coach who I followed literally across the country, from Georgia Southern to Stephen F. Austin (Texas), to Nicholls State (La.) to Southern Utah to Eastern Washington to UC Davis to Youngstown State. And on and on. If he couldn't talk to the media at that point in the process, fine. But how about stopping and saying something to the effect: "Hey guys, I can't talk right now but when the time is right, I'll comment."

Meanwhile, the Bison captains took control of the meeting and asked everybody, including Taylor, to leave the room. They wanted to hash things out for themselves and the main issue was simple: did they want Bohl to coach the rest of the season?

"Some felt passionately they wanted him to go and some felt they wanted him to stay," Taylor said. "They all wanted to know what's best for the team."

At the front of the room were senior leaders Jensen, Jirik, Turner, Smith, Williams, Olson and Grothmann. Five of those players eventually signed pro contracts in the NFL or CFL.

"The younger guys were upset, angry, shocked, all those emotions," Jensen said. "They didn't necessarily want it but it wasn't their decision. It was a senior-led team and any big decision the seniors were going to make. And we were 100 percent on board with coach still coaching us during the playoffs. Grothmann had the most difficult time with it; it rubbed him the wrong way. I think he was the most well-respected captain on the team. He was from a small town (Hillsboro, N.D.) and played a non-glorified position of fullback. But at the same time, we were able to talk through it."

Later, the press conference in Laramie to announce Bohl as the UW head coach was broadcasted via webstream on the Forum's website, so anybody could access it. Certainly, many of the Bison players did.

"It was still difficult for us to see him go and put on that Wyoming hat in the press conference during the playoffs," Jensen said. "At the same time, we understood. It was still hard for us to see that he was committed to us as well as being committed to Wyoming."

Several players wanted Bohl to hit the road to Laramie immediately. Several players played through painful injuries for their head coach and they did it because they were loyal soldiers to the coaching staff. The hard part, some players said, was the fact the coaches who left didn't tell them the news to their face. It goes back to that Dodd Twitter message. Jirik said the captains just wanted to clear the air in the team meeting.

"I would say it was tense," he said. "Anger. Animosity. Confusion. The biggest thing is the younger players were confused. We had so many fourth-and fifth-year players but for the first- or second-year kids for their head coach to leave was a lot harder on them to figure out. College football is a business and it revolves around money."

"Looking back, there was nothing with that 2013 team that was going to distract us from winning," Jensen said. "There could have been you name it, there was nothing that was going to distract that team. We had leadership. That team was on autopilot. The coaches didn't need to coach us, just give us a game plan. Those teams come around just once in a while. I think coach Bohl's decision was easier because he knew we could handle it. There is no good timing but we as seniors understood it more than the younger guys. We know how coaching works."

Some faculty were not pleased, however, as evidenced by an email Taylor got from a high-ranking NDSU professor:

Gene,

I followed all of Bohl's shenanigans last night. I feel very badly for the team and you. This puts everyone in a very difficult situation. It is very hard to believe that anyone could do this to a team and an institution in the middle of what could be historic playoffs.

Good luck to you and all the best as you sort this situation out. You have a difficult road ahead of you and I will be thinking of you. Personally, I think you need to promote one of the coordinators to head coach immediately. Vigen is very intelligent and has grown into a very effective OC, however, his downside is his rather flat personality. Not sure that will play well in the media, interacting with boosters, and players (his two years as recruiting coordinator were two of the worst in Bison history and I think it was because recruits did not relate to him).

Klieman is just the opposite in my view and should be the top choice, but it is obviously your call.

One more small word of advice. Give Kramer a huge raise, NOW! In the opinion of many of your TeamMakers, Kramer's program is the key to the Bison championships and their ability to win in the second half. There are lots of strength and conditioning coaches, but Kramer is the best and he holds the keys. Please do not let Asshole Bohl (I just trademarked this AM) steal him away.

All the Best,
Neil

Neil C Gudmestad
University Distinguished Professor / Plant Pathology
North Dakota State University

A day later, Gudmestad sent Taylor another email advocating that perhaps Klieman would be the best guy for the job. And like a lot of fans, Gudmestad put a high emphasis on NDSU retaining Kramer.

Gene,

I just wanted to wish you all the luck in the world in identifying a suitable replacement for Craig Bohl. Big shoes to fill. I know I sent you blistering emails about him during and after the 3-8 season for some of his bonehead moves, but you clearly demonstrated that patience would pay off as he learned how to be an effective head coach. The dividends for your patience were huge.

I always figured Vigen and Klieman would be in the mix to possibly get promoted but recently heard that Brent isn't interested. I don't know if that is true, but from my perspective, Chris Klieman has to be looked at hard and is the better choice between the two for a few reasons.

Although I have not had a lot of interaction with Klieman personally, I have had email dialogue with him and I like how he carries himself in public. I think he is more gregarious and easy to talk to in public settings than is Vigen, which I think bodes well with media relations, booster relations, and recruiting. Besides, I really think NDSUs traditional football legacy has been built on defense and that was carried on with Solomonson, Hager, and Bohl as head coaches, all former DCs. In that vein, Klieman is perfect.

So, in the for what it is worth department, I think Klieman has to be in the mix and I don't think you can go wrong with that choice in any arena. I think you can save some coaching staff and recruits with that choice also.

Again, good luck. And remember, don't let Bohl steal Kramer. He holds the ***keys to the kingdom****.*
Neil

Neil C Gudmestad
University Distinguished Professor / Plant Pathology
North Dakota State University

The Wyoming position created a division within the coaching offices dividing the assistants that were going with Bohl to Laramie and those that were to stay. There were reports of assistants commandeering recruiting files in an attempt to steer athletes NDSU was recruiting to Laramie.

"Stressful to say the least," Taylor said.

Klieman said the staff communicated with each other when it came to the game plan, but that was about it.

"There were a lot of closed doors," he said. "Those doors are always open in our offices, but there were a lot of closed ones then. I understood. They had to do recruiting. They also had to get their Wyoming recruiting board set to go. At that time, the only one who I knew was staying was Goose (Nick Goeser). We had a lot of conversations, a lot of late nights. Between Goose and me, we would call 14 or 15 guys that were committed to us and we would do that between 7 and 10 at night. Then I would stay here until 1 a.m. to get the game plan ready."

Klieman was asked if Bohl was mad at him.

"I don't know if it was mad, just awkward. But I also don't think anybody knows," he said.

Publicly, nothing really came out. No coach would go on the record in talking about others and "how it's going" inside the coaches' offices. About the best clue was after NDSU's win over New Hampshire in the national semifinals when Bohl couldn't throw enough praise at Vigen, who was going with him to Wyoming, while keeping his answer when asked about Klieman to a few words. Privately, it was a gong show with the biggest problem being Klieman's decision to stay rather than go with Bohl to Wyoming. It was widely regarded that Bohl did not like that and the two spoke only when necessitated.

It was somewhat obvious on more than one occasion when Bohl would speak glowingly of Vigen and no other Bison assistant coach.

"It was odd to me that every time Bohl had a chance, he would talk about how great Vigen was," Mike McFeely said. "He would say 'Brent Vigen was the key to the whole run.' You talk about important people, ' Brent Vigen, what a recruiter.' He went out of his way to talk about him."

It reached the point with McFeely that Minneapolis StarTribune columnist Patrick Reusse phoned McFeely after Reusse talked to Bohl about a column he was writing.

"What the hell is with Bohl?" Reusse asked Mike.

"What do you mean?" Mike replied.

"He kept pumping up Vigen. Kept praising Vigen. Where did that come from?" Reusse said.

McFeely said he asked Taylor about it and he said all Gene did was roll his eyes. "Someday, I'll tell you all about what is going on," Taylor told Mike.

McFeely said his "sources inside the department told me Craig had basically frozen out Klieman because he was pissed off at him, apparently for taking the job. After Craig took the job, it became clear to Gene it was either Vigen or Klieman and that was when Bohl basically said screw you. Klieman told him he was going with Bohl to Wyoming and now he was staying. It was ugly."

Taylor and Bohl made an agreement shortly after Bohl took the Wyoming job that he would not recruit any of the NDSU commitments and try to sway them to the Cowboys. Specifically, the stipulation reads:

"Coach shall not for a period of one (1) year after such termination by Coach or otherwise seek to recruit any high school athlete previously contacted or recruited by NDSU, unless (i) such athlete has been recruited or contacted by the Coach's new employing institution prior to the notice of termination by Coach to NDSU or (ii) such recruit initiates the request to be recruited by Coach at Coach's new employing institution."

But Taylor and Bohl also agreed it would be hard to manage some of the language in the contract. For instance, what was to stop a high school player from contacting Wyoming?

"So we knew we needed a clear black-and-white line," Taylor said.

In other words, players who had scholarship offers or were contacted by NDSU before Bohl got the Wyoming job were fair game despite the apparent intention of the contract. But all verbal commitments were off the table. Even if Bohl violated his NDSU contract, it was unclear if there would be any recourse for the school. Bohl's contract had no section that specifically stated any remedies for violations. Taylor said he would have needed to go to the university attorney to get an answer.

"The only thing we would look to do would be to withhold bonuses," he said.

Meanwhile, the assistant athletic directors went about their business and didn't mettle much into the situation.

"Live for the day, don't get caught up in all the drama," Simmers said. "Life is hard enough."

Women's athletic director Lynn Dorn had an officer next door to Taylor at the BSA, so she saw first-hand the tension he was going through.

"Gene did an excellent job of keeping his focus directed at the student-athletes," she said. "To his credit, he didn't falter. He took relationships out of the formula."

But never were the relationships between the assistants more frayed than when the Bison, in preparing for the national title game, had to travel to Grand Forks to practice inside the Alerus Center. The weather that winter in Fargo rendered NDSU's practice fields unusable and the dome was booked with other events. The players took a bus while the coaching staff took two vans: the coaches that were headed to Wyoming were in one and the coaches that were going to stay were in the other.

Only Klieman and Goeser were in one van. Conor Riley was in the Wyoming van but he later remained in Fargo going from fullbacks-tight ends to the offensive line coach.

"Usually it was the defensive coaches who would get in one van but now it was like the Wyoming van," Jirik said. "It was like, really? What are you going to do, make Wyoming recruiting calls on the way up? As players we saw all of that in practice. You saw one staff that was heading to Wyoming standing on one side and the other staff on the other side. As players, again, we're like really? So the Wyoming coaches don't want to talk to our coaches? I thought we were one team. You used to be able to go up to the coaches' offices and everybody's door was open and everybody was joking around. Then everyone's door was closed and everyone was hiding something from somebody."

But perhaps the big fish who Klieman didn't let get away was Kramer, who the players year in and year out pledged unconditional love and allegiance. If I had 20 bucks for every time a player mentioned "Coach Kramer" after a victory, I would have retired. Bohl wanted Kramer to go with him. Bad.

"Very bad," Jensen said. "He was the first one he offered. But coach Kramer had a family and had a family decision to make, and boy were we lucky to have him."

Kramer, who was divorced, had two elementary-aged children in Fargo with his ex-wife. If he were to take the Wyoming job, that would have meant living away from his children with not much of a chance of seeing them. I knew the family when they first moved to Fargo in 2003 because, well, they lived next door. At first, I thought it was a stroke of luck because here was a guy next door to me who was plugged into the program. Nothing was farther from the truth. For one, Jim is a pretty private guy and wouldn't divulge a secret to the Pope. And two, he works so hard that I hardly saw him.

It was Bohl who helped Kramer through his divorce telling him to always be there for his kids. In probably a conversation that bordered on foreshadowing – and the first evidence that Bohl was looking beyond NDSU with a loaded team and a third national title within reach – Kramer said he and Bohl had a conversation a couple of weeks after the Kansas State upset.

"How tight are you with your kids?" Bohl asked Kramer.

"Very tight," was his response. "You talked to me about that and I've grown very close to them."

Kramer knew exactly where Bohl was going with his questions. If he were to take another position, he was feeling Kramer out on his potential to move with him.

"I knew what he was getting at," Kramer said. "He was thinking ahead. That's what coaches always do and that's what coach Bohl was doing. He stayed focused on the task at hand but he was preparing for that moment of going elsewhere. But there was nothing specific at that point yet."

Klieman, in looking back, said Kramer was his No. 1 recruit that year. Quarterback Easton Stick and R.J. Urzendowski from Omaha were pretty good high school recruits, but keeping Kramer was No. 1 priority for Klieman.

He said everybody just assumed Kramer was going to go with Bohl, but Klieman asked Kramer to meet him at the Bison Sports Arena on a Monday before the Coastal Carolina playoff game.

"I said, 'Jim, what's the plan, what are you thinking?'" Klieman said. "He said, 'I don't know, I'm mixed on what to do.' Intrigued, I said I'm going to talk to Gene right now and inquire about the position and make sure you'll stay. He said, 'If you're the next head coach, I'm in.'"

It still wasn't easy for Kramer to turn down Bohl. Asked how Bohl took the news, Kramer said, "Up front I think he was OK. I think he was upset but he wasn't going to let me see it just because he knew it was a tough decision. He's driven and he has his vision, but he accepted it. There may have been some animosity both ways there. He polished me for this career, I owe everything to him."

Privately, there are those who said Bohl was furious with Kramer for turning him down, unleashing some expletives and giving the "I made you" line to him. It could never be verified with either party.

Kramer wasn't one to throw Bohl under the bus. He liked how Bohl got things done over the years. He liked his aggressive nature in getting the pieces to NDSU's program in place. Some people would call Bohl's methods impatient and rude, Kramer said, but if he wasn't impatient and rude, people would sit back and not move as fast.

The hiring of Klieman, Kramer said, only reaffirmed his stance that he made the right decision to stay.

"I just thought, OK, I made a good decision now," he said. "There was no right or wrong. Either way it was a good decision but it was a tough one with my kids. I did need to look at it. When you get in a career with someone that is that successful you're working with, you have to look at that. The money thing was there, too. But here's the thing: strength and conditioning coaches are not in this for the money. The money and hours don't work out."

That season worked out, of course – the Bison routed Towson 35-7 for their three-peat. The final seconds made for one of the oddest-looking Gatorade-baths in FCS coaching history. Bohl got the customary dousing as most head coaches do. But Klieman, the coordinator, also got his own from Jirik and Dudzik.

"Me and Christian dumped the jug on Klieman, and then we got the evil eye from coach Bohl," Jirik said. "He wasn't happy. Me and Christian were defensive players and to me, coach Klieman was my head coach at that point. We felt he needed more recognition than what he was getting."

***

It's mid-March in 2015 and Taylor is sitting in the lobby of the Hyatt hotel in downtown Seattle. He traveled with the University of Iowa men's basketball team that was playing in the NCAA tournament. Also there: NDSU, which I was covering.

Taylor was candid with his thoughts and reasons on why he was part of an FCS dynasty. It was easy to see, however, the one item of unfinished business: why the friendship between he and Craig Bohl deteriorated from almost 11 years of togetherness and resourcefulness to the final month, where they talked very little. It had been 15 months since Bohl announced he was going to Wyoming and at that point, the two had yet to speak to each other.

Why?

"I don't know," Taylor said. "I honestly don't know why he's mad or what I did to make him mad. And to this day if I were to run into him I would be fine, but just tell me what happened? Why? What did I do? Because we went through some hard times together. Hard times and good times."

Taylor said during the national title run he received feedback that Bohl was mad at him. On the Saturday after the Furman game, Taylor said they were as friendly to each other as always.

"Then he came back Monday and it was tense until the day he left," Taylor said.

No communication at all?

"No, not one word," Taylor said. "I congratulated him at the national championship game."

Taylor said he thinks the reason for the tension was the fact he named Klieman as the head coach so soon.

"I told him what I was going to do," Taylor said. "Both he and Vigs were in the mix. And the day we had the (Klieman) press conference he stormed out so those two struggled that last month. Big-time tension. Chris was pretty good, he said he just wanted to be the defensive coordinator but the guys that were going to Wyoming, they were recruiting already."

"Craig is so intense and focused, too bad it has to be like that," Kramer said.

I asked Gene now that he was away from the NDSU job for about half a year if he was better able to wrap his hands around the four straight championships. He looked out a window facing Olive Street in Seattle, paused and thought about it. He reflected back to a conversation he had with Gary Barta, the Iowa athletic director and a former Bison quarterback.

The two were at the 2014 game in Frisco as fans and during the game, Barta, looking over Toyota Stadium full of Bison fans, told Taylor: "Gene, you have no idea what you've done for this program. I can't tell you how proud I am as an alum."

Taylor got emotional at the thought, still staring at Olive Street; his eyes started to well up, although he was prone to emotional moments during his tenure.

"I guess you don't realize it when you're going through it," Taylor said, "but to hear a guy like that say that, it was pretty cool."

XV. Culture club

For the most part, Craig and I got along just fine in the coach-reporter relationship. He recognized I had a job to do as I recognized he had a job to do and we went about our business year after year without many problems. There were a couple rough areas, however. There always are.

The first issue wasn't even my story; it was a series of three articles written by Forum reporters Dave Roepke and Amy Dalrymple in the fall of 2010 on the excessive number of speeding tickets by the head coach. The list was as follows:

• Sept. 18, 2010; North Dakota citations for driving without an operator's license and speeding in Traill County.

• June 1, 2010; South Dakota ticket for speeding on the interstate; 89 in 75-mph zone.

• May 19, 2010; North Dakota citation for driving 79 in a 65-mph zone.

• Feb. 13, 2010; Nebraska ticket for speeding 16 to 20 mph over the limit in Burt County.

• Nov. 10, 2009; North Dakota speeding citation in Cass County.

• July 29, 2008; North Dakota citation for driving 82 in a 75-mph zone in Grand Forks County.

• May 14, 2008; North Dakota citation for speeding in a construction zone with workers present in Pierce County.

• May 11, 2008; Nebraska ticket for driving 6 to 10 mph over the limit in Dakota County.

• March 28, 2008; Nebraska ticket for speeding 6 to 10 mph over the limit.

• Feb. 12, 2008; North Dakota citation for driving 70 in a 55-mph zone in Cass County.

• June 17, 2007; South Dakota ticket for speeding on the interstate; 85 in 75-mph zone.

• May 16, 2007; North Dakota citation for driving 85 in a 75-mph zone.

• April 26, 2006; North Dakota citation for driving 90 in a 75-mph zone in Traill County.

• Oct. 21, 2005; Minnesota citation for driving 95 in a 70-mph zone in Stearns County.

• Sept. 15, 2004; Minnesota citation for driving 75 in a 55-mph zone in Polk County.

• Feb. 11, 2004; Minnesota citation for driving 89 in a 70-mph zone in Douglas County.

• Feb. 10, 2003; Nebraska ticket for speeding 16 to 20 mph over the limit in Lancaster County.

• Dec. 16, 1996; Nebraska ticket for speeding 11 to 15 mph over the limit in Lancaster County.

• Dec, 13, 1996; Nebraska ticket for speeding 11 to 15 mph over the limit in Lancaster County.

Why did these come to light? Because Bohl became a pitch man for a radio advertisement as part of a Fargo Police Department traffic safety campaign called "Are you getting it now?" If he doesn't do those ads, then we probably don't look into his vehicular background. Fargo police didn't know about Bohl's traffic record when they tapped him to be the voiceover. Fargo Police Chief Keith Ternes told Roepke that Bohl likely wouldn't have been picked had they known of his history.

"It certainly does take away from the message when the messenger might be somebody we're trying to reach," Ternes said.

Ternes told Roepke that the spot would probably be re-recorded with somebody else. However, later that day, Ternes called The Forum and said after talking to the football coach about the matter, the police would stick with the Bohl-voiced commercial. Bohl then told The Forum that his own history of speeding was part of the reason he agreed to lend his voice to the public service announcement.

"This message applies to everybody. I looked myself in the mirror and said, 'I need to slow down,' " he said.

When told Ternes said he would likely pull Bohl's commercials for another voiceover, Bohl declined to comment. That would be the last time for about a couple of months that Bohl would return a call from somebody from The Forum, most notably me. That story pissed him off and the response was to shut off the newspaper as best he could. The only access I got was the same as everybody else – Monday press conference and post-game comments.

And, oh by the way, the story first surfaced in mid-November – right before NDSU's first FCS playoff run. In his defense, some of those speeding tickets were pretty ticky-tacky. And, certainly, some were probably the product of the high-pressure stakes of recruiting. If the head coach tells a prospect he's going to be at the house for an in-home visit at a certain time, the head coach better not be late, so you could make the argument some of those tickets were the result of a coach busting his ass.

They were the product of a head coach who worked harder than most head coaches. Every spring, Bohl would take a week and visit every high school in North Dakota that fielded a football team; just to walk in, talk to the coach and to make his presence if nothing else. It was a genius move that wasn't easy. It took careful plotting and communication, but it probably played a part in Bohl dominating the state in recruiting.

Mark Slotsve, the head boys basketball and assistant football coach at Williston High School, once told me Bohl would walk into his second floor classroom, sit down and start a conversation. The coaches loved it. So, although the number of tickets was excessive, I didn't think it was that big of a deal.

The second issue was the Beck story. Bohl was not happy. And as I explained earlier in this book, neither was I. In the first case of the speeding tickets, Bohl eventually apologized when we sat down before spring football practice of 2011. He said he recognized we are reporters and we'll go about our business of reporting.

After the Beck incident, communication slowly dried up. Part of it was the closing of practice to the media, the direct result of Bohl's paranoia of Kansas State head coach Bill Snyder and the access social media could provide anybody in the country. Bohl knew how Snyder operated going back to his days at Nebraska and that was to find any inch of weakness in an opponent, no matter how he got the information. Certainly, NDSU knew it was going to get nothing out of the K-State camp; it reached the point where a Wildcat depth chart was a hot commodity the week of the game.

It was equipment manager Brian Gordon's job to make sure nobody was looking in on NDSU's practice and he was good at it. At NDSU's Thursday practice in the 2011 title game in Frisco, for instance, Gordon spotted somebody at the Comfort Suites hotel looking out the window through binoculars. This, of course, threw Gordon into cop mode thinking it was somebody from Sam Houston State checking out NDSU's formations. It turns out it was Forum co-pilot Roger Larsen, who was bored and simply observing practice from the title game's media hotel.

Bohl ran a tight ship. With the advances in social media, he wanted nothing to do with images showing up on YouTube or Twitter. So with reporters being banned from practice, I simply hardly talked with him anymore. That dwindled to nothing when he got the Wyoming job.

But what never dwindled was the culture he created with Bison football. Bohl knew what he wanted in a recruit and what type of kid fit into the tough-minded Bison style. It's a style you can find with any of the Tampa 2 coaching fraternity brothers.

Like Gus Bradley.

***

Bradley took over the Jacksonville Jaguars in 2013 and it was a major building job. It was also a 180-degree change from what Bradley had just experienced as the defensive coordinator with the Seattle Seahawks, a team that made the most of its lower-round draft picks, but also found the key to any good team: finding the right chemistry. It's a trademark of Pete Carroll.

Gus and Pete think alike when it comes to framing a football team. Talent? Of course. But it goes much deeper and Pete taught his assistant coach something Gus probably knew all along: the foundation of a successful team starts from within.

It starts with culture.

And nobody was more important in the rise of the dynasty than Jim Kramer. Certainly, Bohl was the architect. Taylor and the university presidents and the boosters provided the support and the resources. But if I were to name a dynasty Most Valuable Player, it would be Kramer. I'm pretty sure most every player would, too.

"He's the heart and soul of who we are, plain and simple," Jensen said. "I could sit down and talk about him for hours. He's the reason why we keep the championship tradition. He instills the hard work ethic that NDSU athletes have. We have a chip on our shoulder because of Jim Kramer. We win in the fourth quarter because of Jim Kramer. He'll never accept any of the credit – he never wants anything to do with the credit – but in all reality it all goes to him. He's the MVP 100 percent."

Of course, Kramer would just as soon gouge his eyes out than listen to a compliment.

"I try to let it go in one ear and out the other," he said. "I guess there's a sense of pride with that, too. OK, how do I keep that up? Obviously I've been a big influence on these young men but I have to make sure if it's that big of an impact, there has to be a positive influence even when I have to be negative with it. I want to make sure I'm having the right influence."

Bohl hired him from the United States Olympic Training Center in Colorado Springs, Colo. Kramer also had stops in football hot spots Northern Iowa, Georgia Tech and Appalachian State. He instilled a no-nonsense, discipline-oriented mentality on the players. After NDSU won its first national title in 2011, a few players were wearing their championship T-shirts around the Bison weight room – and that didn't sit well with Kramer. He made them take them off and it wouldn't surprise me if he burned them.

There was to be no resting on your laurels in Kramer's army. When it comes to this dynasty, his contribution was more than most people ever knew. His value in the 2014 coaching change was immeasurable because the players didn't see much change from the day they got back from Frisco until the first day of spring football when the position coaches were back in front of them. In that time frame, from the second week of January until late March, it was Kramer who was their coach. The same Kramer who was their weight training coach in the previous seasons.

Kramer came aboard the same season NDSU started a Division I schedule and over the years, he was a staple while other assistants came and went. And make no mistake, Kramer may not be listed officially as a Bison assistant coach, but he had as much to do with the creation of the dynasty as anyone.

Like several Bison players over the years, Kramer grew up a hard-working farm kid, with home a 200-acre dairy, hog and beef farm near Platteville, Wis., located in the southwest corner of the state. So many mornings, about 5:30, his father Bud would yell up the stairs to get young Jim out of bed. Time for chores.

"Finish the job. Do it right," Bud always told his son. "Do it with quality. Don't do a half-ass job."

Bud hated taking vacations. The Wisconsin Dells were two hours away and that qualified as one. Going to a Milwaukee Brewers baseball game counted as another vacation. One year, the Kramers went to Lambeau Field in Green Bay, the mecca as they called it, and "we thought that was a trip across the earth," Jim said.

The hardest thing young Jim ever did as a kid was ask some buddies to help him bale hay on a 100-plus degree day. That would mean an admission that he couldn't do the entire chore himself.

A typical day would mean getting up when it was still dark and doing his chores. Then it was off to school and perhaps wrestling practice after school. Every day was 12-plus hours of work of some fashion. Even on Saturdays, Jim would spend the mornings working in the barn and then it would be a wrestling or track meet in the afternoon. And you wonder how Kramer gets that work ethic message across to the Bison players.

Wilford "Bud" Kramer died in 2007, but there's been a lot of Bud instilled in NDSU's football players over the years. The farm is a lot like the weight lifting room: Everybody pitches in and more gets accomplished. Kramer takes a teamwork mindset to training. It's like baling hay in 100-degree weather; you grind it out and push through it.

The goal is to simulate the workouts in the weight room like a football practice. It's not an individual thing. Kramer goes back to his days with George O'Leary at Georgia Tech and the tough-love approach to coaching and leading a program.

"George could chew your ass out but you would go away feeling good about yourself," Kramer said. "How does that work? So I watched how he coached kids. Kids yearn for that discipline. They want that. We coach them hard at NDSU. It's not coaching them negative; it's demanding discipline and perfection. On the football field, that's what it's going to take. When they're tired on the field and hurting … and you try to simulate some of that in the weight room. The mentality of it. You teach them in the weight room to rely on each other and feed off of each other. When one guy is tired, another one who is not as tired picks him up. 'You need to push through this, too. Follow him and he'll take you right along.' It's mental toughness training. No one person is mentally tough but together you're mentally tough. What allows us to win is toughness and togetherness. It's not a drill; it's relying on each other, pulling for each other and pushing each other."

It's why every July and August Kramer would do the heat and humidity rain dance in his head. He wanted his kids to work out in as hot of conditions as possible, especially during the transition when the Bison were scheduling so many Southland Conference teams. He knew playing in the likes of Thibodaux, La., Huntsville, Texas, or Nacogdoches, Texas, would be a test for the northern body. He wanted to simulate the conditions as best he could.

NDSU played in those southern states five times in September or early October from 2004-09 and the Bison went 4-1. More impressive, minus the 2009 loss at Sam Houston, they owned the second half. That didn't surprise Phil Hansen, who from his radio color commentary seat saw it time and again.

"The thing about when we played the teams from the south, every time I think if you lined them up athlete for athlete, you would pick the opponent," Hansen said. "You would say they were the better athlete. The thing that got the Bison over the hump was Jim Kramer. The Bison stuck with it – they would ground out three or four yards and the other teams got tired. Every southern team who puts it on as their armor – 'we play in this weather, it's hot down here all the time, we play in this' – the Bison were in theory at a disadvantage. No, not in the fourth quarter they're not. You could see it every game. We would get a 10-yard run and then we would pop another 12-yard run. Then somebody would throw a punch and we would get 15 yards of penalty. And then we would score. And then it just unraveled. You saw it regularly."

***

In April of 2015, Bradley returned to his alma mater for a speaking engagement at the Hilton Garden Inn in south Fargo. It was the biggest room NDSU officials could find and the 500 capacity easily sold out. Gus, of course, hit his speech on culture out of the park. Earlier in the day, he visited the Bison team room on the lower level of the Fargodome for the first time and saw just how far the program evolved since the days he was working out of a small office in the Bison Sports Arena.

Asked how a team like NDSU can win four titles in a row and he gave that trademark smile and laugh.

"It's a great question," he said. "I don't know, that's why I'm here. This is a two-way street now. There are so many good coaches here who have done so many good things. It is difficult. Obviously the players have a lot to do with it – you have to have guys who are really committed. And we always say if you have trust and cooperation, you have a chance to get better. I think with NDSU you not only have trust within the university but the fan base and support is unmatched anywhere I've been. I know that."

And in the Bison title years, the trust and cooperation within the team was probably unmatched in the FCS. There was a time when I first started covering Bison football in the mid-1990s until that 2009 season that going through the daily police report was a necessity. Was I looking to "bust" players? No, but there is an obligation that when you are a public figure – and Bison football players are about as high-profile of public figures as you can get in that city – that you can't go around breaking team policy. I've said the following many times over the years: I could care less what players do on their own time away from the field, but when they get their name in a public record of some sort, usually an arrest by law enforcement agency, then it is my business.

In those five straight title years, there was hardly a problem with law enforcement that I knew of. The team culture of commitment and dedication to football, and not screwing around, was that strong. It was something Gus in Jacksonville was trying his hardest to figure out – finding guys who fit the team chemistry of his program.

"I think we all talk about it, I know in the NFL we talk about it, it's a commonly used word, especially during free agency. How's your culture?" he said. "What's your culture like? Everybody says it's good, it's great, can't wait to show it to you. You have to meet some of the players, but I think it's deeper than that. There is a lot to culture. I think it's where players really enjoy the atmosphere, they know it's about work and getting better, but it is in an atmosphere where they come early and stay late."

Perhaps Philadelphia Daily News columnist Marcus Hayes said it best about the Seattle braintrust, most notably Carroll: "They love players who consider themselves unappreciated victims whose insecurities fuel a competitive desire that leads to team-first sacrifice . . . or, most of Seattle's best," he wrote.

Bison football coaches can relate. They can always play that you-were-overlooked-by-FBS card. It was part of their culture.

"Culture? I could give you a five-page answer," Klieman said. "Culture to me is the way guys do things on and off the field with great pride, great work ethic and always putting the team first and themselves second."

When Carroll was the head coach at USC from 2002-09, the Trojans won seven straight Pac-10 Conference titles and two straight national titles. They had talent, certainly, but there had to be more than that to sustain such success.

Bradley got a taste of what it was coaching under Carroll in Seattle. On that April day in Fargo, Gus could have sat in the Bison team room and talked about Pete all day; on how Pete found the right mix of players and personality and molded that culture into a Super Bowl team.

"I think you're always trying to find players that fit your personality as a head coach," Bradley said. "We knew in Jacksonville that in the situation we came in that there were going to be some changes taking place. When we were at Seattle, we had over 400-and-some roster changes in a couple of years I was there, and we took kind of that same philosophy at Jacksonville. And it's tough. Football is based on trust and loyalty and brotherhood and when you cut, or make 400-some roster changes, it doesn't bring that type of atmosphere but our guys have done a great job with it and we feel like it's going the right direction."

Bradley, of course, was part of the building blocks of NDSU's Division I dynasty. He was the defensive coordinator in 2004 and 2005, a holdover from Bob Babich's staff. Bohl gave him the reigns to the Tampa 2 defense – a style that got Bradley to the NFL.

Bradley got the quality control position with the Tampa Bay Buccaneers following the 2005 season because he aced a phone call from Tampa defensive coordinator Monte Kiffin.

"I killed it," Bradley told me in his Bison Sports Arena office.

The Tampa 2 trademark is all over NDSU's rise starting with Rocky Hager, who hired Bradley as the Bison linebackers coach in 1996. Babich got the Bison job in 1997 and one of his long-time friends and former college teammate at Tulsa was NFL head coach Lovie Smith, who was an assistant at Tampa Bay when Kiffin was the defensive coordinator.

Kiffin and Bohl both have University of Nebraska ties. So when Bradley got the Jacksonville job, he immediately turned to his Tampa 2 ties for assistants, hiring Babich as his defensive coordinator and former Bison assistant Todd Wash as his defensive line coach. A year later, he hired former Bison defensive coordinator Scottie Hazelton as his assistant linebackers coach. Hazelton called the shots in NDSU's first FCS title in 2011 and then took an assistant position at USC.

"I've been fortunate to be around some really good people, and I mean really good people in college, too," Bradley said. "Kevin Donnalley. Rocky Hager. Everybody had an influence on my career and I think you take pieces from all of them. Monte Kiffin is very special. Here's a guy who is a legend in the NFL and how much impact he's had on the game. He really changed how defenses played for many years in the NFL. But I think if you talk about the greatest quality with Monte Kiffin, it would be Monte Kiffin as a person. He developed a lot of coaches and everybody who worked for him appreciates him."

***

Never was the Bison culture more evident than the difference between the '09 season and the subsequent title teams. The 3-8 record in 2009 taught Bohl there is more than athletic ability that makes for a winning FCS team.

"He made a strategic error saying we need more skill when in fact we were getting kids who were not in the culture," said Pat Simmers. "The culture is to be a tough bastard; to play until the last whistle. It's that old AC (North Dakota Agriculture College) mentality: get up, put your boots on and go to work. So what if you have a group of kids who run faster and jump higher, but they didn't fit into our culture. Then when you're not winning, how many programs are like that? So (Bohl) flipped his model – it didn't work here. And the emphasis was to find kids that fit our culture and, boom, overnight success."

It was that Nebraska model of success in Bohl's background that drew Kramer to Fargo. He came to Fargo when the school was just beginning the Division I reclassification and you have to wonder about the intelligence of that move. Remember, when NDSU was about to make the move, nobody thought winning was going to be an immediate venture like it was. But when Kramer got to Fargo, some of the first people he saw were Justin Monson, Nick Zilka, Rob Hunt and Isaac Snell. They were three offensive linemen and a defensive tackle.

"I saw them and I thought we could step into the Missouri Valley, which was the Gateway at the time, just fine," Kramer said. "I knew we could size up just fine."

His interview with Taylor was first class, he said. What made the NDSU job more appealing than his UNI stint was the resources and personnel. At NDSU, he already had two full-time strength coaches and a graduate assistant. At UNI, it was just him and a part-time assistant.

"And I knew with a Nebraska guy at the helm that strength and conditioning was going to be important," Kramer said. "That's where it all started down there. I just knew there would be a major emphasis on it here."

And with that emphasis, he was able to instill the culture that Bud Kramer taught his son.

"Culture, I don't know where that term came from, the dynasty term, I guess it's just a way of describing the family at NDSU," Jim Kramer said. "At Northern Iowa, there is a tremendous amount of pride and tradition, but it runs so deep here. The tradition runs deep at UNI, too, but it seems like our kids embrace it more. One thing that helps out; they get to interact with former players. When they see them down in Frisco, that makes an impact on kids through the years, that this is bigger than me, bigger than I could have ever imagined and I think they see that. They see that they have something to uphold here."

It didn't take Larsen long after taking the A.D. reins to realize that. There was no need to tinker with the strength and conditioning program. It's not like there are any weight lifting secrets going on along 19th Avenue North. It's not like Kramer reinvented the strength training wheel. It's how he goes about his business.

"I think there are a lot of places where the strength coach is about getting them stronger and getting them well conditioned and not that Jim's not doing that," Larsen said. "I think it's more the tone he sets, the expectation level of being a Bison and what all that means. I think that's his value. Yes, he gets them strong – the 45-pound plate weighs the same here as it does any other place in the country. But I think if you talk to the guys, they don't talk about the workout routine he puts them through. They talk about the intangible things. The lessons. The expectations. The drive to be better. And I think that's what makes him different. It's intense, and most of the time when I see Jim he's quiet and mild mannered but I tell you what: he gets after them. There is an expectation and if you're not going to meet it, it's not for the faint of heart. I think if you ask Chris Klieman, the MVP is Jim Kramer. We start going for a national championship when Jim Kramer gets them in February. That sets the tone. Jim Kramer is not patting them on the back saying, hey, you won a national championship. He's kicking them in the butt saying, OK, let's go for five. So he's very unique in terms of what he brings to the program."

It helps to have kids with the kind of work ethic background that the Bison so coveted in recruiting.

***

In the summer of 2015, I did a four-part series on NDSU's offensive linemen from rural towns. The first stop: Landon Lechler's ranch north of Beach, N.D. More specifically, Saddle Butte Township, N.D. The greeting party was a chocolate Chesapeake Bay Retriever named Lilly, a friendly dog who wagged her tail at any human being who approached her domain. She chewed rocks for fun. I guess the first sign of a tough offensive lineman is having a dog that chews rocks for enjoyment.

Tough and polite; that about sums up life on the Lechler farm and ranch. It's a busy place – and then in a sense it is not. There were 300 or so lambs and 130 cattle and none of them cared that Lechler at the time of the story had three NCAA Division I FCS national title rings. It was a workin' man's place, and the only glory within the 2,500 acres was the beauty of the land itself. Where an English major may look at it as drudgery, Lechler looked at it as his escape from the hustle and bustle of Division I football. Whenever he got a weekend off – and that isn't often in the year-around world of college athletics – Lechler would hop into his white pickup that was once his grandfather's and drive the several hours to the last exit before Montana. From there it was north on Highway 16 for a few miles and then a right turn into a bright red scoria road, where the setting of the house is something out of a painting. A creek ran below the farm facility through a mini-canyon that gives the Lechlers their own mini Badlands.

"I'll leave Fargo sometimes, and it feels like an hour drive to get home," Landon said. "I can come out here and just escape and have everything on my mind except football for a weekend. It's a good way to clear my head, and I can go back kind of fresh and get ready to go."

In 2015, he wasn't the only Bison offensive lineman who could do that. Of the 13 on the roster, four were from rural North Dakota, and all four were essentially lightly recruited by almost everybody – regardless of division. Guard Tanner Volson was from Balfour, tackle Jack Plankers carried a Leonard address and guard Luke Bacon was from Granville. The importance of small-town players in the run of five straight national championships cannot be emphasized enough.

The first introduction offensive line coach Riley had to rural North Dakota players and their tough-nosed mentality was his first conversation with the fullback Grothmann. That was in 2013 when Riley had just accepted a Bison assistant position.

"I asked him what his plans were for that summer," Riley said. "He says I get up and lift, I go to work for my internship, then I go directly to the farm where I have a flock of sheep and then I come back and run that evening. Rinse, and recycle the next day. And I'm going, holy cow and you begin to understand that's the culture, that's the acceptable norm."

The acceptable norm on the Lechler ranch was a long way from the modern, air-conditioned tractors and GPS fields of the Red River Valley. There were eight pickups on the property and the one common denominator is they all ran. Nobody cared if there was a little rust, cracked windshield or empty Busch Lite beer cans in them. Paul Lechler, Landon's father, was a master of engines who had the ability to make something run that has no business running. For instance, a piece of farming equipment called a toolbar used for tilling was dated from somewhere in the late 1950s to early 1960s and it still sufficed in 2015. Landon wondered how farmers who bought the latest in farm equipment could sleep at night, citing the enormity of the costs. By the house sat an old Jeep Wrangler that Paul got for $100 and a case of beer. Yes, he figured out how to get that working, too.

Lechler was a general agriculture major, which is separated into four disciplines: animal science, plant science, soil science and agriculture systems management. During the school year, he worked in the NDSU Sheep Unit near the junction of Interstate 29 and 19th Avenue North which, like the ranch near Beach, gave him a getaway from the rigors of football and city.

"I had a huge adjustment coming to Fargo," said Lechler, looking over the vastness of his farm surroundings. "Living there full-time … I still have trouble now and then."

The recruitment of Lechler was interesting in that he was probably a better basketball prospect at 6-foot-7 than a football recruit, although NDSU almost mastered the art of finding guys like that in the most unlikely of places. For the longest time, he saw himself playing hoops at a school like Gonzaga – until the day Brent Vigen contacted him during his junior year at Beach High School about NDSU football. "I watched the Bison growing up and I was like, 'That's awesome, but I could never see myself coming from Beach and nine-man football to NDSU," Landon said.

Vigen invited Lechler to the annual Bison summer football camp held every June and that's where things took a turn for the better. That's where Lechler met Plankers, a big offensive line prospect from Kindred High School just southwest of Fargo. That's where Lechler figured out he was probably good enough to play at that level after going toe-to-toe with some of NDSU's best prospects at the camp.

"I have a biased opinion," Kramer said, "but the hard hours at the farm – the long and boring hours of doing the same repetitive task over and over again – that mentality helps here, too."

It pretty much summed up NDSU's West Coast offense – a physical style of play that fits into the mold of a small-town rancher. Center Austin Kuhnert could relate. Although from Sioux Falls, S.D., and Washington High School, he spent many summers on his uncle's farm growing up near Rowena, S.D., just east of Sioux Falls.

"We'd haul cattle and fix fence," Kuhnert said, "and if we got into trouble, then we'd really have to fix fence on our own, with no machinery or nothing. Some of these guys work all day long and all night long because it's gotta get done."

He had been to the Lechler ranch, where they did chores day and night and fixed equipment.

The one Bison fixture who didn't make it to the ranch was Bohl, who flew his single engine plane to Beach on a recruiting trip. Usually, those small airports have some sort of beat-up old car for pilots to use at their disposal, but there was nothing around when Bohl landed.

So, seeing the Beach water tower not too far in the distance, he started walking toward town when an old pickup pulled up beside him. It was Landon Lechler.

"Coach, can I give you a ride?" Landon said.

The easy answer, in virtually the middle of nowhere, would be to say yes. But it also would have been an NCAA violation, so Lechler went back to town and Bohl continued walking on the lonely rural road. It was an example of how Bohl followed the letter of the NCAA law, not even risking getting a ride outside of Beach, N.D., about as far from an NCAA investigator as a coach could get. They met at the high school, where Bohl laid out his vision for the big recruit. Lechler was impressed.

***

Finding the Plankers ranch didn't take a plane flight from Fargo, but you needed to follow directions closely, nonetheless. The landmark is the West Prairie Free Lutheran Church on the corner of county Highways 46 and 18 near the Sheyenne River Valley about an hour southwest of the NDSU campus. From there, it's a series of turns where each road is narrower and more primitive in construction. There is newly poured blacktop with a shoulder. Then old blacktop with no shoulder. That turns into a gravel road that can fit two vehicles, but eventually morphs into one lane. Roy and Lori Plankers bought their place in 2005, and if "Little House on the Prairie" wanted a setting to renew the famous TV series, this would be a good spot. The last road into their almost 200-acre abode isn't found on most maps. It's 45 miles from Fargo and you would never know it.

"A lot of people don't know this Sheyenne valley exists for the most part," Roy said.

A lot of people, thousands and thousands, knew their son existed in the sport of football. He was an offensive lineman, a local kid from Kindred High School who was more at home in the woods and hills of his farmstead than most of his Bison teammates would be.

On this 2015 team, he was part of the mold of North Dakota native offensive linemen: the hours aren't long; they're just hours. Jack's typical weekday during the summer looked exhausting: It started at 5:30 a.m. at the NDSU weight training facility. Workout complete, he got in his vehicle and drove the 55 miles south on Interstate 29 to Wahpeton, N.D., where he worked at WCCO Belting Inc., an engineering company that specializes in belts. The eight-hour work day completed, it was back on I-29, where the daily routine included a call from his mother to make sure he was staying awake on the road.

"How he does what he does I don't know," Lori said.

He drove back to campus and was usually on Dacotah Field by 5:30 p.m. (he was habitually a half-hour early for everything) for the 6 p.m. running and agility workout sessions.

"Go to sleep and repeat," Jack said.

Those who know the 6-foot-7, 321-pound Plankers would not be surprised by his daily work habits. At Kindred, he was usually the first person to arrive at school every morning thanks to Roy's schedule. He would drop Jack off at the school around 6 a.m. on his way to work at Wholesale Distributors just off 19th Avenue North in Fargo, an hour commute that in the winter meant driving to and from work in darkness.

When the family first bought the property, Roy walked from one corner to the other and it took him most of the day. Jack, a take-care-of-his-teammates kind of guy, had several players out to the property to hunt, shoot, drive four-wheelers or just hang out.

"They've been out here blowing stuff up," Roy said with a laugh.

Lori wouldn't have it any other way. She's sympathetic to long distance Bison parents who don't get to see their sons as often as they do.

"So I try to be like a second mom and open my house to them," she said. "And Jack is that type of kid. They call him 'Papa Plankers' because he watches over everybody."

The Plankers' are in tune with nature. They once raised pheasants. Deer are regular visitors, and a moose once lived across a road from their property. There was even a mountain lion sighting once, by Lori, when she saw one down the hill in front of what once was a calving shed. It's her area of the country. She grew up in nearby Lidgerwood, N.D., and was the center on the Lidgerwood state championship basketball team that was led by NDSU Hall of Fame player Pat (Smykowski) Jacobson. She vividly remembers going to Bison football games at old Dacotah Field with her father, no matter how cold it got.

Roy is from the Iron Range in northern Minnesota, and the couple and their three boys lived in Fargo for a time. It just didn't feel right. Chuck, the youngest of the three, could qualify as an expert outdoorsman. He and Jack spent a lot of time by the winding Sheyenne River gathering wood.

"I was a construction guy in the summer, but before work and after work, I would go down to the woods and cut as much as I could, split them and sell them to people around the area with wood furnaces," Jack said.

Jack never thought of himself as a Division I prospect, even though he went to the NDSU football camp every summer since he was 11 years old. It wasn't until Vigen showed up at Kindred High school unbeknownst to Jack during his junior year.

"He just started talking to me like he knew me for years," Jack said. "So I was like, 'I really don't know what you want with me, if you're looking for somebody, I could help you out.'"

No, Vigen was looking for a big offensive lineman who had a built-in work ethic and toughness about him. How tough was Plankers?

"He breaks his hand in spring ball," Riley said. "I didn't notice it until I look at him in his stance at right tackle and he has his left hand in the ground. I'm going, 'What's going on?' He says he thinks he may have hurt his hand."

An hour later, NDSU head football trainer Bobby Knodel told Riley that Plankers will need surgery. Riley visited Plankers after his procedure on a Saturday thinking he may be out for a while.

"He was in a soft cast the following Wednesday practicing again," Riley said.

Four practices later, Plankers suffered another setback, this time an ankle injury that put him in a walking boot and caused him to miss the annual Spring Game.

"He tells me the following day, 'Coach, I will be full-go by the time we start summer running,' " Riley said. "Sure enough, we start running (at the beginning of June). He came up to my office to visit and he said he was ready to go, just like he promised. They make up their mind."

And if Jack needed to get his mind away from football, home was just an hour away, even if it took a geography major to find it. The address is actually Leonard, N.D., and if you put it in a GPS it will take you to the middle of an open field.

"You have to be driving here to get here," Lori said. "There are a lot of people that get lost."

But a lot of people know the route to Frisco. Five months after his 12-plus hour summer days, Plankers was part of a Bison offensive line that was effective in beating Jacksonville State for the fifth straight FCS title.

***

For the Bison seniors who had been in the program for five years, the title only added to the collection. For receivers Zach Vraa and Nate Moody, they did something that may never be equaled in college football history: play at least one game during the season on five championship teams. Both took a medical hardship because of injuries – Vraa in 2011 after breaking his collarbone and Moody in 2014 to rehabilitate a nagging knee injury. Vraa returned in 2015 for his sixth year of school, a decision he made after the 2014 title game.

"It's amazing to be part of a team that won five," Vraa said, "and to end my career with the fifth one is just so cool."

The senior class wasn't real big with 13 members, but it had some quality. Vraa left as the school's all-time leader in receptions, touchdown receptions and receiving yardage. Joe Haeg was a decorated first team All-American. Wentz's resume spoke for itself. Cornerback CJ Smith was a shutdown defender who always got the opponents' best receiver, and more often than not won that battle.

And punter Ben LeCompte not only left as NDSU's all-time punting leader but as the fourth-best ever in FCS with a 44.6-yard career average.

Moreover, LeCompte overcame some family medical issues during his career that couldn't have been easy to deal with. They put on a lot of miles together, father and son, getting in their car in Barrington, Ill., and driving to football kicking camps across the country. If you could drive it, Berry and Ben LeCompte wouldn't think twice. They went to cities like St. Louis, Pittsburgh, Des Moines, Iowa, and Waukesha, Wis., the latter of which is the home base of Kohl's Professional Camps – the foundation of LeCompte's standout career. For instance, in high school, they would drive to Des Moines for a camp in January and Pittsburgh in February.

"There was a lot of bonding between me and Ben during those long road trips," Berry said.

Ben was the youngest of five children and the youngest by a minute to his twin brother Bart. The plan was to drive both of them to their colleges in the summer of 2011, with Bart having to go in June. On the way back, somewhere in Michigan, Berry said he felt something get caught in his throat. A few days later, he was diagnosed with throat cancer. Ben at the time was just a few weeks from his first day of football practice at NDSU. But the news of his dad's diagnosis had him thinking otherwise, and he lobbied his parents to stay at home in Barrington. Berry wouldn't allow it.

"He was the No. 1 proponent of me making a commitment to this program, so I had to come up here right away," Ben said. "And that again shows me he had my best intentions in mind, because even though I didn't want to come, he knew it would work out."

Ben's coming to NDSU, however, came with a deal: That Berry would recover and be at Ben's first game the following season. He redshirted his freshman year. Berry endured months of chemotherapy and radiation and did indeed recover. And as promised, on Sept. 1, 2012, he was at the Robert Morris University and NDSU home opener at the Fargodome. Unfortunately, it wasn't the end of the family's struggles with cancer, however. After Ben's sophomore season, his mother Catheleen was diagnosed with breast cancer and underwent surgery in June of 2013. The fears that hit him with his father resurfaced all over again with his mother. How did he persevere? His teammates, for one. It wasn't just the starters and older players, Ben said, but everybody from a backup to a scout team player.

"Nobody batted an eye," he said. "Everybody's door was always open; everybody's phone was always on. I count my blessings every day. The fact I had this football team to turn to was nothing I'll ever forget."

And even if a pro career didn't work out, Berry will always have the NCAA letter of intent that Ben signed to attend NDSU. It's a cherished treasure in the family home.

"I always told him as a kid, 'If you can dream it, you can do it,' " Berry said. "So the Christmas I had cancer, he framed the (letter of intent) and said, 'Never stop dreaming.' That was a lot of motivation for me. It's all I would dream about. I would lie in bed and dream about to be able to watch him play. It was a tremendous motivational factor."

XVI: The fourth quarter

The question is not so much who, what, where, when or why. It's ho How did this program put together five straight national championship How did it become the greatest dynasty in college football history? Ho did it do it just three years removed from becoming playoff-eligible afte going through the five-year NCAA Division I reclassification? How is tha possible?

Certainly, there is no one simple explanation, but after sifting throug just over a year of research for this project combined with 20-plus years c covering the team, I came up with 10 reasons in no particular order o importance, with all 10 that could probably be divided into subsets. If any of thes 10 were compromised, I don't believe five in a row would have been a reality.

1. Culture.
2. Recruiting.
3. Geography.
4. Tradition.
5. Physicality.
6. Coaching.
7. Jim Kramer.
8. Institutional leadership/Team Makers
9. Fargodome.
10. Media-mania.

They are 10 factors that when taken into a singular context is not only a hard combination to master but extremely rare. With the tradition element, fo instance, you can eliminate 75 percent of college football programs in the countr We're not talking about a tradition of winning seasons, but a tradition o championships over almost a six-decade period. Broken down, the 10 factor look like this:

1. Culture.

It's pretty simple, really, when you look at the years the Bison ha consistent issues with players getting in trouble and the won-lost records. The were more warnings than a category five hurricane in the months leading up t the 3-8 season of 2009 and that led to a locker room environment that sor players called troublesome. Culture is not something you can gather data ar write a thesis about; it's a feeling among players during the week and especial 90 minutes before a game when they take the field for warmups. In those fi years of titles, the senior leadership was phenomenal but just as important the

were underclassmen who either followed directions or didn't last in the program. Culture is simply the belief that you're going to win. It begins the first frigid morning in January at the start of winter workouts and it goes until the first game of the season. Culture does not take a day off.

2. Recruiting.

South Dakota head coach Joe Glenn was sitting at the front of a room in the deep bowels of the DakotaDome in Vermillion, S.D., when a post-game press conference was just finished. He was talking off the cuff about NDSU middle linebacker Nick DeLuca, who Glenn tried hard to recruit. Bison receiver Darrius Shepherd, mind you, once verballed to USD but decommitted in favor of NDSU. Glenn would have loved to have Omaha kids like Easton Stick and RJ Urzendowski. "It's just amazing the horsepower they have in Fargo," Glenn said. "They have just been amazing at reloading. Their fans, they get into it. Their facilities are second to none in our league. They do a beautiful job of recruiting. They are positive recruiters. That's been forever. They have really classy people all through my time of going against North Dakota State. It's why they keep being so successful."

With the microphones turned off and the cameras leaving the room, Glenn remained in his chair talking off the record, so to speak. When it came to recruiting, he got right to the point. "They get anybody they want," he said.

Well, not everybody, but close. It's not easy, Craig Bohl learned that following the 2011 title that you just can't go into a recruit's home and say, we won, come to our place. While the Bison were getting ready for playoff games, other coaches were in the homes of high school prospects and it doesn't matter how much you win, there's more of an advantage to being on site to a recruit. So the Bison, in order to beat that system, altered their recruiting philosophy and started offering players earlier, like in the spring and summer. The foundation of the teams in '11, '12 and '13 came from the Twin Cities and bad Gopher teams. The foundation of the '14 and '15 teams came from finding just enough stars in the 2011 and '12 recruiting classes and the resurgence of better recruiting classes in '14 and '15.

And it's just not signing kids, either. Perhaps nobody attracts tougher walkon players than NDSU, with its reputation of physical play on both sides of the ball.

3. Geography.

Funny thing about NDSU's location in Fargo, the first impression is it would kill recruiting because it's rather isolated from the rest of the continental

48. In the words of Lee Corso, not so fast my friend. It's actually an advantage. Let me explain:

Competition for attention is almost nil, since the closest professional franchise is located four hours away in downtown Minneapolis. In the entire state of North Dakota and western Minnesota, it's NDSU football and UND hockey – and that's about it. So when it comes to the advertising dollar, the pool for a season ticket base and competition for in-state recruits, there's not much. You won't see Mid-American Conference schools in small-town North Dakota looking for linemen. Other than Wyoming, the Mountain West Conference could care less about North Dakota or Minnesota. In Wisconsin, if players aren't Badger worthy, there are no FCS schools in the state leaving NDSU as one of the closer schools to play. Three of the four starting defensive linemen on the 2015 title team were from Wisconsin, a position that is probably the hardest to recruit effectively in college football. Also on that team, 14 of the 22 starters in the title game came from North Dakota, South Dakota, Minnesota or Wisconsin – a formula you can trace back to the title teams starting in the 1980s. The fact Carson Wentz from the capitol city of North Dakota had only a few FCS offers is all you need to know that isolated geography can be NDSU's friend.

4. Tradition.

It's rather self-explanatory and really no need to go on and on and on and on about all the victories and titles over the years. It just builds on itself, with each year that is added to the massive banner hanging from the south rafters of the Fargodome like another mark on the tradition bedpost. Where you probably see it paying off is in the fourth quarters, when in a close game the quest for a win is an inner mental battle between doubt and confidence. You know all those rallies that were documented in an earlier chapter in this project? Tradition played a key role.

5. Physicality.

Every FCS team has big offensive linemen with guys 6-3 to 6-6 and around 300 pounds. But there's a difference in being big and playing physical. In 2015, the Bison offensive line, a unit I called a Big Ten offensive line during August training camp, was playing OK at best. But once Wentz went down, the team had a Come-to-Jesus meeting the following Monday on playing with a tougher edge. The offensive line was simply not playing physical. The running backs were not breaking tackles. That changed and there was not a more physical team in FCS in the last half of the season, the core reason why No. 5 in a row was accomplished.

In 1952, a TCU coach named Leo "Dutch" Meyer wrote a book on the spread offense in football, but it really didn't take hold in the college game until the 1990s. In 2004, a version of the spread called "the pistol" came about with Nevada head coach Chris Ault getting a lot of the credit. Ironically, that was NDSU's first year in Division I football and Bohl went against the spread offense trend and installed the West Coast offense that is based off of a power game using a fullback and a tight end.

It turned out to be a genius move in that while most other teams were going to the run-and-gun type of football, NDSU stayed old school. That physical style often wore teams down that were not used to playing power teams. In NDSU's five FCS title games, the Bison outscored their opponents 62-16 in the fourth quarter with only Illinois State in 2014 managing a touchdown. Don't underestimate discipline, either: NDSU had 22 penalties for 173 yards in five title games to its opponents' 32 infractions for 252 yards. Only one of the Bison penalties was a personal foul.

6. Coaching.

Bohl was the architect of the dynasty and there is no disputing that. He put together a plan in 2003, tweaked it over the years until he came up with those two golden recruiting years that produced the guts of the first four FCS championships. But, for whatever reason, he did not want to accept the credit for it. And those came from my brief conversations with him in my research for this project. He certainly did not want to sit down and be a quote machine for the many questions that I would have in store for him. For whatever reason, he chose to ride off from Fargo and look only forward, not behind.

But make no mistake, the coaching of Craig Bohl was the creative force behind all the winning. I thought Bohl made two key philosophical changes from the transition years to the championship years: 1. He started to get away from hiring the fired FBS assistant who was looking to work his way back up. It just didn't make for good continuity since those coaches spent a year or two at NDSU and usually got back to the FBS. 2. He made a better effort to recruit a quality quarterback every year, instead of putting money into a guy every two or three years. The recruiting continuity produced Jensen, Wentz and Stick – the three quarterbacks responsible for the five titles although Stick did not start in any of the first five title games. His 8-0 record in relief of the injured Wentz in 2015, however, was crucial.

7. Jim Kramer.

His job on game days is to get the players properly warmed up and once the game starts, keep players and coaches from standing too close to the field. But for the most part, nobody outside of the team watches his real job.

The weight room is his sanctuary and he'll go down as the story behind the story of the college football dynasty.

8. Institutional leadership/Team Makers.

Thomas Plough was the president of North Dakota State from 1995-98, a period of time when Bison football was still good, but not living in the neighborhood of Division II greatness like the championship teams of the '80s and 1990. Many people pointed to the dwindling maximum number of scholarships in DII, although it didn't help that Plough didn't care much for the athletics and continually threatened to cut funding.

I don't know the exact circumstances of Plough leaving to take the presidency at Assumption College (Mass.), but the fact the athletic department was in the process of trimming 8 percent of its budget for the 1999-2000 and 2000-01 academic years did not sit well with the big dogs in Team Makers. They couldn't wait to get him out of office because it's a simple formula: if you don't have a president that cares about football, then your team is in jeopardy of not succeeding. Joe Chapman changed that mindset in a hurry.

Dean Bresciani was pretty good, too. He rarely if ever missed a game, attending almost every post-game press conference at home or on the road, usually sitting in the back of the room. That's unusual for university presidents across the country and rarely do presidents from other schools attend games in the Fargodome. He came to NDSU from Texas A&M, a Big 12 Conference school that knows the value of a successful athletic department and there is no doubt that whoever succeeded Chapman was going to have to put a priority on a good football team because nobody wanted to go back to the Plough days. My first interview with Bresciani was in the NDSU president's office and this was one of the first things he said when asked about the athletic department.

"I've used the word 'critical' enough times, which probably hints that I think it's very important," he said. "It's something that brings the university community together and it brings a sense of cohesiveness to the state."

Bresciani was all-in on football, he was smart enough to let his captains lead their ship, and it was apparent when NDSU started its title run that the president and Gene Taylor got along very well – a far cry from former athletic director Bob Entzion and Plough.

Speaking of Plough and Entzion, those were the days when Team Makers booster group raised annually around $600,000. That jumped into the millions once Division I became trendy and ask any administrator in the country if their football program could be successful without the right funding and you would get a resounding no. In 2015, for example, Team Makers raised $3.85 million.

9. Fargodome.

In the 2015 playoff game against Richmond, the decibel level of the dome crowd reached 105. When Jensen scored the game-winning touchdown in the 2012 semifinals against Georgia Southern, the meter read 111. It was consistently between 102 and 105 when the Eagles were on offense, a roar that became common throughout the road to five straight titles and a roar that was impressive to ESPN sideline reporter Cara Capuano, who covered games at the biggest of college football venues like Alabama, Georgia and LSU. "I get the same hum in my ear as I do at those other places," she said. "What a wonderful reverberation of noise."

Reverberance is a term I used earlier that week when doing a story on NDSU's home field advantage. For expertise, I turned to the interim chair of the NDSU department of architecture and landscape architecture at a school that has long had a well-known accredited program. Ganapathy Mahalingam earned his Ph.D. at the University of Florida with a doctoral dissertation on auditorium design. His assessment of Bison football games: "Because it has a huge volume and most of the surfaces are hard, reflective surfaces, there's a lot of reverberance in that space. That's what causes the noise level to go up during a game."

It's why the Fargodome can be louder than 107,601-seat Michigan Stadium at the University of Michigan, more popularly known as the "The Big House." The Fargodome is "The Loud House" and it was common to see Bison playoff opponents befuddled by the atmosphere.

"You can't hear the guy standing next to you," Grant Olson said.

10. Media-mania.

This is a result of the geography of NDSU since Bison football is the only big show in town. It may also sound self-serving, but no FCS program gets the media attention of NDSU football and nobody comes close. It wasn't unusual for the sports information director from a school the Bison played on the road to get a tad frustrated on where to put everybody. When the Bison played Jacksonville State in the '15 title game, the NCAA had 29 media requests from folks who cover NDSU. There were three writers following Jacksonville and I'm not sure if there was anybody else. In all for the title game, NDSU sports information director Ryan Perreault fulfilled 150 requests for player interviews, which included two Tuesday media days in Fargo, a Thursday media day in Frisco and some NDSU player hometown newspaper requests by telephone.

The importance of such a media following is the dissemination of information to the fan base across the country. At the time of the '15 game, our audience reach at Forum Communications had never been higher, whether it was from the newspaper, the online version of the paper, the Bison Media Blog, WDAY-TV, WDAY.com, WDAY-AM radio or the digital cable channel.

Compare that to the 1990 Division II national title and interest in following the team was not even close.

This reasoning also includes the national spotlight that consists mainly of ESPN, which became regular visitors to the Fargodome during the playoff run and of course the two-year run of ESPN's "College GameDay." In the world of social media, the Bison became vogue for the likes of the senior producer Lee Fitting to almost regularly tweet something about the program to his 26,000-plus followers.

***

There are other factors, of course, from the fundraising to the senior leadership to the academic support staff. But it's probably a safe assumption that none of this would have happened had Darrell Mudra and a select group of Team Makers back in the mid-1960s not decided that they had enough of losing. The booster group had been together since the 1950s, but it was Mudra who convinced Fargo that it could produce a winner by raising more funds.

And that's what happened.

In 1962, the program went 0-10. Mudra was hired in 1963 and in 1964 the Bison went to the first post-season bowl game in program history beating Western State (Colo.) to complete a 10-1 season.

The final score was 14-13 and, of course, it was NDSU that made the game-clinching play stopping a Western two-point conversion with 2:48 left in the game.

The first national title came a year later.

My father's book gets into the details of how the program was built in the college division and later NCAA Division II. All of those conference and national titles had to contribute to five in a row.

Here's all you need to know about what tradition means to a program and the players that made it go:

Every year in the FCS title game, the Friday practice before championship Saturday is open to fans who want to peer through the fence at the Frisco practice complex. In NDSU's case, it's also Reunion Day for the players.

Bohl started it in 2011 when he invited all of the former players to watch practice. At the conclusion of the one-hour workout, he asked the former players to come on the field along with the current team and he gave the message to the players getting ready to play a title game that the reason they were there is because of those who were there before them.

It was the same theme on the Friday practice in 2012 and 2013. Klieman continued that tradition before the 2014 game when the Bison faced Illinois State. There were 150 former players on hand including NFL players Craig Dahl, Joe

Mays, Marcus Williams, Billy Turner and CFL players Ryan Smith and Sam Ojuri. It numbered around 200 on the Friday before the 2015 game against Jacksonville.

As Bison linebacker Carlton Littlejohn was getting ready to leave practice in 2014, he sought Mays out and the two had a talk. Mays told the Bison senior it was "his time to lead" against the Redbirds. Mays, in fact, was so engaged with the scene that he literally was almost the last one to leave.

With Bison fans milling around during the workout, there must have been at least 300 people in or around the complex. That was for a 2 p.m. practice. A couple of hours later, Illinois State had its Friday walk-through practice. There was nobody around.

"Being around college football the last 22 years as a player, coach and administrator, and traveling all over the country, there is just something special about North Dakota State when you look at the history, tradition and rivalries," Matt Larsen said. "You talk to fans who lived it, grown up here and come full circle the way they have. They used to go to games as a kid with their father or grandfather and now they're the grandfather going with their son and their grandson. The best thing for me to describe it is it's a lifestyle. North Dakota State football is a lifestyle. It's a lifestyle in the community and it's a lifestyle for the fan base. It's hard to build tradition, it's hard to build success but I think it's even harder sometimes after you've had it to keep it alive. I think we've been able to do that. When you go into a locker room after the game, you see the way the guys carry on the same traditions that were carried on 50 years ago. It's about keeping those things alive."

Of those 150 former players in '14, there was no way to count the number of championship rings walking around the complex. Klieman paid tribute to Mudra when he had the football alums gather around the players at the conclusion of practice. In a sense, the program went full circle because Mudra was Klieman's head coach at Northern Iowa in Klieman's first two seasons in 1986 and 1987.

My most memorable full circle story came a year earlier at about the same time, same place. Three weeks before the 2013 title game, Stu Orvik was sitting at his computer typing some words about a man he knew long ago. The more he thought of Jerry Schlicht, the more his eyes began to tear up. Stu was almost 77 years old and followed the NDSU success over the years. The FCS run of playoff games and titles got him thinking a lot about his old friend Jerry.

"I've thought of Jerry many times and how he'd relish these Bison teams," Orvik said.

Schlicht died in the Vietnam War a few years after college, and his name can be found on the Vietnam Veterans Memorial Wall in Washington. Former Bison player and legendary Minnesota high school coach George Thole made note of that in an article he wrote for his hometown Stillwater, Minn., newspaper.

"He was a 'copter pilot who was lost and a terrific young man," Thole wrote. "I saw his name on the Wall and I felt that he knew that I was there for him."

They were there for him that late Friday afternoon on a practice field outside of Toyota Stadium. It was the kind of gathering that Jerry would have savored.

"Big time," said Ardell Wiegandt, who played with Schlicht on the '64 team. "Jerry loved football. He loved life. He would enjoy visiting with his teammates."

Wiegandt and Schlicht were both in the Marine Corps; Wiegandt before he got to NDSU and Schlicht after. Wiegandt told the story of how Schlicht trained another former Bison player how to fly a helicopter and how the military meant so much to all of them.

"Great teammate, good friend, very patriotic guy," said Jim Driscoll, who like Wiegandt was a former Bison player and assistant coach. "I think he wanted to coach after he got out of the service, and I'm pretty sure we would have ended up coaching together. We all miss him of course."

Jerry was an offensive lineman who had big legs and a big heart. This was the same generation that went from a 0-10 program in 1962 to the first national championship in 1965. The reason about 200 former players gathered on that Friday to watch practice is because somebody had to start the football prominence. Not everybody got to enjoy watching all of the titles.

"I remember a group of guys got together and went to his funeral," Wiegandt aid. "I remember it like it was yesterday."

That was a tough day. That Friday was a fun day. There were more hugs than you would see at a big wedding. Mention the name Jerry Schlicht to players from the '60s, and they all made some reference to "good guy."

"Jerry was the kind of guy you'd want next to you in the fourth quarter," Stu said.

In 2011, the Bison found enough guys that you would want standing next to you in the fourth quarter.

In 2012, the Bison found enough guys that you would want standing next to you in the fourth quarter.

In 2013, the Bison found enough guys that you would want standing next to you in the fourth quarter.

In 2014, the Bison found enough guys that you would want standing next to you in the fourth quarter.

In 2015, the Bison found enough guys that you would want standing next to you in the fourth quarter.

The result: the greatest dynasty in the history of college football.

My oh my.

XVII. Epilogue:

The year-by-year Xs and Os

At the conclusion of every season in Division I, I wrote an analysis piece in The Forum to try and best explain what happened during that particular season. In most cases, the stories used an analytical approach backed by statistics and general observation. Some of these were pretty easy; some – like sorting through the chaotic 2009 season – were not.

Looking back, it was interesting how Bohl wondered in 2004 that if NDSU were eligible for the playoffs how far it would have gotten. Looking back, this program was really good right away at this level and I think that fact has been largely ignored over the years. When you think of the dynasty, it's not like the program went from worst to first. A huge share of credit has to go to Bohl and his staff for playing at a rather high level from the first year of a Division I schedule. It essentially took a few leaps and bounds those first two or three years and then it was steady growth from there.

Consider this the print version of the bonus content on DVD rentals.

2004
Sterling season
Stifling defense, healthy team keys to Bison success in I-AA

The 25-7 dismantling of UC Davis last Saturday was a work of speed and power by North Dakota State's football team. The Bison flew back to Fargo late that night with a highly successful 8-3 season.

A few hours later, head coach Craig Bohl was on a plane recruiting for new blood. He didn't have much time to sit back and enjoy NDSU's first season in Division I-AA because of the very reason they played so well: the Bison lose 20 seniors.

"All those guys walking out the door," Bohl said. "It would have been interesting if we were eligible for the playoffs how deep we would have gone."

NDSU peaked the last three weeks beating ranked teams Northwestern State (La.) and Davis. Most people close to the program thought 7-4 would have been a good year.

But 8-3?

"I would have liked to have gone 9-2," Bohl said. "But 8-3 … yeah, it's pretty good."

It was pretty good for three principle reasons: a few players played above preseason expectations, the team stayed relatively healthy and the defense was a work of art.

Defense never rests

Opponents averaged 3.2 yards per carry. They got only 13.6 points per game. They threw 17 interceptions and fumbled 11 times. Several times, the Bison defense bordered on dominant.

"We really worked to make teams one-dimensional by shutting down their running game," Bohl said. "That's when all those other things came about like interceptions."

Eight different players picked off a pass, led by Matt Gorman's five. Safety Craig Dahl had three and linebacker Brian Erenberg, linebacker Jayd Kittelson and safety Jared Essler had two each. The defense really had only two bad series all season: the first drive by Carson-Newman (Tenn.) when the Indians' option offense briefly befuddled NDSU's line and the last drive by South Dakota State when the Jackrabbits drove 80 yards in 14 plays without a time out in the final 2:34 to beat NDSU 24-21. That stands as the season low point for Bohl. "I was disappointed that we underachieved against South Dakota State," he said. NDSU's three losses were by a combined eight points, but Bohl doesn't subscribe to the "what if " theory. "I think it all works out in the end," he said.

Better than advertised

Noseguard Isaac Snell finished with 11 tackles for lost yardage, two quarterback sacks, two pass breakups, three quarterback hurries and 55 tackles. That doesn't include the countless times he disrupted a play with penetration into the backfield. "I thought the makings of a good defense were there," Bohl said. "But I also thought we needed a couple of players to exceed what we thought they could do."

Snell heads that list. Junior defensive ends Alvin Robinson and Isaac Lavant, two junior college transfers, were effective nearly every game. And cornerback Bobby Babich had a solid season leading the team in pass breakups with 10.

Moreover, Babich never got beat deep – something that happened his first two seasons.

On offense, tight end A.J. Cooper was an instant hit. He finished second on the team in receptions with 23.

And perhaps no Bison quarterback has ever had a better backup season than freshman Steve Walker. He eventually took over the starting job and finished

47 of 60 for a school record 78 percent, which topped Chris Simdorn's old mark of 68 percent (34 of 50 in 1988).

For the health of it

With 57 receptions and nine touchdowns, receiver Travis White was a picture of consistency. Bohl liked having running backs Kyle Steffes and Cinque Chapman share most of the carries because it kept both of them fresh over the long haul. Good health, in essence, was a team theme.

Receiver Allen Burrell and offensive tackle Tim Popowski were the only starters to miss games because of injury and their absence was limited. Burrell was out one game but was not at full strength in others because of an ankle strain. Popowski missed a game because of a knee strain. Freshman Nate Safe filled in fine for Popowski and receiver was perhaps the deepest position on the team so their loss was cushioned. The minimal injuries were important because they didn't have to spend time juggling their lineup and depth at some positions was questionable.

A look ahead

The biggest loss is four-year starting center Rob Hunt. Hands down. The Bison also lose left tackle Nick Zilka and, most likely, left guard Justin Monson. He's waiting to hear an NCAA appeal on his eligibility.

Safe and sophomores Jake Erickson and Adam Tadisch are the front runners to replace them.

Although Walker – who took over for Tony Stauss, the program's all-time leader in completions with 345 – has the inside track, Bohl said that quarterback position will be open in spring ball between Walker, freshman Andy Thoreson and redshirt freshman Ryan Parsons.

On defense, junior noseguard Rodney Thompson played well the last few games. Sophomore Justin Frick took a regular rotation with Summerville at tackle. Either Lavant or Robinson may fill in for departed end Travis Ware.

Sophomore Tony Bizal may be the heir apparent to Essler, a three-year starter at free safety. Junior Scott Walter is back at cornerback, and Bohl said he's hoping freshmen cornerbacks Symeon Cabell and Dave Earl mature.

Freshman Joe Mays and junior Kole Zimmerman took regular turns at inside linebacker. The Bison also like redshirt freshmen Mike Maresh and Nick Compton.

But filling holes for 20 seniors will take more than spring football and probably more than fall camp. Considering the competition, the Bison had more quality wins this season than they had in a long time.

"With the schedule that we played, to me, it felt like the program is moving in the right direction," Bohl said.

2005
Bison football season just OK

North Dakota State left Natchitoches, La., the evening of Sept. 10 with a 35-7 win over then 11th-ranked Northwestern State. Suddenly, the unthinkable – the players' preseason goal of finishing in the top 10 of the ESPN/USA Today top 25 poll – seemed reasonable. Two years into Division I-AA football and already the Bison had a highly ranked team figured out on the road. Not so fast.

Reality set in at Montana State, California Poly, California Davis and Southern Illinois – all losses. The Bison finished 7-4 and just missed a spot in the poll. They were 3-2 and tied for third in the Great West Football Conference.

"It's OK," said Bison head coach Craig Bohl of the season. "It's OK. I knew going in that it was a very aggressive schedule. I would say there's going to be no gnashing of the teeth, but the impetus going into the offseason will be to make some improvements."

The 2005 season can be summarized in three parts: good defense, average offense and inconsistent special teams.

NDSU led the Great West in most of the principal defensive statistical categories, like scoring defense, at 13.7 points per game.

Although the offense wasn't a prolific scoring machine – mostly due to the preseason loss of leading receiver Travis White to a knee injury – it did take care of the football. The Bison were a plus-11 in turnover margin and that alone kept them in most games.

"Our offense didn't put the defense in a lot of tough situations," Bohl said.

Injuries to White and fullback Tyler Roehl – a broken leg in spring practice – forced the Bison to alter their offensive attack. Last year, the Bison had sprinter Allen Burrell and White to make defenses respect the deep pass.

This year, only senior Marques Johnson had that kind of breakaway speed. Virtually gone was the threat of the long bomb.

"What became apparent to us is to move the football, it had to be on the ground," Bohl said.

And most of that was done by junior Kyle Steffes. He finished with 1,071 yards rushing on 242 attempts. Because of injuries, it took sophomore Cinque Chapman until late in the year before he found the form that made him a big contributor his freshman season.

More often than not, that left it up to the defense. It responded with shutouts of Weber State (Utah) and Northern Colorado, and held playoff-bound Nicholls State (La.) to 13 points.

The Bison averaged 9.3 points in their four losses.

Still, the offense and defense were for the most part consistent. The same can't be said for the special teams.

It was hot with returner Shamen Washington and punter Mike Dragosavich.

It was cold with a couple of punts blocked and some mental errors at inopportune times.

A blocked punt was the difference in a 20-14 loss to Davis and a bad snap and touching a punt downfield resulted in a 9-0 loss at Southern Illinois.

Kicker Cory Vartanian had an off year, finishing 8 of 18 on field goals.

But considering the tougher schedule than 2004, when the Bison went 8-3, this season can be considered more of a success simply because of the competition. Four foes – No. 8 Cal Poly, No. 9 Southern Illinois, No. 16 Montana State and No. 21 Nicholls State – finished in the top 25. Weber State and Davis also received votes.

The Bison finished 19th in the I-AA.org power poll.

"Unless you play Montana State on the road, Southern Illinois on the road and Cal Poly on the road, you're not going to know what you're shooting for," Bohl said. With 2005 behind them, the Bison are shooting for the playoffs in 2008 – the first year they're eligible. So far, they're on the right road.

2006

Surprising Bison

Team beats long odds with near-flawless season

A record Fargodome crowd witnessed the capping of an unforeseen success story last Saturday night. North Dakota State's 41-28 victory over South Dakota State secured two main Bison goals: a Great West Football Conference title and the retention of the Dakota Marker.

NDSU finished 10-1 and was ranked fourth in the latest Division I-AA playoffs. Say that in August and you probably would have needed your head examined.

It just didn't seem possible because the Bison had: 1) Their toughest schedule in years with games against I-A Ball State (Ind.) and the University of Minnesota. 2) Six games in a seven-week stretch away from home, their most demanding road schedule ever. 3) Questions concerning depth, particularly in the defensive line, where Justin Frick was the only returning starter. 4) Young cornerbacks who had yet to consistently see top-notch receivers on a Saturday basis. 5) Lost their top playmaker in sophomore Shamen Washington (knee) and its most experienced offensive lineman in Justin Buckwalter (back) during fall practice.

6) Their top two offensive weapons – quarterback Steve Walker and receiver Travis White – returning from serious knee injuries.

So much for doubt.

This team exceeded expectations. How? Why?

You can point to generalities like great senior leadership, talent at the skill positions and a potent set of linebackers.

But behind the green and yellow curtain, the secret to this year's success was the uncanny ability to take a third-down play and convert it into a first down.

It's called third-down conversion and the Bison were successful 54 percent of the time.

Not only did it keep the ball in NDSU's possession, but it kept the Bison defense on the sideline for another few minutes. Give that unit some rest and the result was one of Division I-AA's best defenses against the run.

"When you're moving the chains like that, that has an impact on a whole lot of variables," said NDSU head coach Craig Bohl.

Variables like field position, time of possession, time for defensive coaches to make adjustments and momentum. The conductor in all of this was Walker.

In one stretch against Stephen F. Austin and Georgia Southern, Walker completed 11 of 13 passes on third down. He was 7 of 10 against Minnesota and 7 of 9 versus Southern Utah on third down.

For the season, Walker completed 43 of 67 passes with third down staring the Bison in the face – a success rate of 64 percent.

Ironically, his worst third-down passing game was against California Davis, when he was 3 of 7. Yet, the Bison were 10 of 11 on third down in the second half, a game in which NDSU set a team record for biggest comeback with a 28-24 win. The game-winner, a 10-yard touchdown pass to John Majeski with 4 seconds left, came, naturally, on third down.

That clutch play showed this team's poise and maturity. True, Walker was the player throwing the ball on third down, but somebody had to block for him and somebody had to run past the first-down marker and catch the ball.

Against California Poly, the Bison were 9 of 12 on third down. The offense was so efficient that the Bison defense was only on the field for 38 plays.

"That's unheard of," Bohl said. "A lot of times, that's a half of football."

The improvement didn't happen by accident. After last season, the Bison coaches reevaluated pass routes. They took a hard look at their West Coast offense and how they could put their players in better spots.

"We were disappointed last year with the West Coast offense," Bohl said. "Overall, Steve threw the ball with more authority and better accuracy."

Sophomore Kole Heckendorf was Walker's favorite target with 52 catches for 752 yards. Heckendorf also displayed marked improvement from last year, showing a better ability to get open. He benefited from increased strength and conditioning and the return of fellow receiver White, who missed the entire 2005 season with a torn ACL.

With more offensive weapons, the Bison scored 40 times in the 47 drives that reached inside their opponents' 20-yard line. It's called the red zone and never was that more damaging than in the last two minutes of the first half.

NDSU struck in the final two minutes of the first half in seven games this season, including scores with no time, 6 seconds, 9 seconds and 19 seconds remaining. The most notable was a 39-yard "Hail Mary" against Ball State that White tipped to Heckendorf. It cut the Cardinals' lead to 14-13 and set the stage for an upset.

It also set the stage for the season. Although NDSU does not count in the official I-AA statistics because it is reclassifying from Division II, the Bison would have been sixth in scoring offense at 34.0 points per game and fourth in rushing defense at 67.2 yards per game.

An outstanding trio of returning linebackers did their part. As expected, senior safety Craig Dahl set a school record for most career solo tackles. But the rapid development of the defensive line was a pleasant surprise to the Bison coaches.

Frick, a three-year starter, was the anchor. But freshman Mike Fairbairn established himself as a solid noseguard and senior defensive ends Brian Dahl and Alex Kingsley had, by a mile, their best seasons.

Unexpected contributors, veteran leadership, poise and maturity: that's how this team went 10-1.

2007

Banner year

Despite losing to South Dakota State, the Bison football team enjoyed another successful season in its rise to full-fledged Division I status

It was like North Dakota State led for 5,279 feet in the mile run. The Bison were beaten at the finish line – that last foot – by South Dakota State in NDSU's race for its two main goals this season: a Great West Football Conference title and a No. 1 ranking in a national poll.

But 10-1 is 10-1. And you don't get to 10 wins in Division I Football Championship Subdivision without a lot of things going right. In the case of 2007, that was:

• An effective rushing attack led by Tyler Roehl.

- An efficient – and timely – passing offense led by Steve Walker.
- A decent defense led by Joe Mays.
- An adequate kicking game led by Mike Dragosavich.

It was NDSU's second straight 10-1 season, although this one had a different feel. The offense was better than 2006 and the defense was worse than 2006.

The proof was in the statistics. The Bison averaged 39.5 points this year compared to 34.0 last year. On the other side, NDSU gave up an average of 22.3 points this year compared to 13.4 last year.

Whoever coined the phrase "defense wins championships" was right. SDSU stopped NDSU when it counted.

Those stats were reflected in head coach Craig Bohl's comments when asked about his team's strength and weakness this season.

The strength: "I think it was the ability to run the football. In the games that we were able to control, we were able to run the football."

The weakness: "Giving up big plays on defense. And there were times our special teams, even though we had good people in place, didn't perform as well as we were expecting it to be."

That was never more evident than in the 29-24 loss to SDSU last week. The Bison gave up a 94-yard punt return for a touchdown, had a punt blocked that led to another touchdown and fumbled a kickoff that the Jackrabbits turned into a field goal.

But that was about as ugly as NDSU's season got. Most teams would kill to have their season lowlight limited to one paragraph.

The Bison won 10 games starting with Roehl, a converted fullback who turned in one of the most productive seasons in Bison history. He had 207 carries for 1,431 yards and received national love on ESPN on a magical day in October when the Bison beat the Gophers 27-21.

His school-record 263 yards came in front of 63,088 fans at the Metrodome – the largest crowd ever to see a Bison football game.

"During certain games, he was dominating," Bohl said. "In other games, he was effective."

Although not so much dominating, Walker had a very effective senior year. He completed 166 of 248 passes (67 percent) for 2,327 yards and 19 touchdowns. He leaves NDSU with six of the school's major passing records.

And nobody will soon forget his last-second touchdown passes to beat Sam Houston State and Cal Poly.

"At times, he was magical," Bohl said.

NDSU was facing a 1-1 record when Walker took over at his own 46 with just 26 seconds left. People had already left the Fargodome, resigned to a loss.

But Walker hit Kole Heckendorf for 27 yards. After stopping the clock with an incomplete pass, he hit Heckendorf again for the game-winner with 77 seconds remaining.

NDSU 41, Sam Houston 38.

Several weeks later, NDSU was facing its first loss again – only this one looked even gloomier. The Bison had the ball at their own 8 with 1:05 left. A penalty brought them back to the 4.

But Walker scrambled for 16 yards to the 20. On the next play, he hit Heckendorf – who else – for an 80-yard touchdown with 38 seconds remaining.

NDSU 31, Cal Poly 28.

"He's a fearless leader," Bohl said.

He was one of the many reasons Bison fans flocked to the dome in record numbers. NDSU averaged 18,141 fans to set a mark for the second consecutive year. And Bohl doesn't think it will stop there.

"The image of the football program is good," Bohl said, "and I would be really surprised next year if we don't have more demand for tickets."

The Bison finished the regular season fifth in the FCS coaches poll and were third in the College Sporting News Gridiron Power Index behind unbeatens Northern Iowa and McNeese State (La.).

The image hit a peak in the Minnesota win. So, too, perhaps did the emotional state of this team.

That was the game the players had targeted all offseason. It was, after all, the only loss in 2006 and revenge is a built-in motivator for players.

The win came on Oct. 20 – or the seventh game of the year – against a Big Ten Conference team. After that, NDSU played OK in beating Southern Utah, had a solid night in beating Illinois State and had marginal games against Cal Poly and SDSU. Asked if NDSU peaked at the Minnesota game, Bohl said, "That's a fair question. I know our players looked at that game as an important game and we were pleased that we won. I know it's difficult to reach a peak 11 Saturdays in a row." But in the end, even if it was the peak, what a peak it was. And, in the end, 10-1 is 10-1. That's an outstanding season.

2008
Fourth quarter blues
Late-game struggles derail NDSU's big expectations

The first three years in Craig Bohl's tenure as the head football coach at North Dakota State ended at 8-3 and back-to-back 7-4 seasons. Considering the transition from NCAA Division II to Division I, they were met with successful evaluations.

Then came back-to-back 10-1 seasons and No. 1 rankings in the Division I Football Championship Subdivision. There were wins over Football Bowl Subdivision teams Minnesota, Ball State and Central Michigan.

Things were really right with the program.

About the only thing missing was a playoff bid and that was only because NDSU was ineligible because of NCAA reclassification rules. But last week, the Bison lost for the second straight year to South Dakota State and subsequently finished 6-5 – the worst record in Bohl's six years at the school. For the first time since the program went 2-8 in 2002, the follow-up question to the season was this:

What went wrong?

How did the team go from ranked No. 1 in the FCS coaches poll in the second week of the season to out of the national picture:? It wasn't attitude and it wasn't team chemistry, Bohl said. He lauded his team's work habits and said the leadership of the seniors was up to expectations.

This was a team that outscored its opponents 329-211. It had 41 touchdowns to its opponents' 23. Offensively, the team ranked in the middle to near the top in the Missouri Valley Football Conference in most offensive categories and was on top or near the top in most of the defensive categories.

They were not the statistics of a 6-5 team. But consider the following: In the fourth quarter against league teams, the Bison were 25 of 53 passing (47 percent) with six interceptions. Four of NDSU's losses ended with interceptions when the Bison had the chance to drive for a potential game-tying or winning score. The late-game slide started at the University of Wyoming when NDSU was 0 of 6 with one interception in the fourth quarter.

The Cowboys won 16-13 on a last-second field goal.

"When the game was on the line and when we needed to move the ball well, for a variety of reasons, we were not able to do it," Bohl said.

Look no further than third down plays as evidence. The Bison had a 39 percent third down conversion rate, which ranked them sixth in the league and was far below past years, which Bohl admitted "was a little bit off the charts."

"Sometimes, you get lulled into a sense of comfort zone as far as third down," he said. "This year, we were opposite."

Certainly, the inexperience of quarterback Nick Mertens showed. It was the fourth year in the program for the junior, but his first as a starter. He came into the season with only 14 passing attempts.

But there was more to this team's offensive faults than the quarterback. The receivers either ran poor routes or dropped passes at key times, top playmaker Kole Heckendorf dealt with a nagging turf toe injury, running back Tyler Roehl suffered an early-season ankle sprain and the offensive line struggled with injuries and run blocking, especially early in the conference season,

Roehl was a second team preseason All-American pick by The Sports Network. Pat Paschall came in as arguably one of the top No. 2 backs in the league. NDSU's West Coast offense is known as a physical, run-first look, but eventually, a lack of a passing attack cost the Bison.

Teams routinely put eight – sometimes nine – players close to the line of scrimmage in an area commonly known as "the box." Although the offensive numbers were decent, the Bison were never able to make a Missouri Valley team pay dearly for that. That will be an offseason emphasis, Bohl said.

Against Western Illinois, the Bison had five rushing attempts for 2 yards in the fourth quarter. They lost 27-22. But no more was the lack of final-quarter offense more glaring than against the Jackrabbits.

Leading 21-17, NDSU took over at its 44-yard line with 14:45 left in the game. Three plays gained 3 yards. The Bison got the ball back at their own 36. Three plays lost 8 yards. After a partially blocked punt, they got the ball at the SDSU 29 with 8:15 remaining. Three plays netted 7 yards.

In those three possessions combined, the Bison had four rushes for 13 yards. Mertens was 2 of 5 passing for just 4 yards.

"We've got to be diversified enough to move the football," Bohl said. "For us to have the attitude that we're going to pound the football and run it, that's a little short-sighted."

Not all about 2008 was short sighted. Roehl finished with 1,075 yards and ended his career among the all-time leaders on the NDSU rushing chart. Mertens' 2,004 yards passing ranked him third in the Missouri Valley.

The defensive line registered 39 quarterback sacks and the Bison ranked first in FCS pass defense allowing 116.8 yards in the air. In the league, NDSU was first in total defense giving up 254.0 yards per game and first in fewest first downs allowed at 15.1 a game.

The one adjustment NDSU's Tampa 2 defense will address in the offseason is finding a better way to stop an opposing quarterback from gaining too many yards on the ground. The Bison had trouble controlling a basic quarterback-running back option play too many times.

That play perhaps exposed a fault in the Tampa 2, a defense that first became popular in the NFL with the Tampa Bay Buccaneers. But the NFL doesn't have to deal with many running quarterbacks. Colleges like NDSU do. Youngstown State and Northern Iowa were effective getting their quarterbacks some space.

"Those are fairly large schematic adjustments," Bohl said. That's stuff for meetings and planning sessions. And they'll probably involve more than just Tampa 2 talk. NDSU certainly doesn't need a complete overhaul, but some tweaking is in order. "We didn't produce on the field like I thought we could," Bohl said. "The year didn't go how I thought it would go."

2009

Slipped away

NDSU's 3-8 season that started with problems stemming from this past spring's flood can be blamed on 7 plays that went wrong

It was just never smooth from the get-go. The North Dakota State football season started in early August with the first day of practice, but in reality, the season starts in January with winter workouts.

A major flood practically washed out spring football. And rarely did a month go by where there wasn't some sort of player disciplinary matter.

"We're spending a great deal of time with the returning players to establish leadership and make sure we don't have all the distractions that we had," said head coach Craig Bohl. "Character and personal behavior had an effect and it spilled over to the year."

Spilled, indeed. In the pretend world of football do-overs, NDSU would like about eight of them this fall. That's how many losses the Bison endured and in seven of those instances, a case can be made where one play made the difference.

Seven plays. They failed every time.

When push came to shove, the Bison got pushed and, that was the theme of the 3-8 season. Certainly, injuries and youth were factors, but to say that would have made a difference in the victory column is conjecture at best.

The seven plays in order are a 51-yard pass by Sam Houston State, a third-down incompletion against Southern Illinois, a personal foul penalty against Illinois State, an incomplete pass against Northern Iowa, a 3-yard loss against South Dakota State, a fumble against Missouri State and a 1-yard loss against Youngstown State.

Too simple? Perhaps. The irony in the seven plays is six were committed by the offense – and it was the Bison defense that was the weakness this season.

At one point in the Division I Football Championship Subdivision statistics, NDSU was ranked 104th out of 118 teams in total defense. So to pen any blame on an offense that currently has the top-ranked rusher in the FCS, is eighth in rushing offense and 19th in total offense doesn't make sense. At any rate, the good teams make the clutch plays and who's to say if the Bison reversed those seven plays that something else wouldn't have happened. The only game the Bison lost where one play didn't make a difference was the season opener at Iowa State, although Bohl said a Bison fumble on the 1-yard line in the first quarter hurt. They were within 24-17 late in the third quarter, but the Cyclones dominated from there to win 34-17. Otherwise, a season of "what ifs?" has turned to "what now?"

2010
Fast-paced progress
Bison improved, and then some in 2010

The season started with the athletic director saying he needed to see improvement in the North Dakota State football program. It didn't take long.

The Bison opened the season with a 6-3 victory at the University of Kansas of the Big 12 Conference and whatever the doubts the players had from the previous 3-8 season were a distant memory. On Saturday, a stirring run in the Division I Football Championship Subdivision playoffs ended in a quarterfinal overtime 38-31 heartbreaker at Eastern Washington.

Program improvement? Of course, no question.

"At the end of the day, it was a great ride for us," said running back D.J. McNorton.

What the postseason wins over Robert Morris University and Montana State did more than anything is restore expectations to the program. When head coach Craig Bohl took the job in 2003, he said the plan was to compete for a national title by the first year of postseason eligibility in 2008.

In the last four months, belief in a national presence for NDSU has taken a dramatic turn for the better. An outstanding freshman class has the ingredients of making a national title return to Texas. Only instead of the old Division II championships in McAllen, the FCS title game is in Frisco, located just outside of Dallas.

"We have a lot of guys coming back so we'll go after it," said linebacker Preston Evans.

But in order to take the semifinal and final playoff steps, and complete Bohl's title quest, the Bison need to find a complete offense and that means a passing game.

They now have an entire offseason to figure it out.

This program hasn't had successful passing statistics since 2007 when Steve Walker threw at a 67 percent clip. From 2003-07, the Bison West Coast offense had passing percentages of 67, 67, 56, 64 and 67.

NDSU was 161 of 308 this season for 52 percent. It was more glaring in the three postseason games completing 27 of 67 passes for 40 percent.

The Bison were at 55 percent in 2009 and 58 percent in 2008. Keep in mind the top two quarterbacks this year, Brock Jensen and Jose Mohler, were a freshman and sophomore respectively.

Keep in mind Walker was a sophomore when he had his subpar-for-him 56 percent completion season in 2005.

You can't pin it all on the pitchers, either; the catchers had their issues. There was a lack of depth at receiver. The fourth guy on the depth chart did not have a single reception and that needs to be addressed.

We're talking tweaking, not a major overhaul here, either. Semifinal teams Eastern Washington and Georgia Southern completed 57 and 51 percent of their passing attempts. Delaware is at 67 percent and Villanova 66.

The Bison also need to address replacing defensive tackle Matthew Gratzek, offensive lineman Michael Arndt and depth at cornerback. But, unlike last year at this time, there are not a lot of holes to fill. The expectations and subsequently anticipation have returned.

2011

Molding a champ

All three facets of team turned Bison into title contenders

About the only thing missing with this Division I Football Championship Subdivision title season was a tickertape parade. And even that was suggested.

It all came together this season, a plan put in place by head coach Craig Bohl when he took the North Dakota State coaching position in 2003. There were a couple of delays in construction, but the 17-6 victory over Sam Houston State (Texas) in Frisco, Texas, validated what he's been saying all along: This program has the potential to be the best.

It wasn't looking that way when the Bison went 3-8 two years ago. But the rally of talent was almost stunning, starting with last season's playoff run that ended in the quarterfinals.

This will officially close the books on 2009, because you cannot ignore a virtual worst-to-first story.

We'll break it down into three familiar categories: offense, defense and special teams. All three played a prominent role, and any analysis of a championship without crediting all three would be an injustice.

All three areas had players that either performed better than expected or came out of nowhere. For instance, at this time last year, Matt Voigtlander was going through winter workouts as a running back hoping for more carries this fall.

He ended up being the second most valuable player in the national title game. As a punter.

And within the three areas of offense, defense and special teams, we'll further break it down as to why this team finished 14-1.

On offense, the passing game improved. On defense, the Bison found a replacement for graduated tackle Matt Gratzek. On special teams, they found Voigtlander. Team-wise, Bohl cited better depth and good leadership as reasons for the success. "The seniors did a great job of bringing the younger players along," he said. Offense. Defense. Special teams. It all came together in December and January.

Breaking down each area:

Offense

Last year's 46 percent completion percentage in the FCS playoffs served notice to what everybody saw during most of the 2010 season: The passing game needed work.

"It had to significantly change," Bohl said.

It was a point of emphasis last spring when the starting quarterback spot was a battle between Brock Jensen and Esley Thorton. Jensen won the job and then rewarded his team with a breakout season.

He led the FCS in completion percentage for most of the season and finished 219 of 326 for 67 percent. His 2,524 yards set a school single-season record. And he threw 14 touchdowns to just four interceptions.

Plus, that translated into better third-down efficiency; The Bison were 71 of 168 for 42 percent.

"It kept our defense off the field and allowed them to play fresher," Bohl said.

Jensen, of course, couldn't have done it without a steady offensive line and better receivers. Senior Warren Holloway set a single-season school record with 77 receptions for 1,003 yards, just the second NDSU receiver to eclipse 1,000.

"That was an element of our offense that we had not had," Bohl said.

The big surprise, however, was the emergence of Ryan Smith. Formerly a backup running back – like the punter Voigtlander – he moved to receiver last spring and flourished this season with 44 receptions.

Injuries to starter Zach Vraa and regular Trevor Gebhart turned Smith's production from needed to critical. With a real passing game, opponents had to concentrate on more than just NDSU's running game.

"No longer could they put nine men in the box," said Bohl, referring to nine defensive players playing the run.

The result: Sophomore Sam Ojuri and senior D.J. McNorton each went over 1,000 yards rushing.

Defense

Gratzek was a beast in 2010, with Bohl calling him arguably the best defensive tackle in the Missouri Valley Football Conference. It's a crucial position in NDSU's 4-3 defensive scheme because if that spot is soft, other breakdowns are imminent.

A trio of sophomores came through.

Noseguard Ryan Drevlow and tackles Leevon Perry and Justin Juckem rotated at all three spots. They were disruptive. All three were instrumental in the playoffs, and so was the defense as a whole for that matter.

"We played outstanding defense in the playoffs," Bohl said.

James Madison, Lehigh, Georgia Southern and Sam Houston State would agree. NDSU gave up just one touchdown in its last three postseason games.

Linebackers Chad Willson and Preston Evans and safety Colten Heagle led the way with 99, 88 and 82 tackles respectively on the season. But the next three tacklers in line – linebacker Travis Beck, cornerback Christian Dudzik and linebacker Carlton Littlejohn – were all redshirt freshmen in 2010.

Beck went from a role player in fall practice to the most valuable player in the championship game. With a bevy of players rotating everywhere, the defenders collectively led the FCS in scoring defense, giving up just 12.7 points a game.

Defense wins championships. In 2009, NDSU gave up 28.6 points a game.

The Bison intercepted 21 passes – led by sophomore Marcus Williams' seven – and recovered 10 fumbles.

That led to NDSU's plus-18 in the all-important turnover margin.

Special teams

Sam Houston head coach Willie Fritz called NDSU's kickoff coverage team the best he saw this year. Although there were a few blips during the year, the NDSU special teams helped much more than it hurt.

Convincing Voigtlander to concentrate solely on punting was key. The Bison led the FCS in 2010 in net punting average, which translated into a huge field-position edge.

After a slow start, Voigtlander finished with a 41.0-yard average with 25 of his 66 punts landing inside the 20-yard line. The net punting average of 36.6 may have been below 2010's 39.1, but it approached its efficiency.

Not many kickers in the FCS were as efficient as Ryan Jastram when it came to field goals. He nailed 16 of 18, including 8 of 9 from 30-39 yards and 3 of 4 from 40-49 yards. He made his only attempt over 50.

More importantly, he made his last 10 attempts, with his last miss a 46-yarder into the wind at South Dakota State on Oct. 22. Jastram made his only attempt in the FCS title game.

2012
Discipline keys repeat

Passion of the fans surrounded championship team, but players kept it in check between the sidelines

The final NCAA statistics for the Division I Football Championship Subdivision are complete, with the exception of one category: Fanaticism.

It's hard to accurately measure, but North Dakota State led the country on the Passion Scale by virtue of having the loudest venue and also buying the most tickets for the title game before the playoffs even began.

In both cases, it really wasn't close.

They flocked to Frisco, Texas, by the thousands to see their team defeat Sam Houston State 39-13 for the FCS title, the second straight for the Bison. They saw an opportunistic offense that made some big plays and a defense that continued to be its consistent self.

Those are general observations.

But if you were to get down to the statistical nitty gritty, an analysis by The Forum can easily point to the Big D.

Defense?

Not specifically. We're talking about discipline.

Perhaps no category measures that better than personal fouls or unsportsmanlike conduct penalties, the latter of which are usually taunting or disrespectful comments and do not involve physical contact. The Bison did not commit either penalty in their four-game playoff march to the FCS title. In fact, they had just one in their last eight games – a 15-yarder in a regular-season game against South Dakota State. That's discipline. On the season, NDSU was flagged with seven personal foul or unsportsmanlike conduct penalties in 15 games, with three of those coming in one game against Northern Iowa. In contrast, Bison opponents had 19 of those major infractions.

Some of them hurt, like the three Georgia Southern picked up in the semifinals at the Fargodome. That did not include a roughing-the-passer penalty on NDSU quarterback Brock Jensen that came in the Bison's game-winning drive in the fourth quarter, capped by Jensen's 5-yard touchdown run on fourth down.

Another penalty statistic of note: NDSU was whistled for roughing-the-passer just once all season in an age when referees seemingly watch it closer than they used to.

True, the Bison led the FCS in scoring defense, giving up 11.5 points per game. Only 17 teams in the entire division gave up less than 20, with four of them in the Missouri Valley Football Conference.

True, NDSU was first in total defense, giving up 234.5 yards per game; first in first-down defense, surrendering 12.7 a game; second in passing defense at 140.5 yards per game; and fourth in rushing defense at 93.8 yards per game.

But with the exception of Marcus Williams' No. 5 ranking in interceptions, you would be hard-pressed to find many Bison players among the top 100 in any defensive individual categories.

Not many stars? No problem. Team defense takes discipline – the ability to do your assigned task and trust the other defensive players to do theirs.

Moreover, it takes discipline to constantly rotate defensive linemen and secondary players and not lose a beat.

NDSU had no players among the top 100 in tackles for lost yardage. Middle linebacker Grant Olson finished 24th in total tackles, and defensive end Cole Jirik was 65th in quarterback sacks.

The only other Bison players to appear on the top 100 leaderboard in a category were linebackers Carlton Littlejohn and Travis Beck and safety Christian Dudzik.

Littlejohn and Beck tied for 38th in forced fumbles with .27 a game, and Littlejohn and Dudzik tied for 39th in fumbles recovered at .2 per contest.

Yet, opponents found scoring on the Bison very difficult this year.

The offense also contributed to the discipline mode. Overall, NDSU was 16th in the FCS in fewest penalties. The Bison were second in time of possession, keeping the ball for an average of 34 minutes, 21 seconds – just one second behind leader Eastern Kentucky.

Being ranked high in that category takes some clutch third-down plays. NDSU was seventh in third-down conversions with a 50.7 percent success rate.

Like the defense, there were real no individual stars. Jensen was 50th in passing efficiency, down from 23rd a season ago.

Junior Sam Ojuri was 65th in rushing at 74.8 yards per game, although teammate John Crockett was right behind at No. 72.

Left tackle Billy Turner was a consensus first-team All-America pick, but it took Turner and the rest of the offensive line to fuel the second-half onslaught against Sam Houston. In the end, it was 22 starters, a kicker, punter and long snapper and key backups that paved the way to back-to-back titles. It's why football is considered one of those ultimate team games.

2013
Perfect trey

A couple of key areas helped NDSU complete an unbeaten season and its third consecutive national championship

It's been a week since greatness in the NCAA Division I FCS was redefined. North Dakota State completed a 15-0 season with its third straight national title.

The reasons, of course, were many, and you could probably write a book to detail every one of them. The numbers don't lie, though, and here's a couple to chew on:

The Bison gave up an average of 0.9 points in the fourth quarter. Pretty tough to lose a game when the opponents can't even average one point in the final 15 minutes when the game is usually on the line.

The University of New Hampshire had a first-and-goal from the North Dakota State 1-yard line with under a minute remaining in the FCS semifinals. It took three plays, but the Wildcats eventually scored to pull within 52-14.

Two months earlier, Missouri State faced a fourth-and-7 from the Bison 11-yard line. The Bears took timeout. What resulted was an 11-yard touchdown pass with six minutes left in the game to make it 41-26.

Those would be the only two touchdowns the Bison surrendered in the fourth quarter all season. NDSU even fought the Missouri State score by blocking the extra point.

"A couple things," said Chris Klieman, the defensive coordinator who is now the head coach. "One, we're a well-conditioned team. Those kids in the fourth quarter get strong. Second, it shows that our kids have a great memory of what happened to them in the first, second and third quarters, because a lot of offenses are what you see is what you get, and they don't have all the other adjustments. Our kids adjust extremely well as the game goes on."

Third-down excellence

While Marshall took the Randy Moss-led offensive explosive route to its unbeaten season in 1996, the Bison took the defensive path. Although the offense was pretty good, too.

The Bison averaged 12.7 points a game in the second quarter, so in essence – considering the NDSU defense gave up an average of 11.3 points a game – it took the offense just one quarter to better that. The telling point in that is NDSU perhaps made a few adjustments after the feeling-out first quarter and effectively put them into action in the second.

Depending on the flow of a game, the most important down is typically third, where on offense teams can keep a drive alive and on defense can get off the field. NDSU dominated the FCS on that down, leading the country both on offense and defense.

That's unheard of.

"That's really rare," Klieman said.

Its defensive rate of allowing opponents to convert 26 percent of the time easily led the subdivision. Teams were successful 54 times in 205 attempts.

On offense, the Bison converted 108 of 195 third downs for a 55 percent success clip. Those two statistics directly resulted in the Bison holding a 33 minute, 40 seconds to 26:19 average time of possession edge, a figure that put them second in the FCS behind Charleston Southern.

"It shows we're getting off the field on third down and getting it back to our offense, and they're converting those," Klieman said.

Special teams excellence

Football, however, is a game of three phases – offense, defense and special teams. The latter had its share of shining moments, too.

The punting game was a field-position gold mine. Of Ben LeCompte's 52 punts, almost half – 25 – ended up inside the opponents' 20-yard line.

Moreover, NDSU gave up just 21 punt return yards all season, with 12 coming on one return in the title game against Towson. LeCompte, perhaps, was one of the most underrated of the FCS postseason All-America team players this season.

NDSU never allowed a kickoff return for a touchdown and did not give up any momentum-swinging big plays in the punting or field-goal game. Ask Towson.

Colten Heagle's blocked field goal with the score tied 7-7 in the second quarter was the big play in the 35-7 title game win. The Tigers never seriously threatened to score again.

It was NDSU's 24th straight win, which ties an FCS record. It was its 43rd victory in the last 45 games, and the three straight titles ties the FCS mark set by Appalachian State.

The Bison also joined the 1989 Georgia Southern team and the 1996 Marshall team as the only squads to go through the FCS – or Division I-AA until the name change – with unbeaten title seasons.

Leadership excellence

NDSU did it with good players, certainly. But there was much more to the equation, such as leadership and dedication. Klieman said the second-half dominance of his team is a direct attribute to strength and conditioning coach Jim Kramer.

The Bison had the luxury of experience with 24 seniors.

"The leadership of those upperclassmen," Klieman said. "The juniors and seniors had that will that they were not going to have that letdown. We had a couple of poor quarters – I don't think we played well early against Illinois State, Northern Iowa or Southern Illinois – but we always settled in."

In the end, they settled into a national title.

2014

Eye-opening opener

Turning point in North Dakota State's season probably came in first game

Perhaps the turning point came so early for North Dakota State that nobody really knew it was a turning point. Put it this way: The Bison offense looked like a disorganized bunch the first two times it had the ball in the season opener against Iowa State.

There was a fumble by quarterback Carson Wentz, although the Bison recovered it. There was a timeout to beat the play clock. There was a delay of game penalty. There were five rushing attempts for two yards or less.

"Just a lot of mistakes by the guys," said head coach Chris Klieman. "Maybe they were nervous or real anxious for their first college start."

Before the second quarter was a minute old, the Cyclones led 14-0, and it appeared a change in head coaches, the loss of 23 seniors, a new starting quarterback and a new offensive coordinator were not going so well.

It was an early test of the new regime on several fronts, such as making adjustments, handling the haphazard first quarter with poise and stopping the momentum that 54,800 thousand fans were generating at Jack Trice Stadium.

In a season where the Bison went 15-1 and captured their fourth straight NCAA Division I FCS national title, perhaps it was one 80-yard touchdown run by John Crockett that created a shut-off valve to the ISU 14-0 lead that changed the course of the season.

The Bison responded with 34 straight points and never did stop until the final drive against Illinois State in Frisco, Texas, on Jan. 10, 2015.

Klieman passed the leadership test against Iowa State. Offensive coordinator Tim Polasek passed the adjustments test. The defense, with new defensive coordinator Matt Entz calling the shots, steadily got better against the Cyclones. The Bison players passed the poise test.

"That was a great test," Klieman said earlier this week. "Going in, one of the things that was unanswered was could we make adjustments with a brand new staff. We're down 14-0 and not playing well. The staff came together that game."

The staff and players rebounded against Iowa State. They rebounded in the second-round playoff win over South Dakota State with a last-minute, game-winning drive. And, of course, they rebounded against Illinois State after falling behind 27-23 with 1 minute and 38 seconds remaining.

The Northern Iowa loss aside, they showed those attributes all season.

That's reason No. 1 this team won a fourth straight FCS national title: After the first quarter against Iowa State, a new coaching staff and players gelled all season.

"We were comfortable all season long, from the first day of fall camp," Klieman said.

The comfort factor taken care of, you can point to four second-tier reasons NDSU went 15-1: The coming-out season for quarterback Carson Wentz, an effective performance by a rebuilt offensive line under new offensive line assistant coach Conor Riley, Kyle Emanuel and the best punter-placekicker combination in FCS.

1. Carson Wentz

For three years, the junior was the understudy to Brock Jensen in the NDSU title runs. He redshirted as a freshman in 2011 and played sparingly in 2012 and 2013.

Yet, with a 6-foot-6, 228-pound frame, a strong right arm, a football intelligence factor that goes along with his 4.0 grade-point average and his leadership ability (he was named a team captain as a junior), those inside the Bison team walls appeared confident.

It wasn't the best of starts, two interceptions and no touchdown passes after two games, but Wentz grew with the offense as the season went along. He was sensational in the playoffs that included a most valuable player award in the title game.

You won't win an FCS championship unless you have a quarterback who can drive the car.

"We handed the keys to him in the last half of the season and the playoffs," Klieman said.

Wentz finished the season with Jensen-like numbers: 228 completions in 358 attempts (64 percent for 3,111 yards, 25 touchdowns and 10 interceptions. Wentz set NDSU single-season records in completions, attempts and passing yards.

More importantly, he had six touchdown passes and one interception in four playoff games.

2. Rebuilt O-line

The poster child statistic to this run of FCS titles is time of possession. Once again, NDSU was near the top finishing second just behind Charleston Southern, with both holding onto the ball for more than 34 minutes a game.

The Bison were also second in that stat in 2012 and 2013 with the full effect of opposing teams being felt in the second half. It's the product of the physical West Coast offense and you can't do that without a productive offensive line.

It paved the way for talented running back John Crockett, who finished with 1,994 yards and an invitation to this weekend's East-West Shrine All-Star game.

"They were so much above expectations," Klieman said.

That's because NDSU came into the season with four new starters and a fifth, junior Joe Haeg, changing positions from right tackle to left tackle. Haeg escalated his play from an all-conference player to an All-American player.

"He was dominant the whole year long," Klieman said. "The accolades he received were well deserving. He's going to be a top lineman in all of FCS next year."

It was the first year as a starter for sophomore right tackle Landon Lechler, junior right guard Jeremy Kelly and freshman left guard Austin Kuhnert.

The kicker to this group: everybody but center Jesse Hinz, who saved his best and healthiest season for last, and part-time starting guard Adam Schueller return next year. And the Bison will also get 2013 all-conference guard Zack Johnson back from a knee injury that sidelined him all of this season.

3. Kyle Emanuel

All the senior did was turn in the best performance by a Bison defensive end since Phil Hansen in 1990. He set a Missouri Valley Football Conference record with 19.5 quarterback sacks and finished his career in a three-way tie for the school sacks lead at 41 with Hansen (1987-90) and Jerry Dahl (1973-74).

Emanuel became the first NDSU player in the Division I era to win a major individual award when he was named the winner of the Buck Buchanan Award, which goes to the best defensive player in the FCS. The honor, given by The Sports Network and voted on by a national panel of sports information directors and media covering FCS football, showed what Emanuel could do when given the opportunity to play full time.

NDSU was so deep in the defensive line the prior two to three years that talented players like Emanuel were forced to divide playing time.

"He was a game changer in every game," Klieman said. "Whether he made the play or not, there was so much attention to him that somebody else was able to make a play. He was a big reason why we were successful on defense. That was as good of a season as I've ever seen a defensive lineman have."

4. Best kicking combo

One of the unsung heroes in the title game win over Illinois State was the 3-for-3 field goal performance by NDSU kicker Adam Keller. Two of those were 41 yards against the wind in a season where Keller was a sparkling 11 of 14 from 40 yards and beyond.

Along with punter Ben LeCompte, who was second in the country with a 45.3-yard average, the two formed the best kicker-punter combination in the FCS.

"They had great years," Klieman said.

It was quite the culmination to a stellar career for Keller, who set an FCS scoring record this season with 145 points. He went into the championship game tied with Griffin Thomas of Jacksonville State (Ala.), who set the mark last year. He also set the FCS record for field goals in a season with 29 in 34 attempts.

Keller broke the NDSU single season mark of 138 points by Jeff Bentrim in 1986 and Lamar Gordon in 2000.

LeCompte's career average of just over 44 yards a punt ranks him first in Valley history, although he has a season remaining. Indiana State's Lucas Hileman has the record of 43.4 set in 2011-12. Despite that, LeCompte was not named to any of the major FCS All-American first teams, getting named to the second team by The Sports Network.

"Ben is one of the best weapons in all of FCS," Klieman said. "I think he's an All-American. He'll get those rewards next year." For now, a new staff with a team that effectively replaced 23 seniors from 2013 can enjoy a fourth straight title.

2015

No way else to explain it: it was one fine coaching job

For a program in recent years that is used to as many FCS titles as losses, the market took a major correction on Aug. 28, 2014. That's when the University of Montana scored on the last play of the game to beat North Dakota State.

More to the point, the Bison defense that had been so stellar in the four previous national championships looked more like a Big Sky Conference outfit that was used to giving up a bunch of points. The drive for five? Shelve that thought.

They rebounded for a while anyway, getting good defensive efforts against Weber State, North Dakota and South Dakota State. But Aaron Bailey ran all over the Bison in the second half and NDSU followed that with an unexpected home loss to South Dakota.

"A lot of people wrote these guys off," said head coach Chris Klieman. "We were 4-2, sitting in the locker room. We lost the starting quarterback for the season. We didn't know what Easton Stick was going to do. We had a real tough meeting Monday after that South Dakota game. Everybody bought in to say,

'Hey, we're going to make this run, we're going to rally around Easton Stick and concentrate on winning every day."

On the south stage of Toyota Stadium in Frisco, Texas, with green and yellow confetti flying around the program's 13th national championship trophy, there was no doubt that mission was accomplished.

And there's no getting around the explanation: the 2015 season will go down as one of the best coaching jobs in Bison football history, perhaps rivaling the 1981 team under Don Morton that started the year losing 38-0 to Northern Michigan, but came back to reach the Division II title game, or the 2010 team coach by Craig Bohl that reached the FCS quarterfinals, one year after a 3-8 season.

On defense, the Bison had to replace the FCS Buck Buchanan Award winner in Kyle Emanuel, an honor that goes to the best defensive player in the division. Also gone: two starting safeties in Colten Heagle and Christian Dudzik who played a combined 120 games, a veteran linebacker trio in Travis Beck, Carlton Littlejohn and Esley Thorton, although Beck was injured before the playoff run last year and was replaced by Nick DeLuca.

The departure of the veterans was evident against Montana, which torched the Bison secondary with 434 yards passing.

On offense, the running backs were looking rather ordinary in trying to replace John Crockett. A couple injuries to the offensive line early in the season didn't help. And then came the USD loss that produced even more anxiety when quarterback Carson Wentz showed up a day later with a broke a bone in his wrist.

That was the low point.

So how did NDSU rescue the season? We give you other five reasons why.

1. Back to the basics. Again, this was a coaching thing, an emphasis on returning Bison football to its identity of being more physical at the point of attack. There were also a few pointed conversations between the coaching staff and the running backs about what it really means to run harder.

King Frazier was the first running back to go over 100 yards and it took until the eighth game to do it. He had 177 against Southern Illinois, a game in which the Bison rushed for 397 yards. The West Coast, physical offense was back, boosted by better offensive line play.

"Hats off to these seniors for being phenomenal leaders," Klieman said. "Their resolve through adversity this year, unlike any other, has been really special."

2. Easton Stick. The Bison figured they got a blue chip-type of recruit when Stick signed his letter of intent in February of 2014. The Omaha Creighton Prep quarterback had a few FBS offers including Rutgers of the Big Ten

Conference, but kept to his NDSU commitment even with the changing of head coaches from Bohl to Klieman. It didn't take him long to make a difference.

Stick won the backup job in a heated battle with Cole Davis that went from spring football into fall camp. His first carry in his first against Indiana State was a 29-yard touchdown run and what followed was eight straight wins to get the Bison to Frisco. Stick completed 61 percent of his passes on 90 of 147 for 1,144 yards and an impressive 13 touchdowns to four interceptions ratio. He finished third on the team in rushing with 498 yards and was the first Bison back to go over 100 yards on the season.

"We wouldn't be here without Easton Stick," Klieman said, not long after the title game in Frisco. You can tell what kind of person Easton is by the article that came out a week ago about his No. 1 goal was to give Carson a chance to play again. What a great young man."

3. Defensive growth. At some point during the season, DeLuca went from being a player who the coaches harped on showing more leadership to a guy who showed more leadership. The results were noticeable on the field, too. He was simply better in the second half of the season and finished the year with one of the best in the history of the program at middle linebacker with 135 tackles, three quarterback sacks, two interceptions and two forced fumbles.

The kid who grew up the most, however, was true freshman safety Robbie Grimsley. The Minnesota Mr. Football award winner from Hutchinson was a backup at Montana who looked overwhelmed. NDSU moved him into the starting lineup after the Oct. 24 game at Indiana State replacing Chris Board, who was moved to linebacker. Grimsley took ownership in the position.

4. Special teams. Nobody was better at the kickoff return and coverage game than NDSU, which rarely allowed a big return by an opponent. It makes a major difference for a team if it's starting a drive closer to midfield than closer to its own end zone. On the other side, the Bison led FCS in kickoff return yardage with an average of 29.1 yards and were led by true freshman Bruce Anderson, who emerged late in the year as a threat to go the distance.

Anderson may have turned in the play of the year when he returned the second half kickoff against Northern Iowa 97 yards for a touchdown.

5. Playoff pedigree. Call it tradition or whatever coachspeak term you want, something happens to this team at playoff time. Jacksonville State head coach John Grass noticed it in the film room.

"I've said it before, their guys, when the playoffs start, you look at them on film and they're a different team," he said. "They're a different team. They know how to win."

In early August, Klieman said his team's defense will get better as the season goes along, and to not expect too much right away. He was right. The

Gamecocks scored 62 points against Sam Houston State in the semifinals; they got one solid drive all day in the title game against NDSU.

The Bison finished fifth in the FCS in scoring defense at 15.3 points per game, but gave up just 9.0 in four playoff games against teams who were on a roll at the time. Montana had 57 and 54 points in its last two regular season games and beat SDSU in the opening round. The Grizzlies had six yards rushing and just 229 total in the FCS second round.

Northern Iowa had games of 59, 41, 49 and 53 points followed by 401 yards rushing in a second round win at Portland State. The Panthers got just 201 yards against NDSU.

Richmond had 556 total yards in a quarterfinal upset win at Illinois State, but had just 38 yards rushing in the semifinals at the Fargodome.

That defense that the Bison put on the field in Missoula?

It was a far different team in the playoffs.

A few words of thanks:

1. To my two older brothers, who one late night in Frisco said I was going to write dad's sequel and as the youngest albeit most talented of the three, "no" was not an option.
2. To my supportive and loving family, who put up with dad being gone too many days or nights, particularly in the fall.
3. To Forum photographer David Samson, an amazing talent who I would take over any sports photog in the country.
4. To Rob Beer of The Forum for his graphical expertise and patience.
5. To my reporting brother Mick Garry of the Sioux Falls Argus Leader newspaper, the last and forever winner of the Ed Kolpack Media Award in the old Division II North Central Conference, for his reliable proof reading and second set of eyes and ears.
6. To Twila Perhus for her expertise in formatting Microsoft Word.
7. To my employer, Forum Communications, for their acceptance, enthusiasm and data base access to allow me to attack this project.
8. To the Bison players, coaches, administrators and fans who made covering this story a historic one to document.

About the author

The family in front of the historic Fargo Theatre, from L: Ben, Ruby, Brandt, Leah, Jeff

Jeff Kolpack started writing at The Forum of Fargo-Moorhead newspaper in 1990 and began covering Bison football in 1995. It was a time in the program's illustrious history, which essentially was christened in the early 1960s, when all was not going well, with a title drought that began in 1991 and lasted until the first FCS title in 2011. Jeff has won numerous state writing awards from both Minnesota and North Dakota newspaper associations over the years, has a radio show on WDAY-AM 970 with WDAY sports director Dom Izzo and hosts the WDAY Golf Show on 970-AM from April through August.

He is married to Ruby Kolpack and they are the parents of three children: Ben, Leah and Brandt. Jeff is a proud member of the B Team Bicycle Club and the GD Cooking Club, enjoys golfing and an occasional ski trip to somewhere not in flat Fargo. "Horns Up" is his first book – and hopefully not the last.

43108286R00131

Made in the USA
Lexington, KY
24 June 2019